The Mom Inventors Handbook

How to Turn Your Great Idea into the Next Big Thing

Tamara Monosoff

McGraw-Hill

New York   Chicago   San Francisco
Lisbon   London   Madrid   Mexico City
Milan   New Delhi   San Juan   Seoul
Singapore   Sydney   Toronto

1 2 3 4 5 6 7 8 9 0   DOC/DOC   0 9 8 7 6 5

ISBN 0-07-145899-9

This publication is designed to provide accurate and authoritative information in regard to the subject matter covered. It is sold with the understanding that the publisher is not engaged in rendering legal, accounting, or other professional service. If legal advice or other expert assistance is required, the services of a competent professional person should be sought.

> —*From a Declaration of Principles Jointly Adopted*
> *by a Committee of the American Bar Association*
> *and a Committee of Publishers and Associations*

McGraw-Hill books are available at special discounts to use as premiums and sales promotions, or for use in corporate training programs. For more information, please write to the Director of Special Sales, Professional Publishing, McGraw-Hill, Two Penn Plaza, New York, NY 10121-2298. Or contact your local bookstore.

 This book is printed on recycled, acid-free paper containing a minimum of 50% recycled de-inked paper.

Library of Congress Cataloging-in-Publication Data

Monosoff, Tamara.
  The mom inventors handbook / by Tamara Monosoff.
     p. cm.
  Includes index.
  ISBN 0-07-145899-9 (alk. paper)
  1. New business enterprises—Management. 2. Women-owned business enterprises—Management. 3. Working mothers. 4. Intellectual property. I. Title.
  HD62.5.M655 2005
  658.1'141'0852—dc22

                                                                2005015220

Contents

Acknowledgments

I wish to acknowledge the thousands of moms in our www.mominventors .com community who were the inspiration for this project. Their interest, inventiveness, and passion—not to mention their quest for down-to-earth information and answers—was the impetus to write this book.

My deepest appreciation to Soledad O'Brien and Julie Aigner-Clark for providing their generous support to this book and for leading by example, contributing their life experiences, and offering inspiration and guidance to women everywhere.

This book would not have been as rich without the contributions from mom inventors who shared their experiences and important lessons learned.

Contributions from a variety of disciplines were essential to this work; thanks go to publicity expert Bill Stoller, research analyst Marta Loeb, marketing and packaging experts Geoff and Stacia Slick, accountant James McClaskey, public relations legend Ann Noder, One Page Business Plan guru Jim Horan, creative genius Lynn Marguerita, seasoned buyer Cathy Downey, historian Autumn Stanley, and our dedicated patent attorney Stuart West.

Others who shared their knowledge and skills were Art Westman, Enoch Poon, Curt Anderson, Judy Lee, Sue Bettenhausen, and Greg Carson.

My gratitude to Bill and Theresa Armour, Jeff Holland, Ann Rankin, Kevin Fisher and Deborah Donnelly, Dale Law, Bob and Jill Hickey, Chester E. Jay and Debra D. Tiner, April Sheldon and John Casado, and Gioccanda Perez for their unwavering support.

At a recent gathering I looked around the room at my four siblings, their spouses, and my parents. I realized that every single member of my family—my parents, Harris and Geraldine, plus Dana, Christopher, Scott, Kathrine, Lance, Tia, and Thom—had in some way directly helped me. In addition, Brad's parents Virginia and David have been supportive in more ways than can be counted. And to our delightful daughters whose excitement is so nourishing: What can you say about perfection? I have always felt the hands of each of you holding me up.

As for my husband, the love of my life, I am forever grateful for your endless love, your compassion, and your intelligence in moving the aims of Mom Inventors, Inc. forward.

My literary agent, Jessica Faust, believed in this book from the start. Without her, this project would never have been more than an idea.

There are also many people at McGraw-Hill who have embraced this project from the beginning. I truly appreciate their enthusiasm and especially wish to thank Donya Dickerson for her support, encouragement, and editorial guidance.

My editor and friend, Jen Rung, provided that "been there, done that" savvy. There isn't a word in its contents she hasn't read and probably improved.

My appreciation to both President and Mrs. Clinton, who, during my time as presidential appointee at the White House, taught me by example, what it takes to bring useful thought into action for the benefit of others.

Finally, I wish to thank the women, like my mother, who have made way for those of us who have been privileged to follow in their steps. Their work is part of my awareness and I often feel a debt for their service.

Foreword

by Soledad O'Brien,
Anchor for CNN's *American Morning*

When my twin boys Jackson and Charlie were born eight months ago, I was a little overwhelmed, but thrilled. Who knew the most frustrating part of having twins would be carrying them both around? Unlike their older sisters, whom I just threw in the baby Bjorn and walked around, there's no easy, hands-free way to carry twins. I wondered why somebody didn't invent a baby-Bjorn–like carrier for twins. How many times have you been frustrated by the lack of something so obvious and practical that many people presumably need? If not a baby product, it may be office equipment, a kitchen helper, or just a better way of doing something.

Don't be surprised if many of today's and tomorrow's inventions come from moms. Women entrepreneurs already contribute to the economy in a big way—an estimated 9.1 million women-owned businesses employ 27.5 million people, and contribute $3.6 trillion to the economy, according to the U.S. Small Business Administration. There have been lots of changes for women in the last century: Women won the right to vote, to work, to have high-powered positions in the business world, and to lead. Lots of women are still fighting for their opportunities, but it feels as if the fight is shifting in the right direction.

Not to mention that millions more women in the workplace are moms. Many of these women are looking for more control over their lives: By figuring out how to maintain some kind of balance between family, friends, and work, anyone can create a better quality of life. We've seen an explosion in the ranks of women entrepreneurs and women-owned businesses. In just 15 years the sales generated by these women have increased by 638 percent—to over 3 trillion dollars. Everybody wants and needs financial stability—but today more women than ever are doing it their own way.

Not only are women capitalizing on the accomplishments of previous generations of female entrepreneurs, but today women are benefiting by the many changes in the way the world does business. In many ways, the Internet has leveled the playing field. Information that's available to a bank president is just as accessible to a stay-at-home mom. And when you consider that so many of today's stay at home moms are former professionals with strong educational backgrounds and workforce experience, one can only expect these numbers to grow. After all, some of the best ideas can come when simultaneously juggling a 20-pound toddler, trying to answer a cell phone, and opening the mail with one's teeth!

As mothers contemplate how they want to define or redefine their lives based on this new entrepreneurial framework—as well as to find the ever-elusive balance between work time and family time—many will look for careers that spark their interest, challenge their intellect, use their creativity, and call on their problem-solving skills. These women will embrace opportunities that allow them the freedom to choose the way they create their lives.

Most of these careers, though, are not advertised in the help wanted section. That's why so many moms today are harnessing their imagination and creating their own reality—and using their own experiences to design the jobs they want. The result: moms who invent products and services that meet the needs in their own lives—and those of people around them.

But these moms need a roadmap—and that's where Tamara Monosoff comes in. *The Mom Inventors Handbook* is the only book that tells moms how to take an idea from concept to the marketplace: not as a little hobby or a way to fill time, but as a real, income-generating business. Her advice, information, and tone is clear, and the information is ideal for moms who have a great idea or who want to reinvent their lives, but aren't quite sure how to get there. Not only does Tamara provide solid business advice and concrete tips on creating a successful business, she also inspires women who have long dreamed of forging their own way—but who were just waiting for that spark to get them going. Here's your spark—get going!

Prologue

Julie Aigner-Clark
Founder of The Baby Einstein Company

In 1997, I founded a company called Baby Einstein. As a full-time mom and former English teacher, my goal was simply to develop videos I could use to expose my babies to the arts and humanities. Unaware of the journey on which I was embarking, I borrowed equipment, cobbled together supplies, and filmed two videos in my own basement. Soon I was inundated by requests for the videos, and a business was born. Five years, ten videos, and $20 million in sales later, my husband and I sold Baby Einstein to Disney.

Though we had many things working in our favor, along the way there were a lot of questions—and few easy answers. Like many other mom inventors and entrepreneurs, I cherished all the help I could get—whether it was from friends, family, or business experts. Looking back, I can recall many moments when a resource like *The Mom Inventors Handbook* would have been a godsend. The book outlines, in clear, step-by-step terms, how to get a product to market. And it's written by someone who's actually endured the trials and tribulations of inventing and launching her own products—managing the challenges of children and family at the same time.

This book is unique in that it not only demystifies the process of taking a product to market, it also debunks many myths commonly believed about inventing. This frees the inventor of many of her self-imposed obstacles.

Also valuable are the insights shared by other mom inventors throughout the book who, with Tamara, each help guide the way for any motivated inventor. From my own experience, I know this information is invaluable and will help you on your way to making your own dream come true. Good luck, and good for you! In opening this book you're taking the first step in making your business dream come true.

Myth Busting

Myth: Build a better mousetrap and the world will beat a path to your
          door.

Reality: We live in a sales and marketing culture. This means that often
          it's not the best invention that sclls…but instead, the best-mar-
          keted one. Few inventions—if any—are good enough to have
          thc world line up to buy them without being prompted or en-
          couraged. Thomas Edison said it best: "Genius is one percent
          inspiration and ninety-nine percent perspiration." In today's
          world, sales and marketing equals perspiration.

Myth: A patent = inventing.

Reality: People with a new invention idea often believe that the first
          thing they need to do is to file a patent. Rarely should it be your
          first step. It's more important to first determine if your inven-
          tion is marketable. In fact, only 2 to 3 percent of patented prod-
          ucts ever make it to market. Plus, many inventors run
          successful businesses without ever filing a patent. Though a
          patent can be a valuable tool, it should seldom, if ever, be your
          first step in the inventing process.

Myth: Invention idea = a million dollars.

Reality: Earning a million dollars on an invention is highly uncommon. However, there *are* an abundance of ideas worth $50,000 or $100,000! Learn the process and you can find success, especially if you have more than one marketable idea.

Myth: An inventor is not a businessperson.

Reality: Business is about making a profit. Successful businesspeople come from every aspect of our society including arts, healthcare, and science. Inventing is just one of many creative ways to make money.

Myth: An idea is worth money.

Reality: A truly good, useful idea has likely visited many minds. *Action* is what distinguishes the successful inventor, and what turns an idea into a potentially profitable venture.

Myth: Someone else has already patented my idea, so I can't pursue it.

Reality: If another inventor has patented your idea, there are several great strategies that will allow you to still take your idea to market (legally).

Myth: Nobody has ever thought of this great idea before.

Reality: If nobody has thought of it before, it probably doesn't address a real problem.

Myth: If I tell people my idea, they'll steal it!

Reality: The theft of a new invention idea is rare. A lot of sweat equity goes into developing an invention, which is a big barrier to most potential "thieves." When it does occur, ideas are typically stolen only after a product has proved successfully.

Myth: It's not ladylike to talk about ways to make money.

Reality: Money equals freedom and independence. What could be sexier than that?

Myth: Successful inventing is about ideas.

Reality: Creative, inventive problem solving is critical, but to really succeed you must think like a businessperson. Ask, "What is the commercial viability of this product, and who is my potential market?" You're then on your way to determining whether your idea is marketable.

Myth: Invention ideas are worth money.
Reality: Invention ideas are *not* worth money by themselves. Business opportunities *are* worth money.

Myth: The challenging part of inventing is the process of patenting, prototyping, and manufacturing.
Reality: These are actually the easy aspects to inventing. You can hire experts in each area to accomplish these steps. The real challenge is selling your idea, and only you have the power to be your best salesperson.

Myth: I am not a salesperson so I can't sell my product.
Reality: Contrary to popular belief, there's no such thing as a born salesperson. Like any specialized skill, sales ability is learned. Being extroverted can make parts of the process easier, but there are highly successful salespeople of every personality type.

Praise for
The Mom Inventors Handbook

"Have a great idea? Want to turn it into a profitable business with sustainable cash flow? I highly recommend *The Mom Inventors Handbook*! This is the first book I have found that helps aspiring inventors—moms, dads, or anyone, for that matter—to understand all the steps necessary to take a great idea, bring it to market, and turn it into a real business. Tamara Monosoff has taken all of the information she personally researched to create her Mom Invented products … and put it into an easy-to-understand handbook for inventors. This book belongs on every aspiring entrepreneur's desk!"

—Jim Horan
President, One Page Business Plan, Inc.

In *The Mom Inventors Handbook* Tamara Monosoff has not only created a superbly practical guide for women inventors, especially those who are also mothers, but she has written a how-to book that could serve as a model for the genre. The writing is clear, the steps are logical, the facts are straight, and the tone is upbeat without being cute or patronizing. Vivid quotes and specific examples from experience illustrate most points, making the book fun as well as informative. Never again will I be intimidated by the phrase "business plan."

—Autumn Stanley
Independent scholar, historian, and author of
Mothers and Daughters of Invention

Introduction

It Takes a Village …

When I first became an inventor, I discovered a lack of resources that spoke to me directly. Sure, there were books about inventing products and starting home businesses. But none of them addressed the complexity that define a mom's life—juggling kids and family life while simultaneously trying to create a product from scratch, conduct market research, build a prototype, work with engineers, find a factory to produce the product, and sell and distribute it nationally. All while making mac and cheese and reading about Dora's next adventure.

One day during my own inventing journey, I woke up with three important phone calls to make. I wondered how I was going to manage this seemingly simple task with a strong-willed toddler attached to my leg. As each hour passed, my anxiety mounted, and I debated when I could take the chance to make these critical calls—and also ensure a "professional" impression. One was to a senior buyer in a retail store to whom I was attempting to sell my new product. The other was to my patent attorney, where every five-dollar minute always seemed to click away in double time. The third was to the factory where critical decisions had to be made about problems that had occurred during my first manufacturing run.

As the day progressed, I decided to drive Sophia around the block until she fell asleep in the car. If I were lucky, I'd have an hour, tops. So I made the calls, trying to whisper and sound professional at the same time. I knew that if she suddenly woke up my cover would be blown—that I was "just" a stay-at-home mom, not a "serious" businesswoman.

As I spoke to each contact, I visualized them sitting at their mahogany desks, comfortably conducting business on a normal schedule. Little did they know that I was conducting business from our family van, sleeping child in the back seat, a smashed bean-and-cheese burrito on my pants, and a poopy diaper among the stacked papers on the passenger seat! I remember pausing as I was about to dial the first number: I thought there had to be a better way.

Where was the roadmap that related to my concerns about making business calls when, at any given moment, my child could need immediate attention? Where was the book, website, or support group that could understand that I didn't have neat, uninterrupted eight-hour windows of work time to accomplish daily tasks? I didn't find it. It just didn't exist.

So I set out to find other moms who had successfully gone through the process, who might be able to provide encouraging words and a lighted lantern for me to follow. I hoped they could share critical information and contacts, lessons learned, biggest mistakes, and how to actually succeed. I wanted all of this along with the comfort of knowing that they were moms too, dealing with the same challenges and struggles that I was. And I hoped to learn how they overcame their fears and obstacles (real and imagined) and garnered the courage and strength to move forward.

I did find this information, piece by piece and mom by mom. And my greatest discovery—aside from the invaluable practical and detailed information they had to offer—was that the most successful moms had one thing in common—the right mindset to accomplish their goals.

A Message to Those Who Are Not Moms

I am a mom, and it is from that perspective that I became an inventor and developed a community for other mom inventors. However, this book is for anybody who wishes to transform their invention into reality. Throughout the book, references will be made to mom inventors; however, the information and the process applies to any inventive entrepreneur. Even if you're not a mom, you were mom invented (and dad inspired) so turn the page and get started!

Adopting the "Inventor Mindset"

All the time, we tell our kids that attitude is important. We encourage them to think positively and optimistically, and to have confidence in their talents and abilities. Yet often we don't take our own advice.

That's why I believe that the first step in creating that great invention isn't thinking up the watershed idea or researching the market. It is, instead, adopting the right mindset. Often I hear from moms—even those who've successfully launched a product—"I'm just a mom trying to bring my idea to market" or "I don't consider myself an entrepreneur or an inventor—I just want to see my product on store shelves." These women are selling themselves short—not that this is unusual.

Historian and author of *Mothers and Daughters of Invention*, Autumn Stanley, affirms this point: "In the 19th century, and to some extent even today, women hesitate to claim credit for achievements," Stanley points out. "Women are socialized to be generous and giving and may freely pass on their ideas to relatives and friends, rather than seeking to patent and profit from them."

My doctoral research in international and multicultural education supports Stanley's theory. In my dissertation, "Women and Leadership in the Executive Office of the President 1993–2000," I had the honor of interviewing fourteen of the highest-ranking women in the Clinton White House. I focused on the views these women had about themselves as leaders. What I learned was that many of these women found it difficult to consider themselves leaders or expressed discomfort in being called a "leader." However, many of the same women discussed the rewards of being in leadership positions and the feelings of gratification at having an impact on something larger than themselves. In addition to this, some of the participants discussed the management styles they use to produce results. My research found that it was easier for these women to speak about the process of leadership as an external force, as opposed to focusing on themselves as leaders.

So how does research relate to you, the aspiring inventor or home business owner? William James, a prominent philosopher and psychologist who lived over a hundred years ago, said it best: "Human beings, by changing the inner attitudes of their minds, can change the outer aspects of their lives." As a mother, you already have what it takes to be a successful inventor or business owner. Believing in yourself throughout the process will help you succeed.

Your Impressive Resume

No matter what your level of education or experience in the business world, as a mom you have an enviable skill set. Do not underestimate these abilities! It may sound clichéd, but you already have the most important job in the world—raising a child. This job comes with the most responsibility, the heaviest workload (no days off!), and the greatest risks. Coincidentally, these are the characteristics that define an entrepreneur. A successful entrepreneur isn't afraid to take risks—or if she is afraid, she overcomes her fear. She has the skills to establish a business (or learns the skills) and is determined to achieve what she sets out to accomplish.

The characteristics of a successful entrepreneur, then, don't differ a great deal from the characteristics of a successful mom. You've already taken a great risk by dramatically altering your life to accommodate a child. You've learned the skills necessary to raise this child—and, of course, you continue to learn as you go along. And hopefully, you already recognize the great achievements you've made—anything from teaching your child to read to teaching your child to be happy and confident. All the while, you've continued to manage the household, foster loving relationships with family and friends, deal with periodic depression, and possibly even manage a career. Whew! That's quite an accomplishment. In comparison, taking your invention to market should be child's play. No pun intended!

A Roadmap to Get You There

Then why, for so many of us, does it seem less intimidating to raise a child than it does to bring an invention to market or start our own business? Probably because most of us, as women, have encountered child-raising experiences throughout our lives. Taking care of younger siblings, babysitting as a teenager, and absorbing child-rearing strategies from your mother, your sisters, and your friends have probably come naturally in your life. There is also a never-ending supply of books, magazines, and even Websites to turn to for advice. But how many successful inventors or home business owners do you know? If you're anything like I was, very few. And how many books or resources combine the unique requirements of bringing a product to market with the unique needs of being a mom? Until now, none.

That's why in 2003 I started Mom Inventors, Inc.—to provide an online national community of support with the answers that mom inventors (and others who were interested in this topic) were seeking. I wanted to provide a forum that would encourage other moms to forge ahead and access this untapped network of intelligence that already existed in pockets around the country. Like our network of mothers, sisters, friends, doctors, books, and magazines that supplies knowledge for child-rearing, the Mom Inventors network—a Web-based community generating over a quarter million hits per month, with more than 5,000 registered members spanning the United States and other countries—provides similar tools on a more focused scale.

As a community of "moms helping moms," we provide informational resources, a message board, seminars, inspiring stories from our featured moms, our popular newsletter, and a Mom Invented™ online store. In addition to supporting this community, Mom Inventors, Inc. develops, manufactures, and distributes products made for and invented by moms. Each product carries the Mom Invented brand, a brand symbolizing the dynamic creativity of moms everywhere and our potential connection to each other. We also license inventions from other moms who are not interested in running a business, place their photo on the package, and pay them a royalty (percentage of sales) for their idea.

This book is a continuation of my efforts to provide answers. It supplies a simple, step-by-step roadmap to a process that may be largely unfamiliar to you, as it was to me when I first began. In it I share the strategies to succeed—and the pitfalls to avoid—as you go through the process yourself, from the very beginning to the very end. All the while I keep in mind your unique needs as a mother balancing many important facets of your life.

My Story

I am an entrepreneur. While only recently have I become an "entrepreneur" in the sense of starting a business, I now realize that I have been entrepreneurial most of my life. When I was growing up, I lived near the beach in Northern California. After visitors spent the day at the beach, they were tired, hungry, and thirsty. When I was nine years old, I decided to sell chocolate brownies and lemonade on the street corner. On my third weekend, a policeman leaned out his car window and playfully asked, "Hey little girl, are you making any money?" Thrilled with my earnings, I replied, "Yes! $300 dollars so far!" With shock on his face, he said, "Oh my gosh…you need a license for that. You have to go home and you can't do this anymore." I still remember the shock and astonishment of my first brush with the law.

While I learned that there are regulations to follow, more relevant to me was that I could earn my own money and spend it. As a nine-year-old, I felt empowered. I worked every summer from that time forward (busing tables, working in delis and toy stores). Even though I was underage, I found that a store owner couldn't say "no" to a kid that voluntarily wanted to work. I remember fondly earning $8 after eight hours of busing tables at a local restaurant one Saturday. I headed straight for the candy store and bought $8 worth of candy. My mother, who ordinarily wouldn't allow me to eat sweets, chose not to say "no" because she was proud that I had earned it on my own…another powerful lesson about the power of choice when you've earned your own money.

As an adult, my experience at becoming an "inventor" was not unlike that of many other women who had invented new products. I was not sitting around my house looking for something to do. After becoming a new mother, my entire world turned upside down. Full-time motherhood was harder than any other job I had ever had. When I had worked in the White House a few years earlier, often 14-hour workdays, it was challenging and intense, but I still found that I could systematically get through my workload and finish projects on time. As a mother, time as I knew it ceased to exist. Tasks are seldom "finished" when you're taking care of the needs of someone else every minute of the day. This was unexpected. I knew that I would be focusing on my new baby, but I didn't know that I'd rarely be able to complete a sentence, shower when I needed to, or dash out the door to meet with a colleague or friend. Inventing was the last thing on my mind.

However, circumstances soon changed that. After 10 months of motherhood, my daughter began pulling the family toilet paper. At first I thought this was creative and clever. A few clogged toilets later, it lost its charm. I went to the store to purchase the "thing" that prevents kids from unrolling the toilet paper. Unable to find it, I figured I couldn't be the only mom in America experiencing this, so I began asking other mothers about it. The responses I received were surprising: "Lock the toilet paper up in the cabinet until she grows out of it," and "Make sure that the bathroom door is closed at all times." This is ridiculous, I thought. There had to be a better solution for parents. So I decided to "invent" a solution to the problem myself. My product, the TP Saver, is a simple plastic tube with an elastic band attached to it. The tube is inserted into the toilet paper roll, the elastic is extended over the front of the toilet paper securing it in place, and a toddler safety cap locks into the other end of the tube. It was launched into the market 11 months after I began developing the idea, and it is now available in retail stores nationwide.

There is a great maxim, "Believe in your dreams and they may come true; believe in yourself and they will come true." I am an inventor, and I now realize that I became an inventor the moment I conceived of the TP Saver idea. I encourage you to say, "I am an inventor." Try it on. Go ahead and say it!

The Power of Creative Solutions

Part of getting into the inventor mindset is to utilize creative thinking. As a mom, this is a skill that can help you tremendously when juggling priorities and dealing with your unique work environment—a workplace that's seldom quiet and doesn't come with a standard eight-hour day.

In fact, you probably already think creatively without even knowing it. As a mom, with so many unexpected curve balls thrown your way on a daily basis, you are forever devising solutions and strategies to attain your goals. And whether it's finding an efficient way to feed your family three healthy meals a day or devising a strategy to get the kids to all their activities prepared and on time—there's no doubt you've created your very own solutions to accomplish these and countless other family-management tasks.

Plan on tapping into these creative-thinking abilities as you go through the entrepreneurial process, as well. What truly sets a successful entrepreneur and inventor apart is how she handles potential obstacles. When you are confronted with a challenge, don't change your goals—be creative and change your plan of action. After all, when we think that we have only two options, we often find ourselves in a dilemma. In his book, *Profiting from Intellectual Capital: Extracting Value from Innovation*, Patrick H. Sullivan says, "When given the choice between two alternatives, always pick a third!"

I kept this strategy in mind myself when trying to get a job as a political appointee in the Clinton Administration eight years ago. At the time, I was completing my doctorate at the University of San Francisco. I volunteered every free moment at the campaign office in San Francisco, and I identified people in the White House for whom I wanted to work and sent in the required paperwork. I was determined to work for the President. What I couldn't control was the difficulty of penetrating the barriers of communication with the "all-powerful" Office of Presidential Personnel. For months, I left multiple messages every week, yet no one returned my calls. So I decided to increase my options by getting on an airplane from California to Washington, D.C. I figured that if I called saying I was in town for a limited time, they would finally have to return my call. From my hotel room in D.C., I went ahead with this plan. It turns out, my strategy wasn't that unique—not a single returned call. It appeared that my trip was in vain, and I began regretting all the time and money I had wasted by going to D.C. without appointments.

Then I asked myself again, "How can I change my options?" I had learned that no appointment was needed to enter the lobby of the Old Executive Office Building, which housed the Office of Presidential Personnel. I didn't know exactly what I could achieve when I got there, as I didn't even know what the people I was trying to contact looked like. Nonetheless, I decided to go sit there anyway. I observed well-dressed people enter, sit in the chair next to me, and call the person they were scheduled to meet. I realized that they were not dialing entire phone numbers from the lobby, but just a few digits. "Aha! These calls are internal," I thought. "Maybe if I call my contacts from this phone they will pick up thinking I am a forgotten appointment in the lobby."

I took a deep breath and dialed the last digits of the number I had been calling for weeks. When I heard the human voice on the other end, I almost didn't know what to say. I quickly pulled myself together and told him that I was in the lobby and only in town for one more day. I asked, "Would it be possible to meet for a few minutes to discuss my application?" The answer was, "Yes." Rather than change my goal, I changed my approach and increased my options. And I ended up getting the job.

Sometimes it's important to change your environment and do something different. Talk to someone you have thought about approaching, or join a club or association that you've thought about joining. Put yourself someplace you have never been and just hang out and see what happens! There is no way you can know what will transpire until you take a chance. This thinking—constantly creating new options for yourself—should apply during all the steps you'll soon take as an inventor.

Moms Who Know

So how can you adopt the proper mindset? Besides believing in the skills you already do have, it's valuable to learn from other moms' experiences.

Inventors are entrepreneurs who tend to see the world through the lens of problems and solutions. They not only imagine the solution, but go a step further to create the actual means to an end. The mom inventors interviewed for this book had different motivations for starting their businesses. Some wanted to earn money so that they could stay at home with their children. Others wanted to develop an educational tool to help children, or they felt there was a void in the market that they wanted to fill. Still other mothers were motivated by the creative experience or were motivated to make a million dollars to change their lifestyle.

Regardless of why they wanted to bring a product to market or create a home business, one thing was clear: They were all personally motivated to make it happen. Meghan Ritchie, owner of EarlyOn, Inc. explains, "I

Meghan Ritchie, the founder of EarlyOn, Inc.—a company that creates unique products that build self-esteem, educate, and entertain—is pictured here with Caroo, the mascot of her children's video series.

would describe myself as very driven. It's something my parents instilled in me at a very young age. And some of it is inherent. I am one that does not like to sit around for too long, if at all. In fact, I have a need to always be doing something. I joke that it's a curse. I loved always having something on my plate. Yes, I am a 'doer' which really helps if you are someone who wants to start your own business."

Even though becoming an entrepreneur may come more naturally to some, it is a learned skill. It isn't easy, but neither is motherhood. As noted previously, Thomas Edison famously said, "Genius is one percent inspiration and ninety-nine percent perspiration." While a great idea is necessary for success, thought alone will get you nowhere. That's where this book can help. My objective is to demystify and simplify what can seem like an intimidating process.

What to Expect

The chapters that follow break down the inventing process into manageable parts. The book details the steps necessary for bringing a product idea to market, with insider insight from many moms who've gone through it themselves, including details from my own experience. I've found that the easiest way to accomplish a goal is to narrow it down into small steps you can take every day. I believe this is a particularly useful strategy when you're a mom and life doesn't always go as scheduled.

So congratulations! You've already taken the first step by picking up this book. Now adjust your mindset, believe in your ability, and read on— and you'll be on your way to success!

Taking Your First Steps

I have some great invention ideas but no clue where to begin. I'm afraid that one day I'll see my product in stores and say, "Hey, I thought of that!" I don't want to regret not pursuing my dreams. Please help me get started.
—Message e-mailed to Mom Inventors, Inc., 2004.

So you have a great idea. And whether it's been percolating in your head for a week or marinating in your mind for years, the key to transforming this idea from concept to profit is *action*. If it is truly a problem-solving idea, rest assured that someone else has thought of it. Acting on that idea is what will differentiate you! This chapter discusses how to take action by first breathing life into your initial idea—and then taking your idea a step further to develop a business plan. This chapter also offers the skinny on invention promotion companies, organizations that, for a fee, promise to take your invention to market. Are they legitimate? I'll show you what to watch out for.

In addition, this chapter briefly discusses finances, and what to expect during the first phase of your inventing process. While we'll discuss finances in greater detail in subsequent chapters, this provides a quick overview as well as do-it-yourself alternatives if you're on a shoestring budget.

One for the Books

When you're in the idea stage, taking your invention to market may seem like an overwhelming prospect. What exactly should you do next? Talk to people? Get a patent? Search online? Though these steps will become important later, your first step should be to flesh out your idea. Fortunately, this step is simple and inexpensive; in fact, all you'll need is a fresh notebook and a pen. In this notebook you will record your initial thoughts and plan of action, as well as every conversation and phone call you have—in chronological order—regarding your project.

I recommend using a bound notebook or journal that's small enough to stick in your purse, briefcase, or diaper bag so you can take it everywhere you go. The only required element of the notebook is that it contains bound pages that can't be temporarily removed (no loose-leaf binders). That's because this is not simply a warm-and-fuzzy journal; it's also an important business tool as recommended by the United States Patent and Trademark Office (www.uspto.gov). By recording your conversations with others, your dated notebook will act as a record to validate your progress if there are any future problems or discrepancies (or if someone tries to steal your idea). Also, if someone is working independently from you to develop a similar idea, patent rights are granted to the person "most actively developing the product." Your notebook will provide a detailed record of your progress with dates attached to each step you take.

Another important reason to keep this notebook is to honor your milestones. In the day of a mother, it is difficult to remember, much less celebrate, the hundreds of tasks that you accomplish. Once you embark on the inventing process you'll overcome many hurdles and experience small successes that you will want to remember. Your invention notebook can provide more than legal documentation—it's also a measure of your ongoing progress and evidence of your determination. Plus it records all those details, contacts, and information that seem easy to remember now but which you might forget in a month or two.

The Write Stuff

Each inventor's journey and style is unique. But the more you write in your notebook, the better organized you'll be. I recommend including the following topics to provide the foundation for your notebook, but feel free to include anything you think is relevant. To better illustrate exactly what should be included, I will provide examples from my own experience inventing the TP Saver. Because I didn't record as well then as I would now (I didn't have this handbook!), I will provide examples of how I would record information now if I were just starting out.

Describe Your Invention Idea

- *What is your idea?* For me, this was "a device that prevents children from unrolling the family toilet paper."
- *How did you think of it?* In other words, what inspired you and what experiences was it based upon? TP Saver example: My daughter, at age 10 months, started pulling the toilet paper and clogging the toilet.
- *What does it look like?* This should include dimensions, shape, materials, and anything else that is relevant. TP Saver example: It should extend the length of the internal toilet paper tube and stick out a little bit further so that one can hold onto the end while fastening the cap (approximately 5 inches long and 1 inch wide). The current design is similar to that of a hair-permanent rod. It is a long tube with some type of elastic securing the body of the device to the cap. Initially, I think it will be made of plastic and rubber bands.
- *How does it work?* Describe the function of the invention. TP Saver example: The body of the device slides into the current cardboard toilet paper tube and sits next to the metal or plastic toilet paper holder used to hold toilet paper in nearly all current toilet paper holders available on the market. It would not be necessary to remove the metal rod. This device would fit inside the toilet paper tube next to the actual toilet paper holder as it is. No aspect of the toilet paper holder mechanism would need to be removed while attaching the toilet paper saving device.
- *What problem does it solve?* Describe why the product is needed. TP Saver example: There appears to be nothing available that prevents children from unrolling the family toilet paper. It solves the problem of kids pulling the toilet paper and clogging the toilet or making an unsanitary mess on the bathroom floor and wasting paper.
- *Possible product names?* Write down the names that you are considering for your product. TP Saver example: TP Roll Stopper, TP

Roll Guard, TP Roll Holder, Toddler Toilet Paper Protector, Toddler TP Guard, and TP Saver.

Draw a picture of your invention idea.   Don't worry if you're not artistically inclined; this can be a rudimentary sketch. A drawing is important not just to keep a record of your invention idea, but also so that you can better communicate with the machinist, engineer, or product developer what you are trying to achieve when you get to the design or prototype stage (see Chapter 3). An added benefit of an early sketch is that you will be able to revisit it to see how far you have actually come once the product is stocked on retail store shelves!

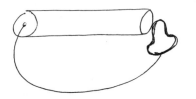

Nov. 2002

Toilet paper protecting device

Fits inside toilet paper roll next to metal toilet paper holder

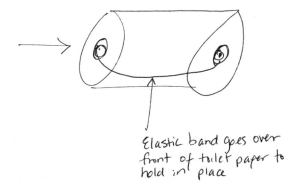

Elastic band goes over front of toilet paper to hold in place

First sketch of the TP Saver in November 2002.

Describe your product's features. According to the American Heritage Dictionary, a "feature" is "a prominent or distinctive aspect, quality, or characteristic." If you were describing a home's features, for instance, you might say three bedrooms, a master bath, an updated kitchen, and hardwood floors. Use this as a guide when determining your own product's proposed features. The TP Saver has the following product features:

- No assembly required
- Simple to use
- No need to remove toilet paper for insertion
- Fits most standard toilet paper holders

List your product's benefits. According to the American Heritage Dictionary, a "benefit" is "something that promotes or enhances well-being; an advantage." In other words, what does this product solve? How can it help someone in his or her daily life? The TP Saver™ packaging states the following benefits:

- Prevents your child or pet from unrolling toilet paper
- Reduces the risk of paper ingestion
- Saves paper, money, and the environment

What makes your product unique to the market? Your idea may be brand new to the market—nothing similar exists. Or, it may be an improvement on something that already does exist, but with unique features and benefits to differentiate it. It can be helpful to include similar products in your list. When I performed my initial research, for instance, there was nothing like the TP Saver on the market, though one major manufacturer, Safety 1st, offered a kit filled with other types of gadgets to lock down the bathroom. I jotted this fact down in my notebook.

Who will buy it? Who is your target customer? It's important to fully understand who will need or want your product. This will help you during every aspect of the process as you move forward—design, market research, advertising, and sales. It is also valuable to figure out the approximate number this audience represents.

For the TP Saver, I determined that my initial target market was parents with children of approximately 10 months to 2 years old who pull the family toilet paper. My research indicated there were 11.8 million American households with children 0 to 3 years old, 4 million new births per year, and 69 million grandparents—a significant market. (You will learn how to retrieve this type of helpful market research in Chapter 4.)

How might your product be expanded to other uses or customers? Create a list of possible markets. When I first developed the TP Saver, I assumed my only market would be parents with small children. However, as time went on, I heard from consumers whose cats and dogs also got into the toilet paper and often pulled it all over the house. I quickly realized that this was an entirely new market, and I began researching to determine how many more potential customers this would mean. I discovered there were 77.7 million households with cats and 65 million households with dogs in America—not too shabby!

Record discussions pertaining to your invention.   You will be amazed at the number of people you will speak to as you go through the inventing process. Be sure to keep a brief record of all conversations you think are relevant. For example, when you speak with an engineer, graphic artist, prototype developer, or patent attorney, write down the date and time of your call. Then, in two or three sentences, summarize your conversation. Not only will this provide a record of details you can easily refer back to (relying on memory can be risky!), you'll also have written documentation to help protect your interests.

Here is a sample of a notation I made after speaking with the machinist:

December 15, 2002—met with Art Westman of Accurate Manufacturing. He gave me a copy of the signed nondisclosure agreement that I had faxed to him. We discussed the prototype for the toilet paper saving device. I showed him my sketch and the hair-permanent rod, and he seemed to understand what I was trying to achieve. He said that he would be glad to hand-make a prototype out of Delrin® plastic. He said that it would be ready in about two weeks and that it would cost about $100. I told him to go ahead and make it.

Continue to update your notebook throughout the product development process.   Record meetings, new developments, and personal stories (if you wish). In addition to having a legal record, remember that this notebook is a measure of your progress. Enjoy it. But also don't feel intimidated by it. In other words, don't feel that you have to write an essay or long detailed accounts. If you forget to make an entry, that's ok. Share stories and write enough to make sense to any sensible person. You may also wish to jot down personal stories to track your progress and provide future reminders about the process.

Here's another sample entry that comes from my own notebook. I wrote it after Sophia, my baby daughter, accompanied me on a business call:

> *Sophia and I went to meet with the president of XYZ Company. I had brought a diaper bag full of toys and snacks. I became so entrenched in the discussion that I didn't notice, until it was too late, that Sophia had smeared diaper cream into her elegant carpet. Right away I dropped to my hands and knees, and with handy wipes desperately tried to get the cream out of the carpet. Unfortunately diaper cream is waterproof! All I could do was apologize. I was embarrassed, but because it had taken so much effort for me to make that meeting I decided to continue. But the president sat stiffly in her chair as we continued our discussion, clearly unhappy; and so it became clear to me that I could only work with people who wouldn't mind having kids around.*

This was definitely a lesson I wanted to remember!

Don't Just Think Outside the Box—Reinvent It!

As you think deeply about your idea and document your thoughts, there are some proven ways to help broaden your thinking and view your project from different perspectives. Roger von Oech is an internationally recognized leader in stimulating creativity and innovation. The following is an excerpt from his book *A Whack on the Side of the Head: How You Can Be More Creative* (Warner Books, 1998, pages 108–112). It's a fantastic look at getting into the creative mindset, with ideas you can use as you develop your own invention—from the beginning stages through to sales and marketing.

Be an Explorer

It's one thing to be open to new ideas; it's quite another to go on the offensive and actively seek them out. I encourage you to be an "explorer" and search for ideas outside your area....To be an explorer you must believe that there is a lot of good information around you, and all you have to do is find it....Many good ideas have been discovered because someone poked around in an outside industry or discipline, and applied what he found to his own field. World War I military designers borrowed from the cubist art of Picasso and Braque to create more efficient camouflage patterns for tanks and guns. Football coach Knute Rockne got the idea for his "four horsemen" backfield shift while watching a burlesque chorus routine. Mathematician John von Neumann analyzed poker-table behavior and developed the "game theory" model of economics. The roll-on deodorant was an adaptation of the ball-point pen. Drive-in banks were adapted from drive-in restaurants.

Exercise: Where do you explore for ideas? What outside people, places, activities, and situations do you use to stimulate your thinking?

TIP: Develop the explorer's attitude: the outlook that wherever you go, there are ideas waiting to be discovered.

TIP: Don't get so busy that you lose the free time necessary for exploring. Give yourself a nontask day once a month or so, or an afternoon every several weeks.

TIP: When you "capture" an idea, be sure to write it down.

TIP: Sometimes the most helpful ideas are right in front of us. As the noted explorer Scott Love once put it, "Only the most foolish of mice would hide in a cat's ear. But only the wisest of cats would think to look there." Ask yourself: What resources and solutions are right in front of me? What am I overlooking?

Getting Down to a Business Plan

Once you've begun writing in your notebook, you'll probably find that you've clarified many issues. Suddenly it becomes easier to talk about your idea, and you can communicate your goals more clearly. This is the time you may wish to take your notebook findings and develop them further into an organized business plan.

A business plan spells out the goals of your business and articulates the steps you need to take to achieve these goals. In order to get somewhere, you need to know where you want to go and figure out the route you'll take to get there. An initial business plan is nothing more than committing these thoughts to paper. Once you write it down, you can follow and refine it, and use it to measure results. It shouldn't prevent you from moving forward, and it can actually save you time and create a sense of confidence over the long run. A written plan has a way of turning an idea or dream into something concrete.

Your business plan is meant to complement your notebook, not replace it. Think of the inventor's notebook as a record of your progress and lessons learned, whereas your business plan is about the future. Your business plan is the map that will provide your project's direction and major highways, while your notebook records the turns and detours you end up taking. One of my goals with this book is to help you increase efficiencies and chances for success. Creating a business plan will aid in that goal.

At first I was reluctant to develop my own business plan. Shortly after conceiving my company, Mom Inventors, Inc., my husband told me that the local chamber of commerce was offering a seminar on business plan writing. He suggested that it might help me start thinking about how to shape the company. My initial reaction was, "Ugh! I have to write a business plan?" I had heard about business plans. They were typically long, incredibly detailed, and took up a great deal of time and energy.

But when I heard that this seminar would offer advice about how to create a business plan in just one page (the instructor was Jim Horan, author of *The One Page Business Plan*) I thought differently and decided to attend. I figured I could handle one page!

As I sat in the audience and listened to the lecture, I could see that this was something I could do. I realized that a business plan can be simple, brief, and even fun to develop—yet still contain all the elements I would need to go forward. Truthfully, I couldn't believe that I was actually feeling energized about creating a business plan. Over the next few days following the lecture, I got to work thinking about the steps. Essentially, there are five elements that you will need to work through to develop your own business plan. Ask yourself the following questions:

- What am I building? Is this a business, service, or product? The answers to these questions will help provide your *vision* statement.
- Why does this product or business exist? What does it aim to accomplish? When you have answered these questions, you have stated your *mission*.
- What are my specific short- and long-term goals? Once you write these specific goals down, you will have a list of *objectives* that you can later measure. For example: By August 2003 sell TP Savers in one store with first year sales of 5,000 units. By August 2004 sell TP Savers in one hundred stores, with second year unit sales of 25,000.
- How are we going to build this company over time? These will become your *strategies*. For example: I am initially going to sell to small independent stores and then move into bigger chain stores by leveraging the sales in the smaller stores. I also want to expand into other markets, such as pets.
- What is the work to be done? Create an *action plan* with specific tasks to be accomplished with due dates.

You can spend five minutes, hours, days, or weeks on the one-page business plan depending on your goals. I found this system to be simple enough to create an initial plan in one hour.

No matter what format your business plan takes, it is an evolving document that changes over time as your product, service, or company develops. I recommend the format of *The One Page Business Plan* because it is accessible and simple yet highly effective; however, you should use a format that feels comfortable to you. There are plenty of books and Websites that will help you on your way. If you are interested in *The One Page Plan*, there is a free online template with which you can get started immediately at www.onepagebusinessplan.com. You can also purchase the more detailed workbook for further support.

The purpose of a business plan is to help you translate what you are thinking into something tangible. Writing it down will help you focus on results. The experience of writing a business plan can help broaden your thinking and give you the tools necessary to clearly articulate your plans for the company. If you have a partner in your endeavor, this process is helpful in unifying your goals and approach. It is gratifying to revisit your plan every few months to see what you have accomplished, to see what you still have to accomplish, and to add any variations to the plan based on changes that have occurred. It is a living document that changes as you and your company, product, or service evolves over time. Your business plan will help you further define your goals, identify steps you need to achieve them, and help create manageable time lines for accountability (accountability to yourself!). Once you have a plan, modify and update it as necessary, and resist the temptation to hire a company who promises to "make you millions" from your idea.

Avoiding Scam Artists

"I paid $5,000 dollars to an invention promoter. The firm promised to bring my product to market within two years, but after I paid them, they rarely communicated with me. After a while they stopped returning my phone calls and e-mails altogether. I should have listened to my own discomfort with this deal. I feel so embarrassed for not realizing I was being cheated. Now there are competing products on the market that came out while I was idly waiting for something to happen."

—Virginia K., mom inventor

As you begin brainstorming your idea and nailing down details, you're sure to get more and more excited about taking further action. You may be tempted to contact an invention promotion company, which promises to take your idea to market in return for a sum of money, which can range from $1,000 to $30,000 plus.

While not every invention promotion company is fraudulent, the industry is fraught with unethical and dishonest firms. These firms often advertise on TV, the radio, or the Internet and in newspapers and magazines. If it sounds too good to be true, it usually is. These firms may offer you the promise of free information on how to patent and market your invention. They may also claim to have special agreements with manufacturers looking to license new products, or they may even claim to represent these manufacturers. They may even guarantee you a successful patent or your money back. If you decide to take this route, be sure to ask for references before you sign a contract. And even then, beware: These companies have also been known to use shills—people they hire to give good testimonials.

The Federal Trade Commission issues this warning: "There's great satisfaction in developing a new product or service and in getting a patent. But when it comes to determining market potential, inventors should proceed with caution as they try to avoid falling for the sweet-sounding promises of a fraudulent promotion firm." (FTC Facts for Consumers: Invention Promotion Firms, www.ftc.gov 877-FTC-HELP.) See the sidebar "Important Tips When Considering an Invention Promotion Company" for additional advice when pursuing this option.

Important Tips When Considering an Invention Promotion Company

1. *If it sounds too good to be true, it probably is.* Anyone who gives you extreme assurances that they can get your product licensed—or is a little too enthusiastic about your product—is probably giving you the hard sell. Licensing is difficult and never a certainty, no matter how brilliant your idea.
2. *Treat this relationship like you would treat any other serious business relationship.* Insist on a written proposal. Read and ask questions about the fine print, and check the company's credentials. Be sure you understand what they are committing to (and not committing to) as well as what is expected of you.
3. *Get references.* If a company has a good track record and reputation, ask to speak to at least two other clients with whom they've worked. Then actually speak to those clients. If a company is in the business of bilking inventors, they can easily concoct fake references. Therefore, it is important to cross-check the validity of these clients. To do so, ask some questions about their success that you can then verify, such as: What is your patent number? When was it issued? What manufacturer licensed your product? Where is your product sold?
4. *Be very suspicious of pay-upfront deals.* For a legitimate operation, a modest upfront payment may be reasonable, if it's clear what the money will be used for and the prices seem inline. An example of this would be $100 to $500 for the creation and duplication of a marketing packet, with which you should be provided copies. However, a legitimate company should be

compensated mainly on its performance and results—usually in the form of a percentage of future revenues referred to as royalties. Beware! Even if they don't charge a lot out of the gate, more upfront fees may be coming. These companies have been known to charge a small fee upfront for a "feasibility study," and then come back with "Great News! Your product can make it big" (this is the hook). They'll then ask you for another payment, ranging from $3,000 to $15,000, which they claim will go toward costs like market research, a preliminary patent search, or identifying licensing partners. I have heard from a number of inventors that once they've paid this money, they never hear from the product submission company again.

5. *Check the United States Federal Trade Commission (FTC) government Website.* I recommend that you review the document entitled, "Spotting Sweet-Sounding Promises of Fraudulent Invention Promotion Firms," available at www.ftc.gov/bcp/conline/pubs/alerts/invnalrt.htm. It illustrates typical claims or promises that invention submission companies make to draw you in, and offers specific responses you can use to address these claims. In addition, the United States Patent and Trademark Office offers a list of companies with complaints made against them. To view the list, visit www.uspto.gov/web/offices/com/iip/complaints.htm.

6. *Refer to the American Inventors Protection Act of 1999.* This law dictates that a firm must present certain provisions to you prior to contracting. These provisions include the number of inventions the firm has evaluated, the number of customers the firm has worked with, the number of customers who have made money, and the names and phone numbers of other invention companies with whom the principals of the firm have been previously affiliated. For a full copy of the act, visit http://www.uspto.gov/web/offices/com/speeches/s1948gb1.pdf.

7. *If you make an agreement, be sure it contains clear time lines.* These time lines should state when the company should achieve certain benchmarks and when they should communicate progress to you. It should also contain a clause that permits you to terminate the agreement if you are dissatisfied, without releasing any of the rights to your invention.

8. *Register complaints with the United States Department of Commerce.* If you have had a bad experience or have been cheated by one of these companies, provide your name and contact information, where you heard of the company, the service they offered, and a thorough explanation of your complaint. Sign it, date it, and submit the letter to: U.S. Patent and Trademark Office, Mail Stop 24, Commissioner for Patents, PO Box 1450, Alexandria, VA 22313-1450. Or fax it to: 703-306-5570. You can also download a complaint form and log it in at the United States Inventors Association Website at www.uspto.gov/web/forms/2048.pdf.

A Few Words about Financing

I've found that as mom inventors begin the process, most of them fall into two categories: They either give very little thought to financing the business, or they're overwhelmed by the prospect and believe they can't move forward. The reasons for this, ironically, are exactly the same for each: They have no idea what expenses (and income) to expect; they're unsure if they can take their concept to a marketable product; and they have psychological barriers to defining their work as a "business."

To the extent that you can do so without it becoming an obstacle, I encourage you to plan. For example, I recently spoke with a mom inventor who was in a difficult position, due largely to the fact that she didn't think through financing early enough. In her case, she had designed a great product and filed a (soon-to-expire) provisional patent. Unfortunately, she had reached a point where taking her product to the next step would require significant resources, which she didn't have, and licensing wasn't a good option for her. If she had thought through the financing scenario sooner, she might have held off on her early investment, taken a different approach, or pursued a different invention idea.

For each step of the inventing process, which is outlined chapter by chapter in this book, you'll find a sidebar titled "What Will It Cost?" that can help clarify what costs you'll likely encounter. In the meantime, here is a quick overview of what you'll need during the first phase of your inventing process (Chapters 1–5), which involves research, preparation, and protection. [The second phase involves production and sales (Chapters 6–9).] In this first phase, you can do much of the work for little money, and much of it can be paid for through your own "sweat equity." Some expenses you may incur in this stage include:

- A computer and an Internet Service Provider to connect you to the Internet.
- Market research. This book will teach you how to do much of this yourself, but you can also invest substantial money with a professional research firm.
- Preliminary patent search. This book will provide resources so you can do it yourself. You can also hire a professional for approximately $250 to $800.
- Prototype development. Again, depending on your product and whether you have the resources and inclination, you can do it yourself. For professional prototypes, the price will vary, depending on materials and complexity of design, and can run you from a few hundred to thousands of dollars.
- Market testing. You can run your own informal focus groups, or you can expect to spend $3,000 to $5,000 on professional focus groups.
- Patent. A provisional patent comes with a $100 filing fee at the U.S. Patent and Trademark Office. Beyond that, you can draft and file for a patent yourself, which can be complicated, or spend approximately $2,500 plus for a patent agent to $10,000 plus for a patent attorney. Patent costs are largely driven by the level of complexity (e.g., patenting a new drug is more costly than a TP Saver).

Don't let the finances overwhelm you. These steps are typically taken over time. In this first phase, most inventors pay as they go and don't require a firmly written plan. And if you've done strong groundwork before the patent stage, you may even be able to attract investors when you begin to face the higher-ticket items. Once you've gone through the patent stage, you'll reach a fork in the road—you can decide to go into business for yourself, which will require a clear financial plan and more significant resources, or you can decide to license your product, which requires fewer resources from your end. We will discuss launching your own business in Chapter 7 and the ins and outs of licensing in Chapter 10.

Once you've taken your first steps and your idea begins taking shape, you'll be ready for the next stage—conducting a market search and preliminary patent search. These topics are covered in the next chapter.

Knowledge Is a Mom's Best Friend

Your next step after formulating your idea is research, research, research. A thorough, defined approach to research is critical because it can save you a lot of money in the long run by preventing you from investing in an idea that's already on the market or on its way to market. Your research may take some time, and the strategies in this chapter are designed to help you make the most efficient use of your valuable research hours.

There are two stages to your research: a market search and a preliminary patent search. The first step, a market search, will help determine if your product—or similar products—are already being sold in retail stores, catalogs, or on the Internet. Fortunately, today's market search is easier than ever, especially for busy moms, because you can complete most of it online. You'll still need to go to a few retailers for a more in-depth search, but the lion's share of your work can be done from home.

The second part of your research, the preliminary patent search, will help you determine if someone else has already made an intellectual claim to the idea or invention (in legal terminology this claim is referred to as *prior art*). This step is important because even if you don't find your idea being sold in stores, it's possible that a similar patent or copyright already exists but hasn't yet been taken to market. For some, the preliminary patent search can be a bit overwhelming, which is why I outline this task in easy-to-follow detail. Much of this research can also be done on the Internet, a convenient option for moms with unpredictable and busy schedules!

The Importance of Research

Moms frequently submit their ideas to my company, Mom Inventors, Inc., in the interest of having us license, develop, and manufacture their products and pay them royalties for sales. Often they claim that their ideas are both new and revolutionary. However, after a quick search on the Internet, I frequently locate their exact products already being sold on the market. On a positive note, they were right about one thing—it was a good enough idea for someone to take to market.

However, when you're presenting an idea to a manufacturer, it's the wrong time to make this discovery. If you want to be taken seriously, it is imperative that you devote the time and effort to find out this crucial information before taking any further steps. And even more important than saving face, good research can help you save money. After all, you don't want to sink time and dollars into developing a prototype, business plan, etc., only to discover later that your product already exists.

Now that you have acknowledged that you are an inventor, you need to take yourself and your product seriously. You are a businessperson, and your invention is a "product in development" (consumers buy products, *not* inventions). As such, you need to make many business decisions, all of which require information. The key decisions you will need to make after your research are whether to (1) abandon the product altogether, (2) modify the product, or (3) proceed with the product as planned.

Extra work at this stage can save thousands of dollars, years of work, and untold frustration. By the end of your market search and preliminary patent search, you should be able to answer the following questions:

- Does the same product already exist? If so, what is it?
- What products are similar, but not exactly the same? (List their specific features.)
- How does your product differ? (List your product's specific features.)

- Which retailers sell these similar products? (List names and contact information, i.e., telephone numbers and addresses.)
- Which manufacturers produce them? (List names and contact information.)
- How are these similar items priced? (List products and price points—e.g., toilet lid lock $6.99 at independent baby stores and e-retailers and $4.99 at national chain stores)
- Based on this information, is there still room for your product? (Write your conclusions or thoughts.)

Make sure to note all this information in your notebook. You will refer back to these details many times throughout the process. Even if all this information doesn't seem fully relevant now, the need for it will become clear as you proceed.

Stage One—Market Research

Your market search comes before your preliminary patent search for good reason. If you discover your product is already on the market, a more complicated patent search may be unnecessary.

A market search is a simple concept to grasp—you're simply researching to determine if there are products on the market the same or similar to your idea. Your everyday shopping skills will be put to good use now. And your first step is to get on a computer with Internet access. If you don't have one yourself, go to an Internet Café or your local library for free access.

Useful Tool

If you have some money to invest, a laptop with wireless connection and battery pack can provide you with an advantage (find out exactly what you need at your local computer retailer). With a laptop, you can work anywhere in the house or in the yard without cables or the need to plug into an electrical outlet. This way, you can steal a few minutes at a time to move your project forward gradually —when the kids are playing outside, or when you're waiting to pick them up. Busy moms generally need to utilize any free time they have!

If you're an Internet novice, note that you will need to pay for an Internet connection service like AOL or a cable service provider for access. From there, you will need to use a browser like Internet Explorer or Netscape to log in, and a search engine to complete your quest for information. Search engines are tools that can help you find out just about anything in the world. There are many free search engines available; here are some of my favorites: Google (www.google.com), Yahoo (www.yahoo.com), MSN (www.msn.com), and Ask Jeeves (www.askjeeves.com). These search engines are all effective and user-friendly. Test out each of these or other search engines to see which one appeals to you the most. To find other search engines, including International specific engines, visit www.searchengines.com.

Your next step is to think about *key words*. These are descriptive words that will help unearth the information you're looking for, to determine ultimately if a product like yours exists.

- Try using specific and obvious terms first, as if you were looking up a topic in an encyclopedia. If you're looking for information on basset hounds, for instance, enter "basset hounds" rather than "dogs."
- Use words you'd expect to see on the site you're looking for. "Italian Restaurant Cleveland" will give you better results, for example, than "places to eat in Cleveland."
- According to Google.com guidelines, the order in which the terms are typed will affect the search results. The first word you type will carry the most importance. You can string items together without having to use the word *and*. Google will bring up pages that include each of the words you type. If you are interested in searching by phrase rather than a single word, put quotations marks around it to tell Google that you want the entire phrase to be found. Quotes can be useful because without them, your search will bring up every instance of every word in your list (e.g., keying in Jenny Adams brings up Web pages that contain the words *Jenny* and *Adams* in any order. Jenny may appear in the first paragraph, and Adams may appear in the tenth paragraph. However, when you put quotes around Jenny Adams, both words must appear together, and in that order.

You may be asking, Yes, but what words do *I* need to look for, for my particular idea? This is definitely a trial-and-error process; you may not know exactly, right off the bat. Be patient. Use descriptive words that ex-

Web Images Groups News Froogle Local

Web   Images   Groups   News   Froogle   Local **New!**   **more »**

toilet paper

Google Search

Advanced Search
Preferences
Language Tools

Advertising Programs - Business Solutions - About Google

©2005 Google - Seaching 8,058,044,651 web pages

The Google homepage search window is a great starting point to perform your market search.

plain what you are trying to find. Often the first word you use may not bring up the information you are looking for. However, another similar word may open up many avenues of information. To help you with word and phrasing alternatives, use a thesaurus. The one that I use religiously is *The Synonym Finder*, published by Rodale. This book will provide numerous alternatives with similar meanings for the key words that you are using. Another resource is www.synonym.com. Type in your key word and it will bring up a variety of similar words to choose from. Although the online resource is quick, convenient, and free, it is still limited. I find that the actual book provides many more choices.

The search conducted by Jennifer Fleece of Fleece Baby provides a great example of this trial-and-error research process. When Jennifer first began searching, she typed "crib sheets" into the Google search box. It brought up a variety of general retailers that sell sheets for the crib. Jennifer then refined her search further by typing "fleece crib sheets" to determine if there were competitive products. When she found that there were, indeed, a few competitors, she refined her search further to include her product's defining feature—safety pockets. She typed "fleece crib sheets safety pockets." Nothing came up. This was one of Jennifer's aha moments. She discovered that her product was unique. Today, five years

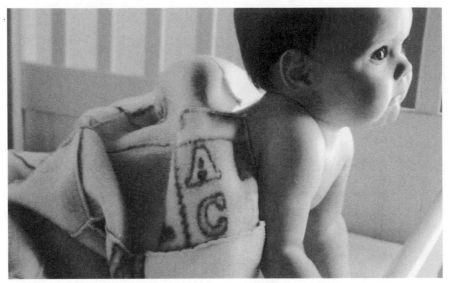

Jennifer Fleece invented her product, Fleece Sheets, to create a softer, more snuggly alternative to crib sheets for her own baby. They're now widely available online and in stores nationwide.

later, you can type in "fleece crib sheets safety pockets" and find numerous listings, all pointing to Jennifer's Fleece Baby Sheets.

Inspired Inventors

Jennifer Hughes, inventor of the Stylease children's clothing line, said, "I was tired of the jammie romper look and wanted a more sophisticated look for my baby—but I didn't want to deal with the hassle of separates." She wondered why somebody hadn't made a one-piece outfit that *looked* like separates. "Since it was the second time in three years that I had said it, it occurred to *me* that it was me that was supposed to do it. That moment of realization was an epiphany for me."

A Way with Words

Throughout the inventing process, you will conduct many more online searches to retrieve the information necessary to support the development

One-piece Stylease clothing, invented by Jennifer Hughes, looks like a stylish two-piece ensemble but offers the convenience of a single piece. Hughes is an ex-private investigator turned mom entrepreneur who was tired of dressing her kids in cookie-cutter romper styles, which is what inspired her to create Stylease.

and growth of your business. Jennifer Hughes, inventor of Stylease, considered herself an experienced Internet researcher (due to her prior career as a private investigator) before she embarked on her own project. However, she found that even she needed extra patience and stamina to find the information she needed online. When she began searching for a manufacturer to produce her product, she typed in a key word that she believed made the most sense.

"I typed in the phrase *garment manufacturer*. I hit wall after wall, not coming up with much," said Hughes. "Then, I substituted the word *apparel* for *garment*. The floodgates opened and I had dozens of manufacturers all over the world to choose from." The lesson: Make sure you try as many possible words for potential products before you reach any conclusion about what is currently on the market.

Once you have completed your initial Internet searches, I recommend that you start brainstorming to determine specific online sites that might sell your product. If you're not sure, ask your friends which online stores they purchase products from. For example, when I was searching online stores and catalogs to find a gadget like the TP Saver, I visited www.onestepahead.com, www.babiesrus.com, www.babyuniverse.com, www.babycenter.com, www.bedbathandbeyond.com, and www.longs.com—stores that focus on baby products, as well as stores with home sections or pharmacies that carry baby-oriented items. These stores are another great resource for determining what is currently available to the buying public. I discovered that each of these online stores sells safety bathroom gadgets but that none offered a product similar to mine (big relief!). I concluded that my product would likely fill a void in their product offerings. I noted how these similar products were priced, which gave me some early insight into how I could price my own product. I made sure to write down all the relevant information that I had found.

Exhausting Your Options

Although you'll never know for sure if there is something that you are not finding, once you've exhausted every combination of key words you can think of—in multiple search engines—you've gone as far as you can on the Internet. That's when it's time to head to the stores to search for the product.

Shop 'til You Drop

Based on my own online search, I began to feel more confident about moving forward. However, I also knew that online stores often carry different items from traditional retail stores. It was time to grab my notebook and baby, put on my detective cap, and baby, and head out for an adventure. This is a step I recommend that you take too, in order to ensure you've exhausted all the retail possibilities before moving forward.

What Will It Cost?

The beauty of market research is that it doesn't have to cost a thing—except for your own time. And by doing your research when you might shop online or in stores anyway, you can tag it onto your other daily errands.

Be sure to take your notebook when you do your in-store research, as you'll be jotting down lots of information. Each outing should be to a different type of store. One day you should visit a big-box store like Target or Wal-Mart, another day a grocery or drug store, and then another day smaller independent or specialty retail stores. Choose the specific stores based on where you believe your product would be sold.

If time is of the essence (as it is for most moms!), keep in mind that this detective work can coincide with your own regular shopping needs—a separate trip is not necessary. Once you are in the store, identify the area within the store that would most likely sell your product if it were available today. To research my own invention, I focused on the safety gadgets and bathroom sections of the stores. While in the store, I was able to peruse the current stock carefully, looking closely at similar items. I looked at toilet lid locks, cabinet latches, and door handle locks. I observed the plastic material these items were made of so that I could later discuss this with my engineer. I looked at the packaging, noting what I liked and didn't like (the brand, colors used, whether they used clam shells, blister packs, or shrink wrap). I read the warning labels, wrote down the prices for these items, and finally wrote down the names of the manufacturers.

You should write down similar information about products related to your own invention. Write down these products' names and prices, reading their features carefully and jotting them down. (If you've got the kids in tow, you can also write down the product's Web address, if available, to study from home another time.) It's valuable to understand the features of existing competitive products in order to either create significant improvements in your product or to enable you to articulate more clearly how your product is different and better. This in-store research will help you understand how your idea fits into the marketplace and also how similar items are priced.

By searching online and in stores for competing items, you'll not only determine if there's anything like your product on the market, you'll also get a feel for your product category in general. Once you've exhausted your market research, you'll be ready to take it a step further by performing a preliminary patent search. This search will help fill in any gaps in your research to date.

Knowing When to Fold 'Em

While I was fortunate that my product did not exist and that I had no competition, you may not have this experience. If you discover that there are similar products out there, and that the market is well-served, it may make sense for you to put your feelings aside and move on to your next idea. As I mentioned earlier in the introduction, inventing is a mindset. Once you start observing your surroundings in a problem–and-solution manner, the inventive ideas never cease. Many people worry that if they let go of their one idea they will not think of another. But if your search reveals that your product idea already exists, you must critically analyze the opportunity or whether it's realistic to continue.

I think it's important to share that the TP Saver was my third idea, not my first! I had to let go of my first invention idea when, during my rudimentary market search, I identified a company that was already well down the road in developing this product. I felt relieved to let it go because it was too technically complex and costly for my first invention. My second idea could have made me a bundle, however; it was a car seat accessory with a plethora of regulatory hurdles, such as car crash testing, and increased liability issues. Again, I let it go. I understand that this can be disappointing.

If your product is currently on the market, then you're already thinking smart. It just so happens that someone else acted first. However, that doesn't mean they created the best product. Think about ways you can improve upon and differentiate your product. The better news is that you are an inventor—and that even if your first idea isn't the best, you're sure to have other great ideas. Keep on!

What Is a Preliminary Patent Search?

You've gone through your market search online and in stores. And you're fairly confident there's nothing like your product already on store shelves. Now it's time to perform a preliminary patent search. This search will determine whether there is already a patent in existence that matches your idea. This step is critical, because you don't want to develop a product that matches an already filed patent in the United States Patent and Trademark Office (USPTO). Doing so would risk infringing on someone else's intellectual property, and it could provide a major legal roadblock if you tried launching your own idea in the marketplace.

During your preliminary patent search, there's a good chance that you'll find a similar patent. But remember, even if there's a similar idea already filed, it is by no means the end of the process. With enough to differentiate your product, you may still be able to develop your idea and bring it to market.

At this point, our goal is to research patents, not file your own. Filing patents is covered in Chapter 5, and typically involves the help of a patent attorney. For now, we'll simply be looking for prior art to determine what already exists in relation to your own idea. This step provides value in two ways: First, you'll determine if anyone already has a legal claim to your idea; second, it will introduce you to the specialized world of U.S. patents—how they're worded and what information they include. This exposure will be valuable as you continue the inventing process. Actually, it's part of the fun.

So what is this prior art, anyway? According to the USPTO, "Prior art is any body of knowledge that relates to your invention including previous patents." There are a few ways you can look for prior art. The first is to go to an official Patent and Trademark Depository Library (PTDL). These libraries are specially designated by the USPTO to both receive patent information from inventors and actively disseminate patent and trademark information to the public. The library offers free online access to USPTO's online collections. You can locate a PTDL in your area by visiting http://www.uspto.gov/go/ptdl. They're listed by state.

Fortunately, busy moms can eliminate this extra trip by doing nearly the same research from home online, at www.uspto.gov. Though you'll only be able to access the last 30 years of patents with this method—those since 1975—you're still likely to find most of the answers you need, at least at this stage. Patents from 1790 through 1975 are searchable only by patent number and current U.S. classification.

As you did in your market search, you will need to use key words in the search box on the USTPO Website.

The 411 on Patents

Patents do expire. The expiration depends on the filing date:

- If the application was filed before November 1999, the patent will expire 17 years from the date that it issued.
- If the patent application was filed after November 1999, the patent will expire 20 years from the date of filing.
- Maintenance fees are due on patents once issued; if you don't pay them, your patent will become abandoned (unenforceable).
- Maintenance fees are paid three times during the life of the patent: at 3.5 years, 7.5 years, and 11.5 years.

(All dates are based on the date the patent is granted.)

The Importance of a Preliminary Patent Search

Even though your idea is not sitting on the Wal-Mart shelves—yet, someone else may have patented the idea without fully developing it. It's important to know this information, so you don't unintentionally violate or infringe on already existing patents. This search will also identify potential issues and opportunities that may arise.

Just as you did in your market search, you may find a product that is similar but not exactly the same. This search will help you determine how your product is unique, and if these differences will deem your product patentable. At this point a patent attorney, who understands the nuances of patent language, can help you determine if your idea is different enough to be considered a newly patented idea.

It can be discouraging to find your idea already filed. However, all is not necessarily lost if you do. Your discovery may afford you a new opportunity. All patents list the contact information of the person who obtained the patent. If that person hasn't further developed their product to bring it to market, you may consider approaching him or her to partner in some way. It's possible that the patent holder would accept money to transfer the patent to you or that you might partner in some other capacity (discussed in Chapter 5). I recommend seeking legal counsel first if you plan to pursue this option. If you do form a partnership, the advantage would be bypassing the entire patent process, a complex endeavor which is covered in Chapter 5.

The Nitty-Gritty on Your Preliminary Patent Search

Before you begin your search, a word of caution: Attorneys with engineering backgrounds write patents. Their legalese usually doesn't make for light reading. Here's one tip to help expedite the process: As you start finding related patents, skip ahead to the diagrams and drawings first, to determine if the invention is remotely similar. Once you study the illustrations, the verbiage is usually more understandable.

Here's a step-by-step guide to help you in your research:

1. Go to www.uspto.gov. On the homepage, click on Patent Search on the left-hand side of the screen. At this point I recommend downloading the free TIFF Image Viewer and Plug-ins by clicking on "How to Access and View Full-Page Images," a link you'll find halfway down this page. This will take you to a page that will walk you through downloading this free software. Click on the option that is appropriate for your computer system and type of computer (based on whether you have an Apple or a PC).

    If you have a PC, you have two software options for downloading: AlternaTIFF and InterneTIFF. If you choose to download AlternaTIFF, click on the upper-right-hand box and choose the option for your particular browser. If you're downloading InterneTIFF, go to the upper-left-hand box and click on "Free." You'll then be led through the appropriate steps. Without this software, you won't be able to view images of the patent drawings. After downloading the software, hit the back button on the top of your page to get back to the search window or just click on "home" to get back to where you started.

2. Under the Patent Button, click on "Advanced Search." It will show you a blank box that says "Query." Type in your key words. For example, when looking for the TP Saver, I typed in the words *toilet paper* in quotes. Note that with the United States patent and trademark Website searches, it is important to make correct use of quotation marks and helpful search terms. See the sidebar for more details. You are also able to select the years that you are interested in viewing. For me, these key words brought up 50 patents to

review. When doing your own patent research, don't stop with the first search. Keep trying as many key words as you can imagine to describe your product, in order to leave no stone unturned!

The Best Use of Search Terms

When using the Advanced Search Page, use the following guidelines for the most effective searching. You can use the terms OR, AND, & ANDNOT to help find what you're looking for. In addition, you can use parentheses to further clarify your search statement. In the absence of parentheses, all operators associate from left to right. (Note that these guidelines are taken verbatim from the USPTO site.)

Example 1

tennis AND (racquet OR racket)

If you enter this query, you will retrieve a list of all patents which contain both the terms tennis and either racket or racquet somewhere in the document.

Example 2

television OR (cathode AND tube)

This query would return patents containing either the word television OR both the words cathode AND tube.

Example 3

needle ANDNOT [(record AND player) OR sewing]

This complex query generates a list of hits that contain the word needle, but does not contain any references to sewing. In addition, none of the hits would contain the combination of record AND player.

3. Once you find patents that are similar to your idea, print them out and review them as well as you can. I know that legalese is no one's preferred bedtime reading. My own TP Saver patent is no exception; here's one excerpt written by my patent attorney: "While

in the foregoing, embodiments of the present invention have been set forth in considerable detail for the purposes of making a complete disclosure of the invention, it may be apparent to those of skill in the art that numerous changes may be made in such detail without departing from the spirit and principles of the invention." This description makes even *me* seriously scratch my head, and I'm the inventor!

Nonetheless, reviewing these patents is important. When doing your own research try to get as much information as you can from the patents you find. Not only will you become better educated about what's out there, but you will save money down the road when you retain a patent attorney. When you present this attorney with the prior art you've found, he or she will better understand what you are describing, and you'll have already done some of the ($250–$350 per hour) legwork!

Is Outsourcing an Option?

It's probably not financially feasible to hire an attorney to do your preliminary patent search. To do a proper search, you'd end up paying an attorney almost the same amount that you would to file the actual patent (a step that comes later and is discussed in Chapter 5). That means you'd have to nearly double your investment—a pricy step at this preliminary stage!

Chapter Wrap-Up

In the early stages of launching a business, particularly an inventing business, it is critical to minimize risk and maximize your opportunities. Knowledge is the key to this. The more you can learn now about similar products on the market and already filed patents, the better equipped you are to make good decisions. Whether you decide to move full steam ahead, to make adjustments and proceed, or to switch to your next invention, good research is time and effort well spent.

If you do decide to move forward, it's time to pull out your hammer, tape measure, and glue gun, and turn this idea into something tangible.

Building your prototype is the next step, which is covered in full in Chapter 3.

Warning: About this time family, friends, or neighbors will begin to gather around your assembled tools. They'll likely ask, "Whatch'a doing?", "No kidding?", or "Have you lost your mind?" Most people are honestly intrigued by creativity of any sort, but if they are less than encouraging you might respond by saying, "Those who dance are often thought insane by those who can't hear the music." (Anon.)

From Your Mind's Eye
to the Palm of Your Hand

Creating Your Prototype

Unless you are a true Renaissance woman—functioning as equal parts attorney, engineer, manufacturer, and marketer (and mom!)—you will need help in communicating your vision to other people. Your invention team, which will consist of everyone who'll help you on your way to market, will make valuable—and often expensive—contributions to your product. The more clearly your team understands your design vision and objectives, the better off you'll be.

At this stage, a prototype is the best way to communicate your unique invention. But what exactly *is* a prototype? And what will it accomplish? In a nutshell, a prototype is simply a three-dimensional version of your vision. It's typically a working model of your product, and it can be as simple as a silicon sticker or as complicated as a refined mechanical device, depending on your idea. This chapter will discuss the ins and outs of building a prototype of your own.

Seeing Is Believing

The advantage of having a full-scale prototype is that it will enable you to avoid potential confusion when communicating your idea. A prototype will also encourage others to take you more seriously. When you arrive with a prototype in hand to meet with any professional, from your own attorney to a potential licensing company, you separate yourself from the dozens of others who've approached them with only vague ideas in mind. Instead, you'll be viewed as a professional with a purpose, as opposed to *just* a mom with a potentially good idea.

Later, when you approach your test market and, after that, potential buyers, a prototype will also prove invaluable. And if your goal is to license your idea rather than manufacture it yourself, presenting an actual prototype can help better articulate your idea's value. Though a drawing may be sufficient to sell an idea to a potential licensor, demonstrating that you have already worked through the design challenges and received valuable consumer feedback will further strengthen your case and help support your sales process.

Form and Function

Your idea works perfectly in theory. It's not until you start physically creating it that you'll encounter flaws in your thinking. That's why another great reason to develop a prototype is to test the functionality of your idea. You'll never know the design issues and challenges until you begin actually taking your idea from theory to reality.

In developing my own invention, for instance, I had to refine my design as much as possible prior to mass production. It was critical to observe the baby-proofing effectiveness of my prototype and have it evaluated for safety. Plus, it needed to be a preproduction prototype (see next section), which is the last opportunity to tweak a product and make final changes before mass production in a factory. In addition, many retail stores wanted to see the final, finished product before committing to ordering.

Your prototype will also allow you to explore an array of materials, which can range from a simple few to a complex assortment for any individual product. Basic considerations for these materials include cost, availability, durability, and safety. My first TP Saver prototype, for example, had a rubber strap. But testing revealed that a rubber strap could easily break, which led me to go with elastic for future designs.

Similarly, Beth Berse, inventor of Table Topper (www.tabletopper.com), a disposable placemat for use in restaurants, worked hard to find the "right" adhesive for her prototype. She was tired of going to restaurants where her toddler would toss aside the commonly used paper placemats, and often had no choice but to see him eat off the germ-covered table or high chair. Having spent time as a waitress earlier in her life, Beth knew that restaurants used dirty rags to wipe off tables. Therefore, she decided to create a plastic placemat that would adhere to the table, but which would be easily removable without leaving behind any residue.

As she developed her prototype, she searched high and low for an effective adhesive. Her aha moment came when she theorized that the adhesive used on Kotex feminine napkins might just work. And after testing this material, she found it worked perfectly! Shortly thereafter, she went into production, and now her product is found at Babies R Us, Target, Toys R Us as well as hundreds of independent stores nationwide.

Beth Berse, a former waitress driven by the knowledge that restaurant tables are often "cleaned" using dirty rags, invented the Table Topper when she had her own kids. Table Topper, a disposable placemat that parents can bring to restaurants to protect their kids from germs, can be found at Target and Babies-R-Us.

Just Your Type

Though there are a full range of prototype formats, from photography to functioning units, I will focus on the two that will likely meet your needs: the presentation prototype and the preproduction prototype.

If you plan on licensing your idea, rather than manufacturing it yourself (more on making this decision in Chapter 10), the presentation prototype is adequate for showing your idea to prospective licensors. But if you plan to manufacture the product yourself, you'll need a preproduction prototype.

The presentation prototype is typically less complex than the preproduction prototype. At times, digital drawings or even hand drawings of good quality will suffice when presenting an idea to a potential licensor. However, it's never a bad idea to create a three-dimensional prototype, to better communicate your idea to all parties involved. While it should look and feel close to your vision, it doesn't necessarily have to include all functioning parts or be at the more sophisticated level of the prototype you need when you are planning to mass-produce the product yourself.

The preproduction prototype, on the other hand, must be a functional version of your final product. All moving pieces and parts (if applicable to your invention) must work, and it must be in near-final phase of development. This is the kind of prototype I used when developing the TP Saver. We'll talk more about developing each kind of prototype later in this chapter.

Haste Makes Waste

If you feel tempted to skip creating a prototype, reconsider. Sure, you might be in a huge rush to get to market, but moving too fast risks compromising your design. Take the time and do your homework, learning as much as you can at this stage and developing a prototype that performs well and looks good. You'll inevitably encounter some bumps in the road, but it's better than losing out completely by taking unnecessary or foolhardy shortcuts.

The Importance of Creating Your Prototype

1. A prototype enables you to test and refine the functionality of your design.

2. A prototype makes it possible to test the performance of various materials.
3. A prototype will help you to eventually describe your product more effectively with your team, including your attorney, packaging or marketing expert, engineers, and potential business partners.
4. A prototype can help communicate your idea's value to licensing prospects, potential investors, prospective consumers, and wholesale buyers.

Developing Your Prototype

So now that you know that creating a prototype is a vital step in your invention process, how exactly do you move forward and actually do it? This stage in the inventing process is possibly the period of greatest learning...and is also my personal favorite. I love the creative exploration that prototyping inspires! This is where your words and thoughts change from, "Can I?" to "How will I?"

Of course, every prototype demands different materials and types of designers, and varies according to your product. Your product may incorporate a range of items such as plastics, textiles, metals, chemicals, electronics, software, and so on. Entire books could be written on developing each of these materials, so my intention here is to introduce basic concepts using the more common elements.

The information presented here can be adapted to fit your individual situation because no matter what your design or materials, there is a universal truth to developing every prototype: trial and error. In the beginning, you probably won't know the ideal combination of design elements or materials. Plus, while going through the process, you may get a sudden burst of new ideas or concerns about your product's functionality. Be receptive to your results and open to change. This is one of the most creative parts of the process, and it is important to let your thoughts unfold freely.

Bob Coker, President of Protosew, a prototype sewing sample manufacturer, tells inventors, "You may think that the design you have in your mind or on paper or even in the form of a working sample is the best possible design for your product. We frequently find that although the unit works and looks nice, the construction is contrary to standard manufacturing protocol and is extremely difficult and sometimes actually impossible to produce. When something is difficult to produce, it of course eats up your labor to produce it, and may be the difference between a very profitable product and complete loser."

Darryl Lenz had her own stop-and-go experience when developing her initial prototype at home. A former flight attendant and inventor of the Ride-On Carry-On (www.rideoncarryon.com), a folding chair that at-

The Ride-On Carry-On was invented by former flight attendant Darryl Lenz to ease stress for traveling families. This attachment for luggage eliminates the need to haul an extra stroller through the airport while traveling.

taches to your suitcase and seats a child up to 40 lb, she confides about developing her prototype:

"It was completely trial and error. We started with children's folding beach chairs. We bought every one we could find until we found one that was the perfect size. Randy, my husband, is quite handy, so he took one apart and reworked it. We talked our design to death and talked to friends. Everyone had their own ideas, and we tried many that didn't work and some that did. As we fine-tuned, we tested each design with our son. When we liked the chair design we had to figure out how to attach it to the luggage."

Darryl said that her husband thought it should be built into the luggage. She felt, though, that luggage is too expensive to expect people to buy a whole new piece, and thought it should be an attachment. Driving home one day she realized that tying the chair to the luggage might just be the solution.

"We tried it and it worked like a champ, and my son loved the ride so much we couldn't get him out of the chair. That was an exciting moment!"

Your prototype is an evolving tool. While your first prototype will most likely be rudimentary, it will become more complex and defined as you develop your idea. So how should you create your prototype? Should you do it with materials at home or hire a professional from the outset? While it may seem easier to hire a professional, developing your own prototype can be a cost-efficient first step that can help to better articulate your vision to a professional. If you can put something together at home first, I recommend you do so.

Getting Crafty

Making a prototype by hand is a great way to start bringing your product to life. Remember, there are no rules! Give yourself permission to experiment. Look around the house and select materials that you can use to test to see if your idea works. If you need a wire coil, pull it out of a spiral notebook. If you need durable yet flexible plastic, cut a piece out of your 2-liter soda bottle. Use modeling clay or your children's modeling compound to make an initial form. There are no boundaries as to what you can find and use. Susan Dunk, inventor of the Toddler Coddler, is a prime example. When developing her comfort travel system for a child's car seat that "stops the slump" by providing toddlers with head, neck, and lateral sup-

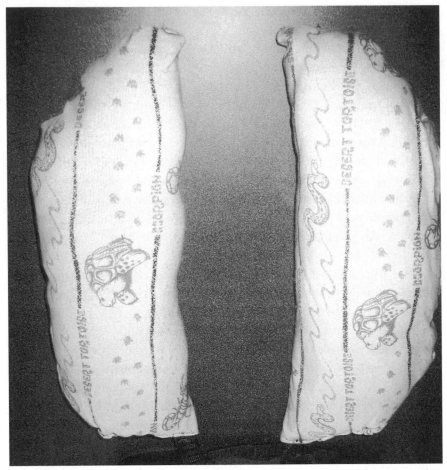

To create her first prototype and test its effectiveness, Susan Dunk glued together the first Toddler Coddler with her own materials.

port, she used whatever she could find to demonstrate her idea. She could not sew so she took two pairs of socks, stuffed them and glued them together. It was not pretty! But it worked well enough as a first step, leading her to eventually produce a better prototype and, later, her finished product, which is now sold nationally. She has also become a spokeswoman for mom-invented products on ABC's *The View* with Barbara Walters.

After exhausting available supplies in your home, the next step is to go shopping! Look for materials in places that you've never considered such as craft, hardware, plumbing, or kitchen supply stores, computer stores, or toy stores. When developing the TP Saver, I was inspired by a hair-permanent rod in a beauty supply store, of all places, which led to my final design.

Susan Dunk's product came a long way from her initial prototype. Here she is with her finished Toddler Coddlers.

Fun New Product

Hot off the production line is a brand-new material perfect for making home prototypes. This unique plastic formulation is called ShapeLock, and only recently has it been made available to the U.S. market. When heated in the microwave or with your hair dryer, it becomes pliable, kind of like clay, so you can mold it any way you'd like. When dry, it becomes a hard plastic. The best part? It's only about $14.95 per container and you can reheat it and reuse it again and again. Find it at www.shapelock.com.

Bringing in the Pros

Once you have developed your prototype as far as you reasonably can, it's time to consider hiring a professional to help you with the next steps. There are many avenues you can take at this stage. You may wish to hire professional prototype developers, engineers, and designers, but others may be able to help as well, including a handyman, a machinist, a student from a local industrial design college, or a manufacturer of similar products, for example. The complexity and materials to be used in your specific product will help drive this decision.

If you decide to go with a professional prototype developer, there are a few ways to find them. I found a prototype developer in my Yellow Pages because at the time, I didn't know what other resources were available. Luckily, I found a good partner. But since then, I have learned about a free resource called www.thomasnet.com (formerly known as www.thomas-register.com), a one-stop resource with all the information you need. I wish I had known about this when I was starting out! It offers a database of 650,000 manufacturers, distributors, and service providers (including prototype developers) to choose from, broken down by state. In a matter of minutes you can find what you are looking for. Simply type your key words (such as "plastic prototype") into the search boxes at the top of the screen. You can look for companies throughout the United States and Canada, or refine your search by state. Immediately, you'll be presented with a list of companies that can provide preproduction prototypes, with descriptions about their specific capabilities. Whether your product is made out of metal, wood, plastic, or wire, www.thomasnet.com has suppliers in all of these arenas, and more.

Machinist versus Engineer

A machinist is a specialized tradesman who can create a prototype. He is often skilled in using a variety of plastics and metals and can hand-tool a prototype for you at a fraction of the cost of an engineer. An engineer is a specially trained professional who is skilled in the technical aspects of designing and building. Engineers are typically trained in specific disciplines such as mechanical, chemical, structural, electrical, and industrial design engineering. Although you can go directly to an industrial design engineer to make a prototype for you, a machinist will often quote you an hourly wage for his services. His services can range from $50 to $100 an hour, whereas an engineer may cost you $200 to $300 an hour for similar work.

There are definite pros and cons of both routes. Starting with a less costly machinist enables you to get closer to your preferred design before you have to pay more money to an engineer. However, an engineer can often help come up with new designs or offer design alternatives that can help bring down mass production manufacturing costs. An engineer understands the bigger picture and can produce the necessary computer-aided design (CAD) drawings you will need to move forward. By handling all steps of the process, from preparing the prototype to improving the design of your product, an engineer can help expedite the process of bringing your product to market.

If you do not have access to a computer on a regular basis, the Yellow Pages will suffice as a starting point. Again, consider hiring a nontraditional designer, such as a handyman, if your product warrants it. If you are seeking to license your product, this may be all you need.

The hottest thing on the prototype scene lately is a process called *rapid prototyping*, which uses a technology called *stereolithography*. This process enables inventors to have prototypes made quickly from CAD drawings by a large machine rather than an expensive injection mold. Rapid prototypes cost a few hundred dollars each, but they're a bargain considering the alternatives. When I first looked into the option of prototyping the TP Saver, for instance, I found that a high-quality preproduction prototype would cost $15,000 plus. It included the cost of building an injection mold tool that would enable me to mass produce my product. We were at a point where we weren't quite ready to finalize our design, but we still needed a few high-quality prototypes of our product. I had a machinist hand-tool individual prototypes (hand-made prototypes almost always have imperfections). I wish I had known about rapid prototyping, which is the perfect solution for this in-between stage of development because within a few days—rather than weeks or even months—you can have a finished-looking representation of your product in hand.

To learn about rapid prototyping or to locate companies that provide this service, do a Google search or visit these Websites:

http://www.cc.utah.edu/~asn8200/rapid.html

http://www.rapidprototyping.net/

http://home.att.net/~castleisland/

http://www.aero3dp.com

Keep in Mind...

As you build and refine your model, you should keep a few manufacturing issues in mind:

- *Labor cost.* When you mass-produce, the general rule is that the less "hands-on" labor required, the lower the cost. For example, during mass production of the TP Saver, a person must hand knot the elastic on each end of the product, which drives up the cost of producing it. Good Bites, the Mom Invented Crustless Sandwich Cutter, however, consists of one simple molded piece. Once it is ejected from the injection-molding machine, it travels on a conveyor belt and drops into a box at the end. There is no additional labor required except for the person running the machine. Mass manufacturing is discussed in greater detail in Chapter 6. But for purposes of developing your prototype, you should keep any labor-intensive issues in mind and avoid them if at all possible.
- *Safety requirements.* Be sure to research any regulatory requirements (see next section) relevant to your product early on in the prototype stage. This way you will avoid unnecessary redesigns of your prototype. When I first designed the TP Saver, for instance, I was unaware of the federal choking hazard requirements. I had already completed my prototype when a consumer offered me some feedback, telling me she would be concerned about her child choking on the cap. When I looked into it, I learned that there are federal safety standards that you must adhere to as a product developer. Because I didn't know earlier, I had to pay an engineer to redesign and re-create his CAD drawings. Luckily, I hadn't manufactured any units yet, but it still was a costly mistake, and one I wanted to share so that you can avoid it.

The 411 on Product Safety Regulations

The process for identifying the right steps to ensure compliance with product safety requirements is usually less than obvious for new inventions. In addition, the environment for companies launching new products, particularly those designed for children, is confusing. Certain items, such as pacifiers, electric heaters, and cribs, have predetermined ASTM (American Society for Testing Materials) standards to which a new product can conform. For other products, however, clear direction is elusive or nonexistent, particularly when it's a brand-new product or category.

This forces inventors and manufacturers to rely on their own common sense when designing and testing products. And, in fact, the "system" for overseeing product safety is more often based on punishment (like recalls or lawsuits) than it is on the creation and enforcement of specific and clearly articulated requirements. While inconvenient, this makes sense. Regulators cannot possibly be expected to guess what products will be invented next. But the good news is that you are not completely in the dark.

Please note: This summary by no means purports or claims to provide all the answers. It is the responsibility of each product developer and company to research and determine the level of compliance necessary for each product, and we can bear no responsibility for omissions or errors in this guidance. For additional help, contact an attorney.

Where to Start

The trade association serving your industry is a good place to start seeking guidance on safety regulations. You can easily find the appropriate organization online. For instance, a search for "pet product trade association" turned up the American Pet Product Manufacturers Association on the first try.

Once you find the proper organization, you may find they provide certain standards or guidelines. For example, the Juvenile Products Manufacturers Association (JPMA) provides a certification program for certain regulated items within the industry. Rick Locker, an attorney for the JPMA, sums up the process as a "three-pronged analysis." First, he says to review the federal standards in the Code of Federal Regulations (CFRs) as they pertain to your product. Second, you should review the voluntary standards at ASTM International (www.astm.org). And third, use common sense, because common law is the regulating force here—think lawsuits. These three prongs apply to most any invention, not just those in the juvenile market.

Federal Safety Standards

To begin researching federal safety standards, first visit the Website of the U.S. Consumer Product Safety Commission (CPSC) at www.cpsc.gov. Under the "Business" link, you'll find another link to "Regulations, Laws and Business Information by Product." This is where you can find federal regulations that may be applicable to your product.

While some specific regulations are listed here, most products don't have their own federal regulation. The current director of children's products at the CPSC said that when an inventor has a truly new item—a product without a regulation or standard—she should look into past product recalls to find out which products and product attributes caused problems. To get data on past product-related injuries and consumer product complaints, you can call the CPSC injury information clearing house at 800-638-2772 and 301-504-7923.

Voluntary Standards Organizations and ASTM International

There are approximately 400 voluntary standards organizations in this country. Think of them as organizations that actively support the development of standards. ASTM International is one of the most dominant of these organizations. It provides a forum for development and publishes standards for materials, products, systems, and services. ASTM standards are accepted and used in research and development, product testing, quality systems, and commercial transactions. ASTM is not a government body but a membership organization (membership is $75). Most of the standards offered by ASTM are in categories where there are established suppliers and products; for example, there are 17 ASTM standards in the juvenile industry, covering products such as bath seats, cribs, and infant bedding.

To use ASTM, first visit their Website at www.astm.org. Click on "standards" and search your category using key words. If a standard exists covering your product, you can purchase it for about $30. If your product is not part of an already established category, try to identify the technical committees listed on the Website that come closest to your item. There are 130 such committees. For the TP Saver, for instance, committee 15 on child safety would be the one to contact. The staff person you contact on this committee can then provide insight into standards or regulations for your item or similar items or can refer you to the proper ASTM staffer.

Note that the International Standards Organization (ISO) is an organization that offers guidance with global standards. This is another organization that you may wish to research.

Test Labs

An independent test lab is another valuable resource to tap into for product safety information. Your industry's trade association can probably recommend an appropriate one. If you decide to test your product at a lab prior to launching, be sure to shop around. In the absence of clear ASTM standards, a test lab may propose a wide array of tests, some of which may not be necessary. Be a good shopper and understand clearly what you're getting for the money you're spending.

State Regulations

Federal regulations may or may not supercede relevant state regulations. Some states do have supplemental enforcements on certain federal laws and sometimes state laws are more restrictive than federal laws. It's valuable to know and understand any state regulations that relate to your product. The proper office to contact varies from state to state.

Labeling Requirements

To determine the labeling requirements for your product, you will likely need to follow the same process you followed for the other safety requirements. Follow the guidance of your trade association, CPSC, voluntary standards, and common sense. Some states will have additional regulations. Another organization, the American National Standards Institute (www.ansi.org) is also a resource. For instance, their voluntary standard Z535.4 addresses label formatting issues, such as font size.

The Possibilities of Plastics

So your product is made out of rubber or metal or chemicals. Then why do you need to know about plastic? Well, not only are many products today made from plastic, but many of the tenets of plastic production can be adapted to your own project.

Plus, inventing is a mindset and you will inevitably have more invention ideas as you go through this development process, some of which may involve plastic. I remember when I was pregnant with my first daughter. I read at least five books on how to prepare for the birth of my child. I scoured every page highlighting important facts, intentionally skipping the chapters on Caesarian sections (C-sections). I felt that I didn't need to know anything about C-sections because I was not planning on having one. Of course, life doesn't always go according to plan. As I was wheeled to the operating room for my own surprise C-section, I remember the fear that I felt, because I didn't have a clue about what to expect. I share this personal story with you because you never know when you might need information in your back pocket (or in my case, hospital gown)!

What Is a Computer-Aided Design (CAD)?

When developing your own product, professionals may recommend you develop a computer-aided design (CAD) drawing. CAD is computer software that enables an engineer to produce three-dimensional drawings (illustrations with specifications and measurements) for a manufacturer to follow to mass-produce your product accurately. CAD is used in countless industries including industrial design, architecture, and, of course, consumer product design. Just as a dressmaker follows a pattern when making a dress from scratch, a manufacturer does the same when producing a plastic product.

Because of its durability, relatively low cost, and ease of use, many products on the market are made of plastic. But just as there are differences among metals like copper, silver, and steel, there is a wide variety of plastics—a.k.a. resins—with different chemical properties. Plastics are often selected over other materials because they're long-lasting, lightweight, and can take a beating. They're also often cheaper to produce than metal. Plus, their lighter weight translates into lower handling and transportation costs.

If you believe your product should be made from plastic, you'll need to research the type and grade of plastic that's most appropriate. (This advice applies to any materials you're considering using, metals, rubber, etc.) For example, because it comes into contact with food, the Good Bites Crustless Sandwich Cutter required a "food grade" polycarbonate plastic that meets food safety requirements. In addition, it needed to be dishwasher safe and virtually unbreakable, so as not to chip when in contact with food. On the other hand, the plastic required for the TP Saver was not nearly as stringent. It did not call for the more costly food-grade plastic, and it didn't need to be flexible. I ended up using high impact polystyrene (known as HIPS), which is inexpensive, lightweight, rigid, tough, and fire resistant.

Knowledge about plastic or any material you anticipate using can save you time and money. At my first meeting with an engineer, he expressed how much he appreciated that I had done my homework. I was equally happy about minimizing my hourly fees. We skipped the education and dove right into our discussion on how to improve my design.

Textiles 101

Many mom-invented products are also made from textiles, which is simply another name for cloth or fabric. Like plastics, you can apply this information to your own prototype development.

When using any materials, try to be open to alternatives you may not have originally considered. For example, you may be convinced that you want to use cotton. If this is the case, challenge yourself by asking "why?" Perhaps another material might work, such as a stretch material like Lycra. Or how about using mesh, canvas, nylon, or leather? What about taking a leap and trying Neoprene (wetsuit material)? There are also higher end and exotic fabrics that might really make a splash when hitting the market. This is the time to say, "what if" and allow yourself the freedom to explore. Put aside your original thoughts. You may end up coming back to them, but at least then you'll know you've made the best decision.

When creating a product from textiles, you'll also need to consider possible attachments—"notions," such as buttons, elastic, zippers, fasteners, and appliqués (labels that can be ironed or sewn on). Visit http://www.notionsmart.com and brainstorm different ways that you can enhance your prototype. Keep in mind that anything and everything you add will increase costs in mass production.

Cheryl Wells is a great example of an inventor who kept an open—and creative—mind. She invented a product called Auto Mobiles, a mobile that hangs from the car's ceiling to provide stimulation for babies in their car seats. During the prototype stage she had difficulty finding the right adhesive that could stick to the interior roof of a car without damaging it. Cheryl shares her aha moment: "My life-changing event was the night I re-

Cheryl Wells invented Auto Mobiles to entertain and stimulate her baby on their many errands driving big sister to school and activities. Her product, which hangs from the headliner inside the car, today comes in many variations.

alized that a diaper tab material was the answer I was looking for to make my product work. I had tried many different materials to get the Auto Mobile to adhere to the headliner of my vehicle. I was changing Tatum's diaper one night when the tab of the diaper stuck to what I was wearing. I cut the tab off the diaper and ran out to the car at midnight. I shouted out loud, 'This is it. I have the material that will make it work!'"

Even if you are an outstanding seamstress and you've created a good-looking product with materials that work well, there comes a time when you'll need to hire a professional textile prototype developer. Textile developers will use your initial design to provide standardized specifications and to create patterns (similar to that of a CAD drawing when developing a plastics product) in preparation for a textile manufacturer.

The Secret Formula

Yet another type of prototype developer is called a *formulator*. This is a chemist who helps create a new formula from scratch. A formulator is used for any number of inventive applications, from beauty products to cleaning agents to pet supplies.

Adena Surabian, founder of Nature's Baby, worked with a formulator to develop a baby shampoo and conditioner with 100 percent plant-derived in-

To help her develop all-natural products for her children using her favorite ingredients, Adena Surabian hired a formulator. She now sells these creations as the Nature's Baby shampoo product line.

gredients. When she first decided to develop an organic shampoo, she never imagined how many renditions she'd need to go through to develop her final product; she worked with the chemist on a prototype for a year. The consistency, texture, smell, and mixture of ingredients had to be adjusted repeatedly. Stabilizers had to be included in the formula to preserve it, and using "all natural" ingredients made this goal challenging. However, she never gave up. Even after the product was finalized they had a new challenge: finding a plastic container that would help preserve the ingredients. If the plastic container let in too much light, the formula would spoil.

Note that you will have to pay a formulator extra money to retain 100 percent rights to your formula. Otherwise, formulators may sell your product to others under a different label.

Ears Open, Mouth Closed

Once you have a prototype, you'll naturally want to start showing it around to friends and family as well as professionals. At this point, it's vital to develop a thick skin in order to solicit—and absorb—valuable feedback.

I can't tell you how many moms have contacted me who were eager to make a million dollars but didn't want to hear feedback about their product. I know other moms with the courage to present their product to retailers, but who'll fall to pieces with one rejection. Yet another mom recently told me that a major buyer in the industry liked her product and was seriously interested in purchasing units from her but wasn't happy with the packaging. Instead of saying to the buyer, "What do you think needs to be changed or modified?" her response was, "Who does she think she is?"

I understand that it can be difficult to hear negative feedback, particularly about something that you've invested so much time, energy, and money in creating. However, provided it's not mean-spirited, negative feedback is possibly the most valuable feedback that you can receive. Retail buyers, when asked for feedback, will more often than not say what you want to hear, and will go to lengths not to hurt your feelings. While it's easy for people to tell you that they like your idea, it's a rare act of courage to look a sweet, enthusiastic inventor in the eye and say, "I would never buy this." Which means you should thank those who impart "honest" feedback (perhaps a little later after you pick up the pieces!). That's because negative feedback will only serve to further enhance your product. I have taken nearly all the negative feedback that I have received about our Mom Invented products directly to our engineers and manufacturers to see if we could make the improvements.

So, if someone says they don't like your product, say, "Thank you for your honest response. I am grateful. I would like to learn more. What don't you like about it? What aspects would you change? If you created this product yourself, what would you do at this point to modify it? Is there any other advice that you are willing to share with me?" I've discovered that when someone sees that I am seriously considering their point of view, they are more than willing to share their honest thoughts. I always say that this is powerful information that you cannot pay for! Use it to your advantage.

What Will It Cost?

Plastic or Metal Prototype

- Engineer $100–$300 per hour
- CAD drawings and product refinement for manufacturability: $1,000–$10,000 depending on the complexity of the product (TP Saver CAD drawings cost $3,000.)
- Machinist $50–$100 per hour (different by state)
- Hand-tooled prototype: $100–$300, depending on the complexity of the product (Each hand-tooled TP Saver prototype cost $100.)
- Rapid prototyping (assuming CAD drawings are complete) $150–$500 (depending on complexity of product)

Textile Prototype

$500 and up (depending on complexity)

Safety Test

Sending your product to an independent safety testing lab will cost anywhere from $500 to $15,000+ (TP Saver cost around $800).

Money Saving Tips

- *Plastics:* Use Shape Lock or a similar product that will allow you to make the prototype by hand. Once you know your product works, you can then hire an engineer to create CAD draw-

ings, followed by a rapid prototyping company to produce fin-
ished-looking prototypes.

- *Textiles:* Use a local seamstress, friend, or family member
  who can sew to flesh out as many of the issues as possible
  before going to a prototype developer.
- *Testing:* Speak to your manufacturer about the items that
  safety labs plan to test; you may be able to avoid unnecessary
  testing. For example, if you have to test for the content of certain chemicals, but your factory can assure that the product
  meets requirements, you may be able to skip this test (and the
  money you'd pay to have it conducted!).

In addition, know the federal requirements in advance, e.g.,
choking hazard standard, and design your product in accordance
with these standards.

Protecting Your Prototype

As you begin showing your prototype around, you might naturally fear that
someone may "borrow" your idea. There are a few steps you can take to
protect yourself without being overly paranoid. If your invention is patented
or has a patent pending, you are pretty well protected (see Chapter 5 on how
to do this). If not, you may wish to consider asking certain parties to sign
nondisclosure agreements (see sample NDA in Appendix) before revealing
your idea or prototype. These parties include manufacturers, engineers,
prototype makers, and graphic artists. Another way to protect yourself is to
be sure to check out these professionals' reputations and track records before doing business with them. Most business people are honest, or they
won't be in business long. But it's good to be cautious, so feel free to speak
to an attorney for further advice about protecting your intellectual property.

Conclusion

Now that you've actually communicated your idea in 3-D and Technicolor,
you've passed a big hurdle—congratulations! Your next step is to formal-
ize your feedback through market testing, which will be covered in the
next chapter.

Put on Your Detective Hat

Market Research

The art and science of asking questions is the source of all knowledge.
Thomas Berger, novelist

By now you must be saying "enough research!" After all, didn't you delve into this enough in Chapter 2 on patents and the market? Well, no. While that research determined if, indeed, your product already existed, the market research in this chapter will give you the information you need to help identify your target market, and to help fine-tune your product to meet this market's needs.

If you plan to read only one chapter in this book, this is the chapter to read! I believe that market research is one of the most essential steps in the product development process, yet interestingly, it is the step most commonly skipped. Even if you're not going to manufacture a product yourself—maybe you plan to license your idea or offer a service—market research is nevertheless critical to your success.

This chapter covers the basic concepts of market research. By the chapter's end you should be able to do your own market research, ranging from gathering broad market information to highly specific product information, to develop the best set of data—and thus the best product possible. I will also describe low-cost alternatives so that you can perform successful research no matter what your budget.

Though this information may initially look overwhelming, it's not as daunting as it first appears. You should have no problem completing your research within a reasonable amount of time, say, a week or two. The key is not to get discouraged! By following the guidelines in this chapter, you'll have an efficient and organized plan of attack.

From Invention to Product

In the beginning of this book, we refer to your idea as an "invention." However, consumers buy products, not inventions. And because you've come this far, your invention is fast evolving into a product! Because my goal is to help you make money, I will from here forward most often refer to your invention as your product.

What Is Market Research?

The term *research* can seem overwhelming. For some, it conjures images of library stacks and technical documents. But if you look at the idea of research in a new way, you'll actually realize you do it every day. Finding out what your child's day was like at school is research. Figuring out the best dentist in your area (often by trial and error!) is research. My hope is to demystify and simplify the research process, which is really just gathering information in the most efficient and unbiased way possible.

There are great benefits to gathering this information. Having a bank of knowledge reduces the risks (and stress) of making business decisions, validates your work, and allows you to continue bounding down your creative path. It offers guidance and shows you if and when you need to take a detour in your journey. Not only will market research help you make important business decisions as you continue developing your product, but it will also provide substantive market data that you can use later when you actually begin selling your product. And because you're researching something near and dear to your heart (rather than, say, medieval history), chances are you'll gain a whole new enthusiasm for the process!

There are two stages to market research: primary and secondary. The process can be compared to assembling a jigsaw puzzle. As you begin any puzzle, your best strategy is to start from the outside in—working on the frame first, with the easiest-to-find pieces, followed by the internal gaps until the image is complete. Think of this research process in the same way.

The outside pieces of this puzzle are your *secondary data*, which is a technical term for information that's been previously gathered and which is now available to the public. This data will give you "big picture" information about the economic feasibility of your opportunity in today's marketplace. The inside of your puzzle is *primary data*, which is information you'll generate yourself through interviews and other methods, specifically about your product or business. This info will help you fill in the gaps that your secondary research didn't produce. The totality of this combined set of data will provide you with two avenues to take. It will either strengthen your case and conviction to move forward, or it can help you determine that your market opportunity is limited (even if your product idea is clever). Either way, you'll be in a better position to decide if this idea is worth investing the necessary time, energy, and money.

From Imagination to Reality

Nearly every day, I hear from a mom who says, "I have the next million dollar idea. I know that every parent in America will buy this product." This type of enthusiasm is wonderful, and she may be right. The first thing I ask is who the product is specifically intended for and how many consumers are represented in this target market. Unfortunately, her answer is often silence. It's this information that your market research will uncover.

I've also heard from many moms who have already completely designed, developed, packaged, manufactured, and patented their product, who'll then say, "I need help! No one is purchasing my product and I spent a fortune!" Unless time and money is no object, *after* you launch the product is not the time to identify your market (secondary research) nor is it the time to gain specific feedback about your product (primary research). You definitely want to gather this information well before you mass-produce. Not only will this information help you launch the best designed product possible, but it will also help prevent your being stuck with thousands of units that are sitting in your garage because your potential market is less enthusiastic or robust than you had imagined.

The experiences of Audrey Storch, inventor of the Huggee Miss You Doll (http://www.huggeemissyou.com), tell us a great deal about the benefits of market research. When she found out she had cancer, she had to leave her two boys behind when she went to the hospital for her treatments. Understandably, her children had a difficult time. At first, Audrey provided her children with a photograph of herself to comfort them when she went away, but she soon realized that it was hard to snuggle with a photograph. Her next step was to create a doll with a place to insert the picture. Audrey has since developed and sold her product nationally and she's also overcome her illness.

Along the way she encountered a few obstacles, specifically when it came to her market research. Before launching, she went through the proper steps, asking hundreds of people different questions about her doll. She was completely open to their suggestions and feedback. She did everything right, collecting and analyzing this information. Consistently, parents told her they would purchase a doll with unisex clothing (she had chosen denim for the doll). She then mass-produced her product feeling confident about her choice. With new product in hand, she attended her first trade show to sell the doll to retail buyers. There, she was stunned to learn that although the retail buyers loved her product, they would not purchase the doll because it came only in denim! The retailers said that they knew their consumer buying trends. They felt that their primary audience, women, overwhelmingly tend to purchase pink for girls and blue for boys. Even with all of the hard work that Audrey had put into this effort, she learned that she should have also interviewed retail buyers prior to going into mass production. Audrey admits that this was an expensive lesson that could have been avoided.

Seek and You Shall Find

So now that you know the importance of market research, it's time to put on your detective cap. Though it sounds backward, you should start by gathering secondary research. Again, this is the information that already exists in the marketplace, which can be accessed or purchased online. This research will provide the big picture on your potential consumers—the number of people in the country that might purchase this product—as well

Audrey Storch created the Huggee Miss You Doll, a special care-giving aid for children, when she was diagnosed with cancer. The doll, which is designed with a place to hold a photograph, provides comfort for children when separated from a loved one. They're now sold in specialty stores nationwide.

as information on your specific industry—the amount of money these people spend on your type of product. Once you've gathered this information, you'll refine it even further with your primary research (focus groups, interviews, e-mails) to find out what improvements consumers and retail buyers would recommend for your specific product.

Here's an example to further define the difference between secondary and primary research. Say you're opening a lemonade stand in a new town. Before setting up your stand on just any random street corner, you'd want to find out which areas have the most foot traffic. Instead of setting up shop on a rural corner, you'd want to be in the center of town, where you'll encounter the most people. Your secondary research finds where this population is and who they are.

Next, you'd want to know if this market prefers traditional or pink lemonade. Perhaps, unbeknown to you, the town has an aversion to regular old lemonade. Again, this is information you'd want to know before you spent money mixing and marketing your lemonade. If there's a greater chance of selling the pink stuff, you'd be much more inclined to take that route. This is the type of information you'd unearth with your primary research.

There are many ways to collect research. I visualize this process as a funnel with the wide end at the top—secondary research—narrowing at the bottom, where the focus then becomes primary research. This may not be a business textbook type of approach, but it is how I envision it.

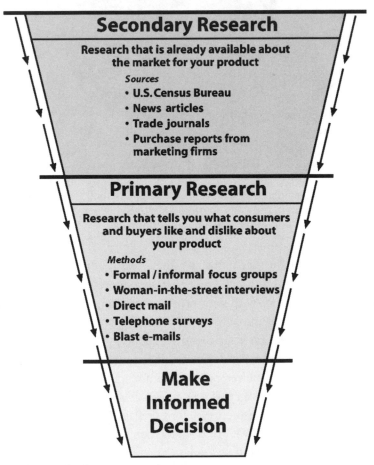

Secondary Research

Research that is already available about the market for your product

Sources
- U.S. Census Bureau
- News articles
- Trade journals
- Purchase reports from marketing firms

Primary Research

Research that tells you what consumers and buyers like and dislike about your product

Methods
- Formal / informal focus groups
- Woman-in-the-street interviews
- Direct mail
- Telephone surveys
- Blast e-mails

Make Informed Decision

Secondary and primary research avenues.

You can do both types of research either by yourself informally or by hiring a market research firm (not an invention promotion company; see Chapter 1) to assist you. Both approaches can be valuable, and the approach taken will all depend on your time frame and budget. We'll talk more about the specifics of hiring a market research firm later. But for now, let's get started!

Secondary Research

With the rise of the Internet, research has become easier. No longer are we forced to spend hours at the library in dark little carrels sifting through piles of original documents. Today, we can perform much of our research from the comfort of home—a boon for busy moms!

The secondary research you'll perform largely on the Internet will help evaluate the market opportunity for your product. This research will help you build the best possible image of your market and the industry by evaluating the data you'll find from multiple resources, including the U.S. census, industry statistics, and business articles. Let's say, for instance, your idea is to develop a "preppy garter" for brides to wear at their weddings, to replace the frilly ones of the past. First, you'd want to research how many brides there are per year—this is your market. Then, you'd delve further into the industry, to determine bridal trends. Suddenly, you find a few articles from bridal magazines that say brides are no longer wearing garters and the tradition of the groom throwing it to his groomsmen has all but disappeared. Certainly, this research would affect your plans to take this idea further, helping you make an informed decision. At the end of the day, your gut instinct still plays a role, but gut instinct combined with good data is a much more reliable decision-making method.

Locating market information relevant to a nonexistent product (invention) can be challenging. Therefore, it is necessary to gather bits of data from as many related sources as possible.

For example, when I was considering developing the TP Saver, I couldn't get information about how many kids pull the toilet paper, but I could get statistics about how many households have children ages 1 to 3 years—7.9 million—and how many new babies are born each year—4 million (U.S. Census 2000). This helped me understand that there was a large potential market out there. Although I intuitively knew that not every child pulls the toilet paper, even capturing a small percentage of this population could make this product viable. Voila! A piece of my puzzle was in place.

To find the information you are looking for, I recommend the following resources, which are discussed in detail further on:

1. Census data (www.census.gov)
2. Internet (key word search using search engines such as www.google.com)
3. Business publications, such as *Entrepreneur Magazine, Business Week, Fortune Small Business, Business 2.0, INC.*, magazine and newspapers, such as *The Wall Street Journal* and *The New York Times*
4. Trade associations
5. Trade-specific publications (*Early Learner* and *Kids Today* are examples from the children's market).
6. Gender or ethnic-specific publications (examples include *Making Bread Magazine, Minority Business Entrepreneur Magazine*).
7. Financial data on important or relevant public companies (www.hoovers.com, www.sec.gov)

For even more resources, talk to retailers and other people in your specific industry about where they gain information and which publications they find to be most useful. Don't forget to jot everything down in your notebook!

Making Sense of the U.S. Census

If you've taken the steps outlined in Chapters 1 through 3, you're now an old pro when it comes to online research. This skill will again come in handy when first determining the size of your market by researching U.S. census data. The United States Census Bureau provides population data that can help you determine how many people are in your target market (the group of people that would qualify to purchase your product).

You will be amazed by the information that is available to you on the U.S. Census Website for free. However, this is where the patience you have gained as a parent comes into play. Conducting research takes time and

should be broken into manageable steps. Here is a quick ⟨
you get started:

- Visit www.census.gov.
- Click on "Subjects A–Z" on the navigation bar along the left-hand side of the homepage. This lists all the reports available by subject in alphabetical order. Read through the titles of the reports to familiarize yourself with the topics that are covered and to identify additional key words to add to your list. By reviewing this list, you will have a better understanding of how the U.S. Census organizes its information. There may be reports that you want to download and read right from that list.
- You can also start by using key words that you already have on your list. (Make sure that you write this list in your inventor's notebook so that you remember the process that you went through to find this data and avoid repeating yourself.) Click on "American FactFinder" (I find this more efficient and easier than clicking on their general search button.) Then click on the search button along the top navigation bar. A window will appear asking you for three things: (1) Select a year and program, (2) Enter keyword(s), and (3) Select a Subject.
- Select a year and program (they provide a list; however, I recommend selecting "All years and programs" unless you specifically need to limit your search.)
- Next, you'll need to narrow down what you're looking for. Let's say that your product is intended for preteens (ages 10 to 14 years old) but you have no idea how many preteens there are. To find this information, it helps to think more generally. I typed in the word *family* into the key word box.
- Using this search word generates several reports. I clicked on "Profile of General Demographic Characteristics 2000" and found that our population was broken down by age. This gave me exactly what I was looking for: There are approximately 21 million preteens in America.
- In addition, I recommend that you tick the "use synonyms" box. This will bring up words similar in meaning to the specific key words that you originally typed in the search box, thus broadening the scope of your search. If you're finding this challenging, click on

the link next to the search box that says "Search Tips" which provides useful strategies.
- If you really don't have any idea where to start, go to "Select a Subject." This will provide you with a drop-down list to begin your search. This will show you how the Census labels the subject headings and will help point you in the right direction. For instance, where you might use the word *children* they might use the word *juvenile*. Reviewing these headings and clicking on links to view different reports is also a wonderful way to familiarize yourself with the data.

The key is not to get discouraged! I know this can be challenging, particularly if you have a limited amount of time. This is the type of work that I typically do when the children are asleep so I can search without interruption. Consider yourself a detective trying to sleuth out information. Finding the facts or reports that help validate your product makes the process well worth the time and effort.

Getting to Know Your Industry

Now that you have your general population data, it is important to learn as much as you can about this group's spending habits in the industry related to your product.

Here's an example of what I'm talking about. When Amy Bergin decided that she wanted to create an organizing system for coupons that would save users time and money, she thought it was a great idea, but wanted to make sure that people would be interested in purchasing her product. Before developing the system, now called the Couponizer and sold nationally, she needed to determine whether there was a large enough market to support her product. Specifically, she needed to know how many people commonly used coupons. She started her search for industry statistics on the Internet. She learned from the Promotion Marketing Association's Coupon Council that $336 billion dollars in coupons were distributed in 2002. Approximately 3.8 billion were redeemed for a total savings to consumers of $3 billion. This means that $333 billion dollars in savings went unclaimed. In addition, she found that 79 percent of consumers used coupons. This knowledge surpassed even Amy's expectations, and confirmed that there was a large market that could potentially use her product and take advantage of the huge deluge of available coupons.

Amy Bergin figured that a better system to organize coupons would help people use them more frequently and easily and thus save more money. That's what inspired her to invent the Couponizer, which will launch on QVC in 2005.

Finding your own industry-specific information will take time and perseverance. Again, use key words applicable to your product and look into publicly available data that comes up in your search. You may also encounter sites and organizations that offer research reports with relevant data for a fee. While it's your choice to purchase such data, you may find yourself buying reports without fully knowing if the data you'll receive is of value to you, specifically. I recommend exhausting your search for data in the public domain before taking this route. (I'll go into more detail on purchasing info later in this chapter.) Keep in mind that you can find information based on gender, ethnicity, and age, etc., by using key words in Internet search boxes.

Reading between the Lines

If specific industry research is not readily available or too costly, news articles can be easier and more cost-effective to find. They often reflect the most current information and therefore potentially the most accurate data available in the market. Fortunately, there are publications covering nearly every geographical region, industry, and interest, no matter how large or small. There are publications about knitting, snowboarding, cats—you name the topic, someone publishes information about it. Once again, these articles can be found on the Internet and also at your local library. If you're having trouble, note that a librarian can be a phenomenal resource. To the librarian, few things are as exciting as the challenge of finding specific data using the tools at their disposal. And, their services are free!

If you're searching on your own, look in local business papers, national newspapers, such as *The Wall Street Journal, New York Times*, and *USA Today*, national small business magazines, such as *Fortune Small Business, Business 2.0, INC. Magazine*, and my personal favorite; *Entrepreneur* magazine. Then, look into niche publications related to your industry, gender, or ethnic group. Most of the larger publications have online versions that you can search; usually they'll offer articles for free that go a month or two back. Beyond that, you can typically pay a small fee to view articles from the archive. To find publications specific to your industry, do a general online search first. For instance, if you've got a product designed for dogs, search online for "pet magazines" and see what turns up. Then you can research to determine if the magazines that have turned up offer information or articles online; if not, you'll already have a list to look up when you go to the library.

Even your general local business newspaper can turn up some research gems. Here is one excerpt that shows the kind of information I found about my own target market—moms. In it writer Alf Nucifora examines women as consumers and offers the following valuable data:

> *Today's woman is both a moving target and a movable feast.*
> *Women head 40 percent of the households in America, make 85*
> *percent of the consumer buying decisions and run 40 percent of all*
> *companies in the United States. They earn $1 trillion per year and*
> *control 51 percent of the nation's private wealth. More impor-*

tantly, their spending power is estimated at $2 trillion per year. In truth, women make the majority of decisions in household purchasing. And the power of their pocketbooks is matched by the authority of their mindset. As a cohort that has become more sophisticated in its decision-making, women have "grown into themselves" and have become comfortable in that role. They've gained the decision-making power and they like it.

From "Thinking Pink Has Different Color Now,"
East Bay Business Times, August 6, 2004.

Information in another article in the February 2003 issue of *Entrepreneur* magazine added a missing piece to my puzzle.

The big news about online retail in 2002 was the emerging dominance of female shoppers. Women now make up a majority of Internet users, and, given the fact that women disburse the bulk of all dollars spent in retail, that is good and important news for e-commerce. It's good because it portends future growth, and it's important because women don't shop like men, and they don't buy the same things.

While neither article completed my puzzle, they reinforced that women represent a huge consumer growth market, and verified that they're also shopping online. In addition, I was able to use these writers' resources, which they cited to support their facts, to find additional data they chose not to include in their stories.

As you perform your own research, be sure to leave no stone unturned. Use any information and quotes you find to lead to additional information. Think of your research as a treasure map—each piece of information will lead to the next great clue.

Trade Secrets—Joining an Association

Another place to look for market and industry information is the trade associations serving your industry. A trade association is an organization that professionals in a certain industry join to keep up on industry knowledge and provide a network of resources. Thus, trade associations will often provide valuable statistics for their membership. If they don't, they can tell you which publications write about the industry. If you'd like to join an association, but you're not sure which makes the most sense, you can visit the Website of The American Society of Association Executives (www.asaenet.org) for a free list of associations nationwide broken down by industry. You can call and request a hard copy of this list at 202-626-2723 for $160. In addition, I recommend that you speak with buyers or owners of the specialty or independent retail stores you would expect to see carrying your product, and ask them which trade organizations they belong to. Also ask them which trade-specific publications they read.

Going Public

There is also a wealth of information you can find via stats from public companies that are related to your industry. Public companies are companies whose stock shares are bought and sold on a stock market such as the New York Stock Exchange, and their information is free and available to the public.

For instance, let's say you have created a new type of bedding product. It would be useful to read about other companies that make and sell bedding, to determine sales figures, quantities, and their top sales channels (e.g., Wal-Mart, Target). To find public companies related to your industry, visit www.hoovers.com to identify these companies and find out their stock symbol. Then visit www.sec.gov (the Website of the Security Exchange Commission) to read their financial reports. In addition, these companies' financials and annual reports are often available on their own Websites.

Here's an example. Go to www.hoovers.com/free. Select "Industry Keyword," and in the search field box write key words for your product, for example, *toy* or *coupon*. A list of companies will come up, which you can read about and determine their stock, or ticker, symbols. Then, on the Securities and Exchange Commission (www.sec.gov) site, you'll find even more info. You will be amazed what you can learn about a public company and its activities, down to the salaries and prior year's bonus of its top executives! In addition, many public libraries offer access to free corporate information databases such as ReferenceUSA through the library Websites. Normally, all that is required is your library card.

Generally Speaking...

There are also market search resources that don't fit any of the standard categories, like magazines, newspapers, or associations. These are general Websites or publications that cover some aspect of what you're interested in finding. One example of this type is *The Bloom Report* (www.the bloomreport.com). Philip A. Bloom is a consultant to global retailers and manufacturers and publishes this report. It is a "trade-specific" Website with a weekly compilation of news articles and press releases from different sources relevant to the retail toy industry. Nearly every week, I find an article with information that is relevant to my business.

Fee-Based Market Research

I have never purchased market research data. However, it would have been helpful if I had and I would not rule it out in the future. There is a wide array of research and analysis firms from which you can purchase market information. They can easily be found by keying "market research" into an Internet search engine such as www.google.com.

These Websites normally list the research data they sell, with a brief summary of each report. If you find a research report that seems close enough to your needs, you can save a tremendous amount of time by purchasing it, which will validate your assumptions and add to the information you have already cobbled together yourself. However, there are two principal challenges to buying research. First, if your invention is truly unique, it may be difficult to find a report specific to your target market. Second, these reports tend to be quite expensive and you don't normally have the opportunity to read them first to decide if they are worth the money. So my advice is buyer beware!

Primary Research Testing Your Specific Market

Now that you have gained your big-picture information through secondary research (and nothing you have found has told you to abandon the project), it is time to narrow your focus and zero in on the consumer—people who are most likely to purchase your product.

There are several ways to gather this type of more personalized data. The method you choose will depend on the specific information you're seeking and the size of your budget. Examples of primary research include focus groups (formal and informal), intercepts (stopping people in their "environment"), bulletin boards (Internet), e-mails to friends and family, direct-mail surveys, and phone interviews. Some methods require a financial commitment; however, most of the information can be gathered on a shoestring budget.

After Amy Bergin learned that $3.8 billion dollars in coupons were redeemed by consumers each year (secondary research), she thought that her market was large enough to move forward developing her product, the Couponizer. But now she needed to determine what individual consumers specifically wanted. Primary research would allow her to test her product and get concrete feedback to help refine her product before mass-producing it.

"I decided it was time to test it," Amy said. "In July 2002, I summoned 21 people to test the product. I put together a tester's packet which included a Couponizer I created from my own printer, a CoupStacker-pre-sorting mat for the coupons, a testing journal, a pair of scissors, and a carrying pouch. I asked for a one-month commitment to the testing process, which included using the system tools and recording their savings in the journal, and I promised in the end a celebration. The support from this group of people was amazing and to this day these friends are some of my biggest cheerleaders."

Specifically, Amy had people in four states and in different demographics participate in the test to ensure a well-rounded process. She encouraged each tester to be honest and forthcoming with constructive criticism and new ideas to make the product better. At the end of the month, she set up individual debriefs with each tester. If they lived close by, they'd meet at Starbucks to discuss the results and Amy collected the test journal. If they were out of town, she conducted a phone interview and they mailed in the tester's journal.

After talking with all the testers, hearing their stories, and learning their experiences, she confirmed that her product really did solve problems associated with coupons, and that it was something that people liked and would buy, given the chance. She then compiled all the feedback, improved the product, and shared her outcomes at the celebration. She also awarded a $50 grocery store gift certificate to the "Top Shopper"—the person who had the best one-time savings from her coupon experience. The person who won saved $76 dollars in one trip to the grocery store. Everyone else received a certificate thanking them for their involvement, as well as drinks and appetizers for the evening.

This method worked for Amy and was a cost-effective way for her to retrieve the data that was critical to refining her product and filling in data gaps. As you saw with Amy's example, her investment was limited. She spent money to produce the testing packets for her subjects to review, paid for postage and telephone calls for certain test subjects, and spent money on the $50 gift certificate and the evening celebration. In the broad scope of market research, she gained a lot of information for a very small investment.

Amy's approach is what's called "focus group" type of research. This and other types of research are covered more thoroughly in the next section.

Primary Research—Understanding Your Options

Before you determine which primary methods you should use to fill in the gaps of your secondary research, it is important to understand clearly what pieces of information you still need.

Marta Loeb of Silver Stork research, a market research firm specializing in the U.S. "mom's market," states, "It is valuable to sit down and take the time to carefully think about what you want to get out of your research. Think about not only what questions you want answered, but also the information you hope to have in your hand after the research is done and what decisions you'll make with this insight."

Following is a worksheet created by Silver Stork Research to help prioritize your research strategies, focus on your key information needs, and assist you in spending time and money wisely.

Research Audit

If you're considering research, following are the key questions to ask yourself before you begin planning or launching your research efforts.

1. What are the top five things you hope to get accomplished with this research?

2. Why is research important now?
3. What business decisions do you want to make from this research?
4. Who do you think you should talk to?
5. If you could only get an answer to one question, what would it be?

Source: Silver Stork Research (www.silverstork.com) 2005

Once your research goals and requirements are clear to you, you will need to determine the data collection methods that will be most effective and appropriate.

An Eye on the Bottom Line

In addition to the type of information you're seeking to gather, budget will also be an important consideration for deciding upon your market research. I have found that survey subjects are generally happy to share their opinions and enjoy participating in these kinds of projects, providing they don't consume an inordinate amount of time or effort. Informal focus groups, woman-on-the-street interviews, online bulletin boards, and e-mail blasts are some low-cost primary research methods. If you are fortunate enough to have money to spend on research, direct-mail and telephone surveys are some additional options.

Informal Focus Groups

The idea here is to get a group of people together who will share their feedback in an environment where answers can be clarified and shades of thinking and opinion can be dissected.

Procedure

- Plan a group of get-togethers with friends and acquaintances who represent your target market, and ask each participant to bring someone you don't know. You may also wish to tap into a group to which you belong for participants (mommy's group, religious group, or club).

- Prioritize what you want to get accomplished.
- Tell your participants that you value their feedback, both positive and negative. Make it clear that you are looking for serious consumers, not cheerleaders, and that their candor is essential.
- Have participants sign a release form (see Appendix B for a sample release form).
- Before the participants arrive, think about what questions are important to you. Keep in mind that some of this data will be helpful in the future as selling points. You can later quote participants in your brochures and product sell sheets.
- List the questions you plan to ask. Your questions should be unique to your product. Start general and get more specific. Here are some examples:
  - Have you seen anything like it before?
  - How have you dealt with this issue without this product?
  - Would you purchase this product? How many?
  - If not, why not?
  - What do you like about it?
  - What would you change?
  - What colors would you prefer?
  - How much would you pay for it?
  - Where would you expect to buy it? (Name specific stores you shop at.)
  - How would you expect it to be packaged?
  - How many per package?
- One person should be assigned to take notes and another one or two people to ask questions and moderate the discussion.
- Follow-up questions to clarify information are important and provide one of the unique benefits of conducting a focus group.
- You may want to record the event on tape.

Benefits.   This method provides an opportunity to go into greater depth than other styles of research. The participants can add to your support network. The process can also be a lot of fun.

Drawbacks.   Coordination is more challenging than in other types of research, and personal acquaintances may be less likely to verbalize negative feedback.

Woman-on-the-Street Interviews

By stopping people in their environment, you can get great feedback. These kinds of interviews are informal, and they can often help you focus on key issues to help refine your product design.

Procedure

- Choose a public place where your target market spends a lot of time. For instance, if you wish to interview moms, some effective locations include playgrounds, supermarkets, and the mall. If it's pet owners you're after, try the dog park or your local pet store.
- Be sure to identify yourself and have a business card on hand to help the people you're talking to feel more comfortable and more eager to offer information. For example, I was enjoying an ice cream cone with my daughter outside an ice cream store one afternoon. As we were sitting there I realized I had a captive audience of parents and children. I leapt to my feet and surprised everyone by introducing myself, my new product Shoe Clues (stickers that teach children their left from right), and asked for their advice. I whipped off Sophia's shoes to show them the stickers inside, then pulled out more samples to show them (which I happened to have in my purse). I asked for honest feedback about the packaging, how much they would pay for the product, and where they would expect to purchase it. I also asked the children which of the pictures on the stickers they liked the best. This was an impromptu intercept and it was fun for all and informative for me. I handed each child a packet of Shoe Clues to express my gratitude. It lasted for no more than 10 minutes.
- List questions on multiple preprepared forms so that everyone you speak to answers the same questions in the same order.
- Rehearse your approach and each question. Keep it under 5 to 10 minutes.
- Explain the product quickly and simply. According to a QVC buyer, you should be able to describe your product in one sentence.
- Ask questions and write answers.
- After the interview, make a few notations about each person for later reference (e.g., mom with two kids in tow).

Benefits.   Anonymity and unbiased feedback.

Drawbacks.   The discomfort in approaching a stranger, shorter interviews, less feedback, and no opportunity for follow-up.

Online Bulletin Boards

The Internet is a fantastic—and free—place to collect information. There are countless Websites with message boards and bulletin boards, where very diverse groups can be found with whom you can open a dialogue.

Procedure

- Visit sites with interest groups and bulletin boards related to your product. Again, if it's for children, try sites like www.parentsoup.com, www.windsorpeak.com, www.babycenter.com, www.ivillage.com, www.clubmom.com. If it's a wedding-related product, try sites like www.theknot.com or www.ultimatewedding.com. The seemingly narrowest of topics have bulletin boards to support them—I recently found one on hamsters! No matter what your subject, you will discover useful boards as your journey on the Internet expands.
- Join in and participate in other ongoing conversations
- On the bulletin board, create a new topic, tell people exactly what you are doing (developing a new product and what it does) and that you would value their advice and feedback.

Benefits.   Can be done from home at anytime; you can change and add new questions all the time.

Drawbacks.   You have no way of knowing if your respondent even remotely fits your target customer. You can't verify their gender, age, ethnicity, economic status, or any other traits that can be verified in direct settings.

E-mail Blasts

Create an e-mail campaign and send it to your network of family, friends, and business associates.

Procedure

- Compile any sources of contact information you have. Get out your address book or contact list. Pull the business cards out from the bottom of your purse, diaper bag, and desk drawer. Use professional association directories.
- Send out a request for information. Describe the consumer or target you are looking for and specify clearly in the e-mail who you want to speak with (e.g., "if you know any women currently planning a wedding, please forward"). Then include your questions in the actual e-mail body so it is easy for people to respond. In other words, don't send an attached document.

Benefits.   Requires little planning.

Drawbacks.   You don't know if you are going to get one response or many. You have little control over the people the message is forwarded to.

Direct-Mail Surveys

A direct-mail survey is a traditional paper survey sent to a mailing list of your target consumers.

Procedure

- Purchase mailing lists from media outlets (e.g., magazines) or list brokers (easily found on the Internet—use Google and type "list brokers" into the search box).
- List the questions—keep it short but complete—that you'd like to have answered. These questions should be in yes/no or true/false format.
- If your budget supports it, hire a research professional to develop your survey; then field and process the responses.
- Make sure to include a self-addressed and postage-paid return envelope. You may also increase your response rate by offering an incentive for completing and returning the survey—a gift certificate to a popular retailer or online store, for instance. It's also nice to send a follow-up thank-you letter.

Benefits.　You're polling a large survey group and you have the opportunity to ask many questions and collect a wide range of information.

Drawbacks.　Uncertainty as to response rate versus investment, and no opportunity to interact or clarify anything that is unclear.

Telephone Surveys

There are many research organizations that have call centers designed to facilitate phone interviews. A phone interview is ideal for close-ended questions (e.g., Yes/no answers, multiple choice, etc.) and should be limited to less than 10 minutes to collect true insights. Market research firms all over the country can script, field, and process the results of a phone survey. Phone surveys are ideal for making final decisions on a product such as pricing or choosing a name. This is an efficient way to gather a lot of data in a short amount of time.

Procedure

- Do an Internet search to identify companies that conduct telephone surveys and collect data. I typed "call centers" and "telephone surveys" into the search box at www.google.com to get started.

Benefits.　You can reach a large number of people, you can get specific information about the person being interviewed, and you have the opportunity to get more refined answers to questions.

Drawbacks.　This can be expensive—several hundred dollars for a small survey and thousands of dollars for an extensive survey.

What Will It Cost?

Research data reports: $500 to $5,000, depending on the industry and depth of the report.
- Save money by finding published media articles that use the same research data

Focus Groups: A few hundred dollars to thousands of dollars, depending on the length, complexity, and marketing firm you hire to conduct them for you.

- Save money by hiring a less expensive professional or someone you know; by borrowing facilities (a board room at a friend's office); rewarding participants with gift certificates ($50 at Target) rather than a larger sum of cash.
- Save more money by asking a community group with which you're affiliated if you can attend one of their meetings and survey their members about your product.

Woman-on-the-Street Interviews: Salary of the person you hire to do this for you.

- Save money by doing these interviews yourself.

Direct-Mail Surveys: Depending on how elaborate, these range from $1 to $5 per mail piece, including development, graphic design, handling, and postage.

- Save money by using your own mailing list, using a letter on plain paper, and mailing it yourself.

Telephone Survey: Your calling list—the names and phone numbers of your target market—will cost from several hundred to several thousand dollars. You will also need to pay the labor costs of personnel who make the calls, as well as the telephone bill.

- Save money by using your own lists or making telephone calls yourself.

Chapter Wrap-Up

Your findings from market research are critical because they will help you make good business decisions. Not only will your research help determine whether there's a viable market for your product, it will also help you hone and tweak your product to fit consumers' individual needs. Though your research may not fill all the gaps, especially under the constraints of a tight budget, you will nevertheless dramatically improve your ability to make decisions, which can mean the difference between profit and failure. This information is extremely important to have before you take your next steps of patenting and manufacturing, where you can expect to invest more significant dollars.

Protect Yourself

All about Patents,
Copyrights, and Trademarks

Watch any invention infomercial and read many invention Websites and you'll undoubtedly hear the same message repeated over and over—get a patent! Many of these "experts" imply a grave sense of urgency to file your patent application before your idea is "stolen." While the reasons for filing patents are often valid, the patent process is by no means universal, nor should it be the first step in your invention process. In fact, by focusing on patents too early, you may spend unnecessary time and money on a product that either doesn't require a patent, that isn't quite ready for patenting—or worst of all, won't sell. The startling fact is that only 2 to 3 percent of patented inventions ever make it to market. Unfortunately, the 97 percent of inventors with patents who *don't* get their products to market are the owners of an expensive ($5,000+!) wall hanging.

On the flip side, because the patent process is expensive, hopeful inventors are often discouraged because patenting feels like an impossible and unaffordable first step. This may cause them to abandon their invention altogether, which can lead to a missed opportunity and a lifetime of wondering What if?

My own view differs from the conventional "rush to patent." I am not suggesting that you should never get a patent. In fact, I have filed patents for most of my products. But I do believe filing for a patent shouldn't be your first step, which is why I've left this topic for Chapter 5. Before you even consider filing a patent, it's critical to evaluate your product idea as a business opportunity and to understand fully your product, your target market, and your competition. Only then will you truly know if your product is commercially viable or not. As we discussed in prior chapters, this decision goes far beyond your gut feelings and encouraging comments from friends and family; it's based on solid market research and attention to product development. You should thoroughly consider the following factors before even thinking about applying for a patent:

- Make sure your idea isn't infringing on someone else's patent. (You began this process by searching for prior art during your preliminary patent search, covered in Chapter 2. An attorney may be necessary to ensure you're within legal requirements, even if you decide not to file a patent.)
- Develop a basic prototype to determine your product's functionality. While you don't need a prototype to get a patent, it is an important step to determine if yours is a viable business idea.
- Define your market and determine how large it is.
- Determine how much it will cost to manufacture your product.

Then, once you've ascertained that your product does indeed have promise, it may make sense to apply for patent protection. The objective of this chapter is to give you an overview of your legal alternatives so you, with your attorney, can make informed and smart decisions about the future of your product.

What Is a Patent?

A patent is a right granted by a government to an inventor, giving the inventor the exclusive right, for a limited period, to stop others from making, using, or selling the invention without the permission of the inventor. When a patent is granted, the invention becomes the property of the inventor. A patent—like any other form of property or business asset—can be bought, sold, licensed, etc. Patents are territorial rights. That means that a U.S. patent will give the holder ownership rights only within the United States. This includes the right to stop others from importing the patented products into the United States.

To Patent or Not to Patent?

Even if you determine your product has great commercial potential and is ready to launch into the marketplace, it's important to note that not all products on the market are patented or patentable. Just as many inventors patent their ideas and never take them to market, thousands of products on the market aren't patented at all. This is a decision your patent attorney can help you make. In addition, your attorney may recommend filing for a copyright or trademark in addition to a patent, or in lieu of a patent, if that's more appropriate. These options are outlined later in the chapter.

There are many misconceptions about the need to patent. It is common to hear statements such as "I just saw something in the stores that I thought of 10 years ago but I didn't do anything with, because I couldn't afford a patent." To me, inventing is about turning an idea into real money—not buying expensive patent protection for a product that may or may not go anywhere. Patents, copyrights, trademarks, and nondisclosure agreements are merely legal tools that may or may not be useful, but the perception that you must take this step first should never be an obstacle to your progress. While legal protection is important, the other steps to getting your product to market are equally important.

When deciding whether you need legal protection, you should base your decision on your ultimate goals, your timeline, and your budget. The pros and cons to patenting are outlined here.

The Benefits of Patent Protection

There are many obvious benefits to protecting your invention legally. If you are interested in manufacturing and selling the product yourself (as opposed to licensing it to another company), a patent can help you better justify your investment in design, production, and marketing. That's because you'll have the comfort of lead time over those who might knock off your product and the peace of mind that your invention is protected by law and that this protection can be enforced if someone infringes on your rights.

If your goal is to license your product to another company rather than manufacture it yourself (see Chapter 10), a patent can be an equally useful asset (provided it's a quality patent filed by a reputable attorney). During negotiations, a patent can help expedite the prospective licensing company's decision, and it can provide leverage to ask for a higher royalty payment (because you've reduced their upfront legal costs and their risk). Your patent also gives them some confidence that they will not be infringing on another patent if they license your idea. Further, many manufacturers are unwilling to consider outside inventions that lack a patent or patent-pending status.

The Negatives of Patent Applications

If you have unlimited time and money, there are really no negatives to applying for patent protection. However, in the real world you'll typically need to weigh other considerations when evaluating the decision to apply for a patent. Moreover, while a patent provides legal protection, that protection is limited to the extent that you're willing to enforce it. Unfortunately, there are no "patent police" out there ensuring companies don't steal your idea. Even after spending the money to file a patent, you'll have to spend even more in legal fees to enforce that patent if you find someone violating your rights!

I learned this tough lesson at my first trade show when launching the TP Saver. Like many new inventors, I was surprised to hear several stories about companies that seek out, copy, and sell new inventors' products. And whether these products are patented or not is often irrelevant!

I don't want to exaggerate your fears, as the stories of idea theft are the exception…yet they are much more frequently told than when "nothing bad happens." Once you start networking within your industry, it won't take you long to learn which manufacturers cannot be trusted. And while imitation is the highest form of flattery, that flattery can be awfully frustrating when you're trying to develop a successful business. Though a patent-pending statement on your product may act as deterrent to these copycat companies, most of them know that patent enforcement is a time-consuming and expensive process, and they use this to their advantage. In addition, once your patent is published your product idea is easy for copycats to obtain—and then design around.

We know some inventors who have adopted the view that the cost and time involved in filing a patent is better spent on designing and launching their next product. They feel that the quicker they get to market, the sooner they'll make money. Then, if they're copied, they can focus on outmaneuvering the copycat in the market rather than fighting them in court.

Jan Childress of J. L.Childress (www.jlchildress.com) is one such example. She developed her first product nearly 20 years ago as a solution to a challenge she was experiencing—saving, rather than wasting, the breast milk she expressed while at work. And, in fact, she became one of the first to create a product, the Express Nursing Bag, which would adequately store mothers' milk. When she initially launched the business, she considered patenting the new product but her patent attorney advised that a patent

Twenty years ago, nothing existed to preserve a mother's milk once she expressed it. That's why Jan Childress invented the Express Nursing Bag, a special storage bag to help working mothers who were still breast-feeding.

wouldn't adequately protect it. Shortly after launching the Express Nursing Bag, Jan experienced what many inventors fear—her product was knocked off by a well-known company. They copied her product exactly, including the style of packaging. The only difference was the product name.

Jan soon realized that she could spend her money on patenting and hiring attorneys to prevent others from infringing on her rights, or she could spend the money to produce other high-quality products and great marketing. After years of experience, she now believes that if she gets an innovative product to market quickly, she'll gain more by obtaining a large market share early than by investing that same money in patent protection. Then, if someone decides to knock off her product, she'll already control a strong share of the market and already be working on her next money-making idea.

Weighing Your Options

If you must choose between legal protection and making your product, your money may be better spent on the design, production, and marketing of your product. In the end you should always rely on the advice of your patent attorney. If your product should hit big, for instance, you'd be wise to have a patent. Not only would your revenues give you the resources to fight any copycats, you'd also have more incentive than ever to protect your product and future revenues. Note: Whether you file for a patent or not, it is important not to infringe on other patents.

As I mentioned earlier, many licensing companies prefer an already patented idea; however, there are certain instances in which they'd prefer your idea wasn't patented. For instance, some companies would rather pay you a lower royalty to cover their own legal costs, or they would prefer having the flexibility to change the function and design of an invention. If the patent has already been filed, they can't modify your patent; their protection may be limited to the version you have already filed. Determining whether or not to patent your product prior to presenting it to a prospective licensing partner is completely dependent on your own personal situation. If you intend to pursue a licensing agreement, and you're able to afford a patent, it may give you more bargaining power. However, through your licensing research (see Chapter 10), you may end up identifying prospective licensing partners who do not require a patent. Doing your homework will help you to make an informed decision.

Understanding Your Resources

A number of legal resources are available to you during the patent process, including patent attorneys, patent agents, and patent search firms. There is more than one type of patent available as well as legal alternatives that may be more applicable to your product than a patent, such as copyrights and trademarks. The following provides an overview of your options when pursuing legal protection. While it is meant to inform, it's not meant to advise. Again, your best bet is to obtain the advice of a legal expert before making any final decisions.

Know Your Patents

There are two types of patents: utility patents and design patents. (There are also plant patents, but these are in a different class and don't generally apply to our purposes.) A *utility patent* protects an actual idea, regardless of its appearance—it deals with the structure and operation of the product. For the TP Saver, I obtained a utility patent, which means that its very function is protected. A *design patent*, which is much less complex and less difficult to obtain, deals only with the exact appearance of the object. The drawback of a design patent is that it allows room for another developer to produce a product that performs the same function as your product, as long as it doesn't look the same.

Your third option is to obtain a provisional patent. This is an alternative available in the United States but not in most other countries. The *provisional patent* application basically consists of a written description of your invention with drawings. Note that a provisional patent will never become a patent unless it is followed by a nonprovisional (utility or design) patent application. The utility patent application must be filed within one year of the provisional application.

A provisional patent application can be filed in lieu of a utility patent application when time and money are short. However, be aware that if you plan to eventually file a utility patent application anyway, it will be more costly to take two steps. A provisional patent can be beneficial when it's just not possible to prepare a utility application within a given time frame, or it's not financially feasible.

Finding a Patent Attorney

The legal field of intellectual property is so complex that it is essential to use an attorney who specializes in this field when considering a patent. There are two types of attorneys: One is the patent attorney, who must have an additional degree in a field such as engineering or science and who must pass two bar exams: their home state's and a federal patent bar exam administered by the United States Patent and Trademark Office. The other type of attorney, intellectual property attorneys, do not require training beyond law school and passing the state bar. We recommend using an attorney registered with the USPTO. They can be found by geographic region by visiting http://www.uspto.gov. In the upper-left corner click "Patents." Then, in the upper-left corner again, click "Registered Patent Attorneys & Agents." This brings up a search tool allowing you to input a zip code to find attorneys registered in your area.

Open Your Mind

Patent attorney Stuart West, founder of West & Associates, a northern California firm specializing in intellectual property, says there's one mistake that's very common during the patent process—thinking too narrowly. "Many times inventors sit in front of me with a focused image of exactly what the final product should or will look like," said West. "With regard to patent applications, inventors need to broaden their minds to all possibilities and possible looks, shapes, appearances of their invention."

West continues, "For example, say that an inventor comes to me with a widget that has two parts that are attached with a screw. I'm going to ask, 'Is the screw necessary? Can it be replaced with anything else? What is the purpose of the screw? Could I glue the pieces? Do they have to be able to be separated? Can I make it out of one piece instead of two attached pieces? Would three pieces be appropriate? Would it still work without the screw?'"

Ask yourself these kinds of questions regarding your design before you see your attorney. In the end, your patent should be as expansive as the patent office will permit. A broad scope will make it more difficult for others to find a way to design around it.

What to Expect in the Patenting Process

Once you find an appropriate attorney, you'll probably want to know how to prepare for your first meeting, how long the patent process will take, and how much it will cost.

Meeting with Your Attorney

The very first question you should ask your attorney is "Is a patent appropriate for my idea?" According to patent attorney Stuart West, your attorney can advise you on the best path—whether it's to apply for a patent, a copyright, a trademark—or nothing at all. Next, you should ask your patent attorney to explain the entire process of obtaining whichever form of protection is appropriate.

To give your attorney the best mental picture of your invention, be sure to bring all records related to your idea to the meeting the more organized the better. You can never provide your attorney with too much information. If your idea does end up requiring a patent, bringing a prototype, drawings, a written description of the invention, a list of the inventors, and any notes you have related to the development (dated in a bound notebook) will be extremely helpful.

Give Yourself Credit

Make sure that your name is included on the patent. Sometimes helpful husbands or partners will "take care of" the patent for you and mistakenly leave off your name as the inventor, only including their own because they are filling out the paperwork. Note that you will *not* have an opportunity to add your name later.

The Time for the Process

Expect to wait a while. The time it takes for the issuance of a utility patent depends on the complexity of the technology. For simple devices it takes approximately 24 months at the minimum. However, for more complex devices it can take over three years from the date of filing. Under special circumstances, paying extra fees (e.g., the presence of a terminal illness or being a certain age), can expedite this process.

For a design patent, expect issuance in about 6 to 12 months.

A new patent filed on or after June 8, 1995 expires 20 years from the date of filing. Maintenance fees are subject to change and are due for a patent at 3.5 years, 7.5 years, and 11.5 years from the date of the granting of the patent. Check the USPTO (www.uspto.gov) Website for updated fee schedules.

You do not have to wait until your patent is issued to start selling your product. Once officially filed, you can mark your product and packaging "patent pending" which makes it clear that obtaining a patent is in progress.

Filing Costs

The cost of filing a patent is subject to a number of factors, two of which have a particularly large impact. The first factor is whom you hire to file it: a big-city firm with staff attorneys specializing in everything from real estate to initial public offerings to intellectual property will generally cost a great deal more than a smaller local firm, a boutique firm specializing in intellectual property, or a patent agent. The second factor affecting cost is the complexity of your product: A widget that has many moving parts, sophisticated engineering, and extensive design variables will cost more than, say, my TP Saver, a small plastic tube with elastic strap and cap. We have paid anything ranging from $1,700 for a provisional patent filed by a patent agent, up to $10,000 for full patents filed with the help of an attorney.

The Scoop on Patent Agents

A patent agent, plainly and simply, writes patents. While anyone—(including you—though I don't advise it!)—can write a patent, the patent writer must have the ability to understand the format requirements and understand the implications of using specific language and terms to present an invention adequately so that it is fully and nonrestrictively described. That's why a patent agent, with the experience and know-how to provide this service, can be helpful—at a cost that is sometimes substantially lower than a patent attorney. It's important to note that like attorneys, patent agents' level of expertise and knowledge varies by individual. Carefully evaluate an agent's background before hiring the person.

The possible downside to using a patent agent rather than an attorney is that this person is not able to defend or enforce a patent in court, should the need arise. In addition, a patent agent may have less experience than an attorney and may write patents that are perceived by some as carrying less force or sophistication than an attorney's. Understanding an individual's specific experience and background is critical if this is a direction you're considering.

The Skinny on Patent Searches

If you're considering skipping the patent-filing process, you'll still need to ensure that your product doesn't infringe on someone else's patent rights. While this is a step that's built into the traditional patent-filing process (the patent office will perform a search once your attorney files), you should take this step independently if you decide to opt out of filing a patent.

Though you've probably already looked for similar patented inventions during your preliminary patent search (in Chapter 2), you may wish to take it a step further and purchase an expert search. You can purchase a basic search performed by experts who use the same databases as the examiners at the USPTO for approximately $250 to $800 dollars. To find a reputable company, visit The United Inventors Association (www.uiausa.com). In their "Resources" section, this association lists companies that can help conduct patent searches.

Don't Give Up!

Anissa Fiore's story illustrates how you shouldn't give up on your idea too soon—even if you find it's already been patented.

"One month after our daughter, Isabella, was born," explains Anissa "we began to bottle feed her. I searched the stores for a baby bottle holder—one that would give me a free hand while feeding, so I wouldn't have to hold the bottle constantly. I couldn't find anything like it. So I created my own bottle holder by sewing my hair scrunchie onto one of Isabella's stuffed animals. I used it often and Isabella seemed to enjoy snuggling with it as well.

"Approximately three months after I designed my own bottle holder, I came upon the same product being sold via a Website called www.bottletenders.com. The site's owner, Rebecca Gammelgaard, had already come out with this product and patented it. Rather than give up, I decided to contact BottleTenders. I explained that I had thought of this same product idea and I found her Website through an Internet search. I told her how wonderful her products were and she told me her own amazing invention story. After asking why BottleTenders wasn't yet available in every store in the country, she explained that she has been doing well with Internet sales but had run into a few stumbling blocks in penetrating the national retail market. After exchanging a few ideas through phone calls, we discovered our business skills were complementary. My background is in licensing, marketing, sales, and product development and Rebecca has 15 years of experience as a designer. We soon realized we could combine our unique skills to form a business that could help bring

Anissa Fiore and Rebecca Gammelgaard formed a unique and creative partnership—taking full advantage of each of their strengths—in order to launch and sell Bottle Tenders.

BottleTenders to the next level. I decided to present a business partnership concept to her. We hired an attorney to draft up a business agreement."

Patent Alternatives

An alternative to the traditional patent may make better sense for your particular product. Your attorney can advise you on which route is most beneficial; however, until then, here is an overview to help you understand the fundamental differences between patents, copyrights, and trademarks (or service marks).

Copyrights

When you want to protect a traditional idea or invention, a patent is most appropriate. However, when you want to protect published or unpublished literary, scientific, or artistic work (in a full range of expressions), a copyright is generally the way to go. In some cases, your attorney may advise you to use both forms of protection.

Whether your creation is an essay, a play, a song, a funky original dance move, a photograph, HTML coding, a computer graphic, a recording on tape or saved to a hard drive, it may be appropriate for copyright protection. Copyright laws grant the creator the exclusive right to reproduce, prepare derivative works, distribute, perform, and display the work publicly.

Advantages

The benefit of a copyright is similar to a patent, in that it gives you legal protections against infringement, and provides a warning to those who might otherwise feel unhampered in copying your work. If you've ever rented a video, you have seen the FBI warning at the beginning that warns you not to violate the copyright. While an individual must rely on the state to prosecute a case of copyright infringement (rather than suing the perpetrator herself), the benefit is the penalty. Unlike civil penalties relating to patent infringement, copyright infringement has an even greater deterrent—possible jail time.

Common Mistakes

The most common mistake an inventor can make is seeking a patent when a copyright is actually more appropriate. And, fortunately, a copyright is also far less expensive! Your attorney can advise you on the best route to take. Though you may pay $300 to speak to an attorney for one hour, if you learn that a copyright is more appropriate for your product than a patent, you've just saved yourself thousands of dollars!

Preparation and Advice

When consulting with a copyright attorney, bring clear evidence of the history of your work. Ancillary information, such as whether anyone else was involved in creating the work (an employee or a work-for-hire agreement, for instance) can be helpful to your attorney.

Timeline and Cost

A standard copyright application typically takes approximately six months and currently costs around $250 if filed by an attorney. (Filing it yourself directly with the copyright office costs $30.) If you choose to expedite the process, you can pay more—approximately $800 for a four- to six-week turnaround—if filed by an attorney.

Trademarks

Trademarks and patents serve very different functions. Trademarks identify a source of goods or services (such as a brand name), while patents protect utilitarian inventions. For example, the Apple trademark identifies the source of the computer, but a patent would protect the internal circuitry of the computer (never the name).

You're probably familiar with many trademarks: iPod is a trademark of Apple; Band-Aid is a trademark of Johnson & Johnson; and Kleenex is a trademark of Kimberly-Clark. No one else may use these trademarked brand names. This is why even though everyone looks or asks for "Band-Aids," a generic term such as "adhesive bandage" is used on the packaging of manufacturers other than Johnson & Johnson. Having this type of trademarked brand equity is a big advantage.

A service mark can be the name of a company (and commonly is) but is not restricted to that. Some examples are 24 Hour Fitness and all their "branded class" formats, various carwashes and their different "branded" levels of service, and banks with their levels of service. Apple is actually a trademark *and* a service mark in numerous different classes of goods and services.

The trademark does not identify or describe the goods or services. In fact, it is very difficult if not impossible to obtain a trademark registration for a descriptive word or phrase. For example, it would be almost impossible to get a trademark for a "Telephone" brand telephone. However, it would be fairly easy to obtain registration for a Uniden or AT&T brand telephone (assuming you are Uniden or AT&T).

The ® symbol on a packaged product, rather than the ™ symbol means that the trademark is a federally registered trademark. While some trademarks are issued through your state, the federally registered ® offers the greatest protection because it's protected nationwide, while state registration may not confer that broader protection.

Obtaining a Trademark

Preliminary search.   Just as you would when filing a patent, it's imperative to discern whether the name you want to trademark has already been filed at the USPTO. While it's not mandatory to do this before filing a trademark (the search is included in the cost of filing) it might save you a few dollars if you find an exact match and decide you'll need to come up with a new name.

You'll need to conduct a search not just for federal trademarks, but also for state and local usage. Any mark currently being used may impact your rights. To first search for federal trademarks, go to the United States Patent and Trademark Office site (www.uspto.gov), and under the heading "Trademarks" (on the left-hand side of the screen) click on the search button. This opens the Trademark Electronic Search System (TESS) page. Click on "New User Form Search (Basic)." A form with an empty field will open up. Type the name of your goods or services into the Search Term field and click on "Submit Query." It will bring up a list of similar names or the exact name if someone already has the trademark. If the record of the name you searched comes up, don't lose heart right away. Make sure to scroll to the bottom of the page to check if the mark is Live or Dead. If it is Dead, you may still have the opportunity to use this trademark yourself.

However, it's also wise to determine if your trademark is registered on the state level or used on a local level. To find this, note that each state maintains its own trademark database. However, not all these databases are online. Thus, you either have to subscribe to a database service or actually go to the facility where the state maintains the records, and search using the computers there. Local trademark information can really only be obtained from a Google or Yahoo! search.

It's important to note that in the process of getting a federal trademark, it's possible that a state or local trademark can block your registration. For example, if you are trying to obtain a federal registration on the mark "XYZ" and someone in California has been using "XYZ" as a trademark (either registered with the state or unregistered) for the same type of goods or services, the Patent and Trademark Office will likely refuse to register your use of the "XYZ" mark. Nevertheless, you may still be able to use and register your "XYZ" mark in your home state or area, provided your territorial use does not overlap or interfere with the other person's territorial use of the "XYZ" mark. Trying to compete using the same mark is *not* recommended. If you are successful and the other mark is still being used, you will not be able to register your mark, or use it where the other person's product is being sold.

Common mistakes and advice.   Most first-time inventors don't realize that they can begin using a trademark symbol immediately, prior to actually filing any formal documents. You actually *should* start using the symbol prior to filing the paperwork. Mr. West advises, "Keep detailed records regarding the date the mark is first used in commerce—this is of critical importance to the attorney filing the trademark application paperwork. One of the requirements prior to registration of a trademark with the USPTO is that the person seeking the mark should provide a date that the mark was first used. Additionally, by placing the trademark symbol next to the desired mark, you acquire some common law rights in the mark (these rights vary by state)."

Time and cost.   Once a trademark application has been filed, it takes anywhere from 16 to 20 months for formal registration. It can take much longer if there are problems with the registration, such as opposition from another party, or if you have to appeal.

The cost depends on the complexity of proceedings. However, you can estimate spending about $925 to $1,075, depending on the type of mark (text versus stylized) and how much your attorney charges per hour. In addition, you may pay more if additional legal time is involved due to unforeseen issues that arise with the mark. (We paid approximately $1,500 for each of our trademark filings.)

Nondisclosure Agreements

Another form of protection is the nondisclosure agreement (NDA). It is a tool that's used between two parties who will disclose confidential information to each other.

Although there's no "standard" template, a typical NDA simply binds two parties to agree to keep secret information confidential (provided it's not attainable by any other public means). The benefits of an NDA are twofold. First, it protects your patent rights. This is especially true with regards to foreign patent rights, where your right to file a patent is immediately forfeited if you publicly disclose information without a patent application on file or a confidentiality agreement in place.

The second benefit of an NDA is that it binds the signatories to refrain from sharing with a third party the "privileged" information they learn about each other. This protects business secrets, product information, and other plans or problems that may be revealed to the other party in the course of business. This can be important if you don't want a potential competitor to know that your product is about to hit the market.

If there is a possibility you will file a patent in the future, then an NDA can be a valuable tool to use. Further, if you're disclosing sensitive information, such as design or marketing plans, an NDA will enable you to share information with the confidence that the other party will not reveal the information for fear of being sued by you. See Appendix B for a sample nondisclosure agreement.

Understanding the NDA

It is important to understand what a nondisclosure agreement will *not* do. A typical nondisclosure agreement does *not* mean that either party agrees not to steal, produce, or otherwise move forward with a similar idea. In other words, a nondisclosure agreement is not a patent, copyright, or trademark so it provides no protection of the invention itself. It simply prevents disclosure of such information to a third party. Some nondisclosure agreements will include a clause that commits the signators to refrain from copying products or competing in the area of discussion. This is called a *noncompete clause*. Noncompete clauses within your NDA can help protect you further; however, the enforceability of a noncompete clause varies dramatically from state to state and many companies, probably most manufacturers, will be unwilling to sign an NDA including this clause.

We regularly work with the same set of vendors, which has allowed us to have a blanket confidentiality agreement that covers all our information sharing. In practice, you will likely find some people who will refuse to sign an NDA. This is often the case if they see little incentive to make a legal commitment for which they could later be sued. And you may also feel uncomfortable in certain situations asking individuals to sign an NDA. For example, during market research it may be a bit awkward to request an NDA signature from someone offering free input. Therefore, in practice, when you cannot get someone to sign an NDA, ask that they agree to keep your conversation in confidence and then document this verbal agreement in your bound notebook.

Taking on the World

Unfortunately, even if you do file for a U.S. patent, you'll only have exclusive rights to your product within the boundaries of the United States. Your patent provides no leverage in preventing others from copying and selling your identical product in other countries.

It makes financial sense to focus upon the U.S. market first because it offers the largest economy and largest potential market with spending power. However, you may also become interested in pursuing international markets and thus in securing protections available in other countries. It bears repeating that this is an area where you will want a professional's help, but I will address some key considerations for protecting yourself when going global.

Loose Lips

There are fundamental differences in intellectual property protections throughout the world. For example, the United States is the only major developed country in which an inventor has a year from the time an invention is publicly disclosed to actually file a patent. In the rest of the world, once an invention is disclosed publicly without an nondisclosure agreement or a patent filing in place, the patent rights are lost (there is an exception relating to the PCT Treaty covered in the next section). That doesn't mean you can't sell your product in those countries, it just means that you won't be able to file for a patent. It's good to be aware of this when pursuing international options.

Proper Protection

To file for patents in most foreign countries (those that are members of the Paris convention), an inventor has one year from her U.S. patent application date to do so. (You can find a list of current contracting parties here: www.wipo.int/treaties/en/ShowResults.jsp?lang=en&treaty_id=2.) There's one option that can buy you more time: applying through the Patent Cooperation Treaty (PCT). Over 120 countries around the world adhere to this treaty, which preserves your right for a period of time to file patents of the same invention in other countries. It also provides centralized filing procedures and a standardized application format. To determine if your country of interest is included in this treaty, go to http://www.uspto.gov/web/offices/pac/dapp/pctstate.pdf.

While a PCT application is commonly referred to as an "international application," it is important to note that there is no such thing as an international patent. Patent rights are country or region specific. A PCT application simply preserves your rights to file in other countries or regions for up to 30 months (31 months in some regions). It will never become a patent itself. In order to retain patent rights in a particular country or region, you still must file for a specific patent in that particular country or region, even after filing a PCT application.

A PCT application is not mandatory; you can file in each country specifically without using the PCT process. But it may be helpful under certain circumstances. For instance, I filed a PCT application for the TP Saver. I wasn't ready to spend the money to file individual patents in separate countries, but I wanted to protect my rights to do so in the future if I felt there was a need at a later date. The PCT gives you that option. It was expensive, at a cost of approximately $7,000, but after much thought, I felt it was worth the investment.

While you do not need a foreign filing license to file a PCT application, you will need one if you file for a patent directly with a foreign country. According to the USPTO, "Under United States law it is necessary, in the case of inventions made in the United States, to obtain a license from the Commissioner of Patents and Trademarks before applying for a patent in a foreign country." Again, this is a highly specific area and I recommend you work with a qualified professional.

International Copyright Protection

Unlike patents, copyrights are a bit easier to protect; they're recognized by all treaty member countries (most of the world with very few exceptions). However, rights to sue for copyright infringement vary by country. In the United States, generally speaking, you must register your copyright with the copyright office before you can sue someone for infringing on your copyright. The U.S. copyright office can be reached at www.copyright.gov.

International Trademark Protection

International trademark protection is as complex as international patent protection. According to attorney Stuart West, there are two routes you can take to protect your trademark outside the United States:

1. File in individual countries directly.
2. Use the Madrid Protocol. This protocol includes filing an application similar to the PCT application for patents. It's a little bit more efficient than a PCT application in that filing one application gives you trademark registration in multiple countries (the International Bureau handles filing in individual countries). However, each country will conduct its own examination of the trademark. The process typically takes 14 to 18 months.

What Will It Cost?

I've outlined projected costs for patents in the chapter. In an effort to save money, however, remember to consider the following points:

1. Would a provisional patent satisfy your immediate needs, enabling you to defer the higher cost of a utility patent?
2. Would a smaller law firm or individual practitioner charge less than a larger firm?
3. Can you find a registered patent agent with the skills and experience necessary to write your patent?
4. Is writing the patent application yourself an option? (While I don't recommend it, it can be done.)
5. Are there nonprofit or other trade groups that can offer free help? (Note: www.lccr.org is one such group with offices in San Francisco, Chicago, and Boston. They're more likely to help if you already have a business plan.)
6. Are you willing to take the risk of *not* filing a patent?
7. Can copyrights or trademarks fulfill your needs? Copyrights and trademarks are less expensive to register and can be put into use before official registration, free of charge. At the end of your name or symbol, simply place a © for a copyrighted item or a ™ for a trademarked item. Record the date you begin using these symbols in your bound notebook. No permission is required. (To create the © symbol in most word processing programs, place the letter *c* between two parentheses, and to create the ™ symbol, place the letters *tm* between two parentheses. Once you begin using them, you can officially register your marks at any time.)

Chapter Wrap-Up

A patent is not essential to take a product to market, and the ability to afford one should not be a deterrent to your progress. You'll find a significant number of products sold are not patented. Consider your attorney's advice, but the final decision rests with you. Either way, a basic understanding of patents, copyrights, and trademarks is important because they're potentially valuable tools at your disposal. Understanding the key points early in the process will enable you to know what options you have, as well as how to avoid potentially costly mistakes.

While there are a number of do-it-yourself publications and other shortcuts to take during the patenting process, I highly encourage you to use a qualified expert should you decide to file for intellectual property protection. It can be expensive or even impossible to correct mistakes that a professional could have helped you avoid in the first place. Remember the old adage: "It can be very expensive to hire a cheap lawyer."

Once you've made your filing decision, it's time to move on to your next important step—manufacturing. All the fundamentals are covered in the next chapter.

Getting the Goods

Manufacturing

Now that you know your product doesn't exist, you've made a successful prototype, and you've completed your market research, you're ready to move forward and manufacture your product. Even if you plan to license your idea to someone else, it's still useful to understand what goes into the manufacturing process and to determine the costs and manufacturing parameters of your own product. This will put you in a position to negotiate the best deal for yourself. (Learn more on licensing and negotiating in Chapter 10.)

This chapter goes into depth about choosing the right manufacturer—including the pros and cons of domestic versus overseas manufacturing—as well as what to watch out for during the manufacturing process. This chapter also covers information on tariffs, freight-forwarding, and customs, should you decide to manufacture overseas. Without a guide to follow, I learned a lot the hard way during the manufacturing stage, and I'd like to help you avoid the same mistakes I made. The purpose of this chapter is to save you time, money, and untold frustration.

Though entire books are devoted to the subjects of manufacturing and importing, my aim here is to shed light on the process and give you a framework by which to move forward. By the end of this chapter, you will know exactly how to find answers to your manufacturing questions. It will help you make your next big business decision—which manufacturer will produce your first run.

What Is Manufacturing?

Manufacturing is simply the process of making things. Companies manufacture nearly everything that we consume in our daily lives, right down to the food we eat. The manufacturing process can include any combination of industrial machinery, raw materials, and human labor. We are so accustomed to having and using these items every day that we don't even think about the effort it took to produce them. You are about to find out.

Who's the Manufacturer in This Scenario?

There's a confusing use of terminology in the industry that I want to clarify before we start. While you think of the "manufacturer" as the factory with whom you contract to produce or fabricate your product, it's important to note that retailers— to whom you will sell your finished product later—will refer to *you* (and your company) as the manufacturer. For purposes of this chapter, we'll still refer to the factory as "the manufacturer." But later, think of your factory as an extension of your company; together, you are the manufacturer.

Pinpointing the Right Manufacturer

There are countless types of manufacturers, producing adhesives, electronics, chemicals, hardware, machinery, tools, metals, plastics, rubber, and textiles, to name just a few categories and materials. The key is narrowing your search to an appropriate organization—one that specializes in the materials from which your product is made, in the volumes that you need and at a price within your budget. For instance, you wouldn't approach a manufacturer that specializes in plastics to make a luxurious pillow.

To begin narrowing down factories, use the same process we discussed in Chapter 3, when you were seeking a prototype developer. This means first identifying your options on www.thomasnet.com (formerly known as www.thomasregister.com), where you will find a network of 650,000 factories to choose from domestically. You can search by materials (vinyl, wire, cotton) and by state (see Chapter 3 for more detailed instructions on how to search this Website).

To locate an overseas manufacturer, try searching www.alibaba.com. Other good resources include the offices that many countries have set up to attract foreign business, such as the Hong Kong Trade Development Council (www.tdctrade.com). This organization offers up-to-date business information about working with companies in Hong Kong and China. Most countries also have an American Chamber of Commerce that can be a great resource. To find specific contacts, visit www.uschamber.com, scroll down the page to the "Full Site Directory," and under the "International & Trade" heading, click on "Find Chamber Abroad." (See more on choosing a United States or an overseas manufacturer further on.)

There are other ways to find a manufacturer, including a telephone book search for factories in your area or a more general Internet search. Word-of-mouth is also one of the best ways to assure that you are working with someone reputable, so I recommend asking fellow inventors to share their resources. (One good place to talk to other inventors is the message board on my Website, www.mominventors.com, where fellow moms collaborate and share resources and information.) Don't be surprised if people are somewhat reticent to share these contacts—it's kind of like sharing the name of that great babysitter. They may not be willing to jeopardize their relationship by casually passing out contact information to people who are not serious.

Once you have identified several companies that seem appropriate, start by visiting their Websites so that you are better informed about their services before you call. I suggest that you interview at least three manufacturers before settling on one to partner with. Knowing the right questions to ask to compare and contrast different companies is important. Here's a list of questions to get you started:

1. What types of products do you make?
2. Do you have reference customers I can contact?
3. What is your strength? (textiles, plastics, metal, etc.)
4. Do you have minimum requirements? What is the smallest manufacturing run that I can do for my first order?

5. Do you charge extra for samples? How long does it take you to produce samples, and when can I expect to receive them?

6. Is product packaging included in your pricing? Or do you outsource or subcontract the packaging?

7. If your product involves plastic, do you make plastic molds? If so, how long will it take to produce a new mold? Note that a company typically won't offer a price quote at this point, without seeing either a prototype or computer-aided design (CAD) drawings.

8. If your product involves fabric, do you make textile products? Do you work with my particular textile (i.e., cotton, canvas, silk)? If not, do you recommend any alternatives? How do you want product designs communicated? Do you expect a professional pattern or will a hand sketch suffice?

9. If you are contacting an overseas manufacturer, ask if they comply with any particular standards. For example, are they ISO certified? (This is an international standard that applies to good business processes.) Or have they been inspected and approved by any other bodies or private companies? (Wal-Mart and Target are both known to inspect and certify overseas manufacturers for their compliance with human rights and quality control standards.)

10. How much do you charge for your services? How do you break down your costs (e.g., cost of mold, per unit cost, packaging)?

11. What are the payment terms?

12. How do you handle damaged or defective product runs? Is there a percentage of product that must be damaged to reimburse my money or to justify a new production run?

I offer up these questions because as a novice, I learned some tough lessons. Having specific questions in hand would have helped a great deal and might even have enabled me to avoid the terrible experience I had with my first manufacturer. When I received the first 30 cartons containing thousands of packaged TP Savers, I eagerly ripped opened the first carton...only to find that the product packaging was falling apart. Although the production of the product itself was excellent, the plastic on the blister package (which houses the product and is glued to the backing card) was not adhering properly. Because we were launching our product at a trade show just three days later, my husband and I stayed up nearly all night regluing the blisters onto the packages. (It wasn't pretty!). We ended up gluing 1,500 pieces by hand. In addition to this "little problem," I discovered that the hang-hole on the package was centered. This seems logical; however, because of the design and weight of the product, the package hung crooked on a peg. The last thing a retailer wants is a package that hangs incorrectly on their store pegs. Therefore, I was also forced to hand-punch an additional hole on the top of each package in order to distribute the weight properly. Needless to say, I let go of our first manufacturer.

On a positive note, it was a valuable lesson learned—I found out what to ask and what to watch for. This enabled me to approach the second company with a few more questions and a lot more sophistication. Proving once again that if you understand the process and know the facts, you can make sound business decisions.

Fringe Benefit

One of the benefits of using a manufacturer that specializes in your industry or with similar products (say, toys) is that they'll likely be familiar with labeling and other U.S. regulatory requirements. This is information you've also likely uncovered when researching safety requirements during the prototype stage (see Chapter 3). Be sure to address and plan for these safety issues with your manufacturer.

First Things First

Before you actually choose a manufacturer and go into production, there are a number of additional issues you'll need to address: communicating your design to the factory and deciding between domestic and overseas production.

Design, Drawings, and Prototypes

Just like you wouldn't whip up a complex soufflé for the first time without a detailed recipe, your factory needs detailed instructions to manufacture your product. And because most manufacturers are not product designers, you should assume they know nothing about your specific product or design.

Depending on your invention, the best and most commonly used tools to communicate product design to your manufacturer are CAD drawings and an actual prototype. (CAD drawings work well for items that involve plastic or metal, but do not apply to textiles.) It may cost a little bit extra to produce these, but they are key to a successful manufacturing run. No matter where you've decided to manufacture, I recommend that you have these tools developed in the United States, to facilitate easy communication and get the ball rolling on a local level.

Whether you are creating a product-ready textile prototype or CAD drawings with a plastics engineer, the refinement process is the same. You'll start out with a hand sketch, discuss it, refine it, and then work with the engineer to create a production-ready design. Though you may be able to take some of these steps directly with the manufacturer, doing it correctly first—with an engineer or a prototype developer—will likely save time and possibly avoid costly errors, especially if you're working with an overseas outfit.

True story: a few times I have heard from surprised inventors about poorly made samples they received from overseas factories. These, they told me, were exact replicas of the rudimentary sketches they had sent—including replication of the flaws in the sketches! The lesson here is that you cannot assume that an overseas manufacturer will understand your design, or help you refine it. To avoid disappointment, design it right in the United States first, and then expect your manufacturer to replicate your exact designs.

The Great Debate

I've already alluded to it—and you may already be weighing the pros and cons. One of your big decisions during this process is to decide whether you want to produce your product domestically (in the United States) or overseas.

Talking strictly from a business standpoint, there are benefits and disadvantages to both. From a political standpoint, the issue often inspires heated debate. In this section, I will mainly discuss this issue from a business perspective; see my own story and decision-making process in the sidebar "More Than Meets the Eye."

More Than Meets the Eye

While companies are often vilified for "outsourcing American jobs," I can tell you that this issue is much more complex than this simple statement suggests. I have no intention to inflame anyone with strong views on the subject, and I'm not inclined to argue the issues in depth here. However, new inventors are often conflicted about the issue and come to me for advice.

This is what I tell them: Developing and launching a product is expensive. The combined costs of design and development, production, transportation, distribution, and marketing are substantial—before you have paid yourself a nickel in salary. For example, three years ago I sought out U.S. manufacturers to create a simple injection mold for my first product. A highly reputable U.S. company told me it would cost $15,000 to produce. I then found I could purchase the same mold in China for $1,500 or less. Because of my financial constraints at the time, the first option meant that I would have to abandon the project altogether. But if I pursued the overseas option, I could afford to give it a try. In the end, I was actually able to produce the mold—and my entire first run—for less than half of the cost of the U.S. mold alone!

It's true that by producing my products in China, I have helped pay the salaries of hard-working Chinese workers in lieu of deserving American workers. However, since the time I launched my company, I have also spent thousands of dollars employing American workers who provided technical design, wrote my patents, created my packaging and branding, developed my Website, handled my bookkeeping, set up my computer system, managed my warehouse, handled my shipping, and the list goes on. Had I abandoned the project, none of these additional dollars (at least five times the amount of money I've spent on manufacturing) would have found their way into the pockets of any American workers. And I would have forfeited my own income, as well.

Some might see this as focusing on profit over living by a moral code. Obviously, I disagree with the very basis of this position, but I am not looking to convert anyone. If you feel strongly about manufacturing in the United States, then by all means, do so. Many American factories are coming up with new ways to compete on cost with overseas manufacturers, and they may just provide an option that benefits your bottom line.

Domestic Manufacturing

There are definitely benefits to working in the United States. Without a language barrier, and with minimal time zone challenges, working with an American company can reduce the frustration factor. In addition, delivery time frames are shorter, there is no involvement with customs and freight-forwarding, and order minimums are generally lower. Plus it can be comforting for a beginner to work with another party that is subject to the American legal system, with all the caution and understanding that goes with it.

While American factories have taken steps to compete on price with overseas factories, they are typically at a disadvantage due to the higher cost of U.S. labor and materials. But even though the production costs may be higher, you should still evaluate all factors to determine if it might still make sense to manufacture in the United States. For instance, if you want a relatively small manufacturing run, paying more early on to a U.S. company might make sense, because you can receive feedback and evaluate demand prior to saddling yourself with a huge inventory. (Overseas manufacturers often require larger manufacturing runs.) In other words, if you order 200 units and your product is selling well, you may want to increase your run to 400 units for the next order, and so on. Once you see that there is strong interest in your product, you may then consider lowering your production costs by producing larger quantities overseas—which will increase your profit margin and your overall income.

What Is an Injection Mold?

If your product is to be made out of plastic, your initial professional prototype will most likely be hand-tooled by a handyman, machinist, or an engineer. This prototype will help you create a functional product. The TP Saver went through eight hand-tooled renditions before it was perfected and ready to take to the next stage. It was at this point that I needed an injection mold to allow for mass production. A *mold* is a block of steel with a cavity that is created in the shape of your product. A machine is programmed electronically with the specifications from your CAD drawings to cut the cavity out of the steel (this is why good design specs are so important!).

Once you have your steel mold, plastic pellets are put into the mold and heated until they melt, turning into hot liquid. This hot liquid then settles into the mold, forming the shape of your product. When it cools and hardens, the product is ejected out of the mold and the process repeats itself until you have completed the number of parts you are manufacturing. A single mold can be designed so that many parts can be produced at the same time. This is sometimes referred to as a *family mold*.

Manufacturing Beyond the Borders

There are, of course, also benefits to manufacturing overseas, but to many, this prospect is daunting. With differences in language, culture, currency, time zones, and distance, this fear is rational. However, because you're working with people who are economically motivated to make the process work, the greatest challenge is less a meeting of the minds than it is of logistics.

The greatest benefit to manufacturing overseas is, as I mentioned earlier, cost. Labor and materials are simply less expensive. And if you can produce your product for less money while maintaining high quality standards, you will have a better profit margin in the end (that is, if your product sells!). The greatest disadvantage to overseas manufacturing is that it adds another level of complexity to your business. Besides understanding all the manufacturing issues, you'll also need to understand the fundamentals of freight-forwarding, tariffs, and U.S. custom payments. Moreover, communication issues can be frustrating, and you must trust your vendor implicitly because there are so many more unknown factors.

But be reassured knowing that thousands of companies have good experiences with manufacturers in foreign countries. This is evident by the predominance of products on our shelves made abroad. Regrettably, the stories about positive experiences attract much less media attention than scandals and corruption. (Imagine how little media interest there would be in a press release headlined, "Chinese factory delivers exactly what was agreed to.") The bottom line is that when you're choosing a factory to work with—either at home or abroad—you should use good shopping practices. Look at the factory's body of work, speak with references, and make sure that you understand and clearly agree on the expectations of the job and the terms.

Once you learn the steps and you have all the systems in place, working with an overseas manufacturer is as simple as any of the other processes that you put into practice when running a business.

If you do take the overseas route, note that there are a few international-specific issues to understand—like tariffs, freight-forwarding, and customs brokerage—discussed next.

Totaling your tariffs.   You'll most likely have to pay a tariff when you import the product you've manufactured overseas. A *tariff* is basically the tax you pay to bring items into the United States. A specific tariff is assigned to your goods when they go through customs. It's important to know in advance the amount you will be taxed, so that you can include this figure in your overall budget. The most efficient way to find this information is by visiting the Website of the United States International Trade Commission (www.usitc.gov). Under "Tools & Links" on the right-hand side of the screen, click on "Tariff Schedule." Scroll down until you see "2005 HTSA—by Chapter." Click on that link and you'll find a breakdown of tariffs by categories.

Unless you have time to go through the small print, I recommend that you scroll all the way down the page until you see the actual Harmonized Tariff Schedule. This document has headings, article descriptions, and general tax information. For example, one of our Mom Invented products is made out of high-impact polystyrene and the other out of polycarbonate. By clicking on plastics, I learned that I will be taxed 6.5 percent for the value of the goods that contain styrene and only 5.8 percent for the value of the goods that are part of the polycarbonate family!

Creating your calendar.   There is often a lag in shipping when utilizing an overseas manufacturer. However, it's not usually due to simple distance. It's more often the result of a lack of knowledge about how each of the steps in the manufacturing, shipping, and delivery process relate. For that reason, you need to establish a clear list with all of these steps, each of which has its own time requirements. It's also important to know which steps are dependent on the completion of prior steps and which ones can be done simultaneously. For example, the production of your product may be able to coincide with the printing of your packaging. Once you do this you can take your interdependent list of tasks, add up the number of days each task will take, and forecast a date of delivery. Transportation and customs clearance may affect your time frame.

Freight-forwarding. Freight-forwarding companies are service providers that offer help with transporting goods overseas and in the United States. *Freight-forwarding* refers to moving cargo from one location to another using every kind of transportation available: air freight, shipping, rail freight, and trucking. Freight-forwarding companies also oversee logistics management, customs brokers, and export documentation.

A quick Internet search will reveal many companies that offer this service. But if you feel more comfortable going with a well-known brand name your first time around, Fed Ex now offers door-to-door service from countries around the world to the United States through their Fed Ex Trade Networks (www.ftn.fedex.com). Note that using freight-forwarding companies can be expensive, so shop around if you're not going to go with the big brands. And once you choose a preferred company, save money by going with a "consolidated" shipment, which means you'll share a large container—and thus share the costs of shipping —with other importers. In industry terms, this is called *LTL* (less than load container).

Customs brokerage. Just as when you cross international borders and must show your passport for clearance, the products that you import must also pass muster to enter the United States, going through U.S. Customs for approval. Though some freight-forwarding companies offer their own custom brokerage services, you may need to contract with a separate customs broker to handle the paperwork and help clear your shipment at the port when the vessel containing your shipment arrives.

There are certain documents required for your shipment to clear U.S. Customs. The following are the basics; your particular product may require more. A customs brokerage firm can help you determine if this is the case.

- *Packing List.* This document outlines the contents of your shipment, including the number of cartons and description of your goods. It's prepared by the factory that manufactures your product and is given to the shipping company.
- *Bill of Lading.* This outlines the contents of your shipment, and is prepared by the shipping company and given to you. It should exactly match the manufacturer's original packing list. In other words, if 22 cartons left the factory in Xiamen, China, the same number should be listed on the bill of lading headed for Long Beach, California.

- *Arrival Notice.* This is a document prepared by the shipping company that announces the arrival of your goods. This will be sent to you, usually via fax, upon the shipment's arrival. When you receive this fax, be prepared to send a payment immediately so that the shipment can be moved right after it clears customs. Delays in moving your goods will often result in penalties, unless the shipping company has the capability of warehousing your goods. Be sure you know the logistics of this before your shipment arrives at the port.
- *U.S. Dept. of Treasury Customs Bond.* Your customs broker can prepare a customs bond. This document is required by U.S. Customs, so they're provided with "insurance" for payment upon arrival. For instance, if U.S. Customs has difficulty getting payment from you, the importer, they want to be assured that someone will pay the duty and any fees. It's a relatively simple (one page) application.

Your customs broker will ask you for copies of these documents and will be physically present to shepherd your shipment through customs. It's also possible to do your own customs brokering; for an outline of the process, along with the appropriate forms, go to www.customs.gov. However, this experience can be frustrating and challenging. You may find yourself at the docks without proper documentation or information, which can delay taking possession of your goods. I believe a customs brokerage firm is well worth the money. They handle absolutely everything and usually charge between $95 and $200 per shipment. This amount is paid in addition to the U.S. Dept. of Treasury Customs Bond. Your tariff is also due at this time.

Cost-Cutting Measure

A common mistake when manufacturing for the first time is the belief that you'll only need one shipment per year. But, if your product is wildly popular and you need more inventory, you'll soon need additional shipments. Note that you are charged duty on every shipment. It is also mandatory to purchase a U.S. Department of Treasury Customs Bond. Your choices include Single Entry Bonds, purchased for each individual shipment, or an

Annual Entry Bond (approximately $500 for coverage of up to $50,000). If you anticipate more than one shipment per year, I recommend the Annual Entry Bond because it allows for unlimited shipments throughout the year.

Manufacturing Know-How

Now that you've weighed the pros and cons of domestic versus overseas manufacturing, and you've evaluated your choices and hopefully chosen a partner, there are a number of issues to be aware of as you go through the production process concerning materials, labor costs, samples, specifications, and packaging.

Making the Most of Materials

While doing your market search and developing your prototype (Chapters 2 and 3), I mentioned paying particular attention to materials. This was because I believe it's helpful to show the manufacturer samples of the material you would like to use. However, it is equally as important to keep an open mind.

In the end, your initial materials may present problems when it comes to mass production. For example, I am developing a new product right now. I found a plastic material that I thought would be appropriate for this product, so I sent it to the manufacturer. He came back to me with production pricing that would not work. Based on my target retail price point, I realized that by the time I spent money to have my product produced, shipped, and sold, there would be an insufficient profit margin. (See the discussion on calculating margin in Chapter 8 to understand how to determine pricing.) When I told my manufacturer that the price points didn't work, he worked with me to develop a solution. He proposed that if we used a thinner grade of this material, I might not lose the integrity or quality of the product…and it could bring the price back in line with my projections.

While you should have a general idea of what materials might work for your product, don't be too hasty when finalizing your decision. Once again, you'll need to do some research on pricing, suppliers, durability, and quality. Even if a material costs more, you could end up saving money elsewhere. For instance, nylon may be more costly per square yard than cotton, but perhaps the nylon supplier is in your region, thus cutting down on shipping. Or maybe nylon sews 20 percent faster or stuffs 50 percent easier, saving labor costs. And, be aware that some regions or countries have better access, and pricing, on certain types of materials. Therefore, keep an open mind. You can turn to your manufacturer for advice and expertise, but don't always take your initial information at face value.

Learning about Labor

The cost of labor can significantly influence your production costs. Just as it does when you get your car repaired, labor costs can often dwarf the cost of materials and parts when it comes to manufacturing your product. For instance, a typical U.S. manufacturing shop will charge anything from $15 to $40 an hour for labor. Say it takes exactly two minutes to assemble your product. If you go with a shop that charges $15 an hour, your per-unit labor cost is 50 cents. If you go with a shop that charges $30 (a typical figure for excellent quality work), your labor cost per unit is $1. Obviously, a 100 percent difference in labor can change your profit margin significantly.

However, be aware that when it comes to labor, you usually get what you pay for. Even though you think you're getting a deal with a $15-per-hour shop, in reality it may end up costing you more. For instance, if the work is sloppy, you may end up with a percentage of products that can't be sold or that are returned from the consumer. Add in shipping costs for returns, and suddenly your cost advantage may disappear. So if the labor costs seem too good to be true, they probably are! Use caution when choosing a manufacturer strictly on the basis of price.

Getting Samples

Before you mass-produce your product with your chosen manufacturer, you'll want to examine samples of the product with the final materials you've selected. This will give you a true picture of what the final product will look like, and it will raise a red flag about any last minute design flaws or issues with the materials. For instance, if you are manufacturing a fabric item that you wish to be washing machine-safe, make sure that you test it repeatedly to see what happens to the materials. When I was testing the

TP Saver sample, I used all my strength to try to break the product. When I couldn't, I was satisfied.

Do good quality samples ensure that the quality of your entire production run will be maintained? Not necessarily. Even if you see high-quality samples, there are no guarantees that the quality will be maintained. However, if you have an initial sample that you both agree to, you have something to fall back upon if a substandard run is later delivered. Be sure to get in writing what your recourse is, should you receive poor-quality product. For instance, if the factory ships you 40,000 units of damaged goods, what are your remedies? An honest company will have no problem signing such an agreement, because they stand behind their work. This is especially important when manufacturing overseas, because you can't visit the factory to oversee production yourself.

Get It in Writing!

Missy Cohen-Fyffe, inventor of the Clean Shopper, a fabric cover that protects babies from shopping cart germs (www.cleanshopper.com) learned her own hard lesson, after trusting an importer from the U.S. who facilitated production in Asia. While her first few production runs turned out great, she later received two large container loads of goods that were completely defective.

"By the time we realized the extent of the damage, we had unknowingly sold more than 2,000 defective units," Cohen said. Her importer had switched factories without telling her, and when the damaged product arrived, refused to compensate her for damages. She had no choice but to temporarily close the business while searching for the solution. She ended up trucking all boxes of product, stacked to her ceiling, to a U.S. facility known for fixing product defects. She also began the process of recalling product that had been sold, and answering consumer inquiries.

"It took three months to get the company back on track, but now we are a stronger company, with a new and reputable Asian supplier and better quality systems in place. The entire process taught me to have agreements in place, and to consult my attorney frequently," Cohen said.

The Clean Shopper, invented by Missy Cohen, not only helps protect kids from shopping cart germs that collect after repeated use, it also keeps kids comfortable and cozy in the cart.

Manufacturing and Printing Specifications (MAPS)

Before you send your manufacturer the first purchase order, essentially, the go-ahead for them to mass-produce your product (see the sample purchase order in Appendix B), make sure the company has the proper specifications that explicitly spell out the details you and the manufacturer have agreed to. These specifications are in the form of a manufacturing and printing specifications (MAPS) document (see Appendix B for a sample MAPS) that contains details in categories relevant to your project (e.g., printing and packaging, product quality and traits, and packing and shipping).

Specifics you may wish to include in the printing category for example are trim size and card stock of your packaging, digital art that details your packaging designs, colors (see sidebar on Pantone colors for more on the universal language of color), front of backing card, back of backing card, and press proofs.

For the product itself, you'll want to clarify details like color, style, material used, process notes, and numerous other items. For packing, you'll want to pinpoint how many units should go into an inner carton, and how many inner cartons should be included in a master carton. And shipping information should include all delivery requirements.

Unfortunately, many people do not take the time to create MAPS documents for their manufacturer. But I highly recommend that you do, in order to have an organized record of the entire process, as well as the terms you both agreed to. Once your manufacturer agrees to the terms of your MAPS document, you'll be able to send your first purchase order to officially start the process.

What Are Pantone Colors?

The Pantone Matching System is the worldwide standard for color reference. By referring to Pantone color guides and mixing formulas, designers and printers across the world and across language barriers can clearly communicate exact color requirements and expectations. You can purchase your own Pantone Formula Guide by visiting www.pantone.com.

There are many variations of each color, and each color is assigned a number. The Pantone standard ensures that everyone is on the same page. For instance, if I told my manufacturer that I want my product to be red, he would choose whichever red he liked—it might be an orange-red, pink-red, or blue-red, while I expected a fire-engine red. Choosing a specific Pantone color can eliminate any miscommunication. Pantone also offers color chips that you can rip out of a chip book and send to your manufacturer.

Proper Packaging

First-time inventors are often so consumed with the production of their product that they leave the packaging decisions until the last minute. But packaging is an integral part of your process, and you need to give it special consideration. In many cases, the packaging is more complex than the development of the product itself. After all, you have less than three seconds to get the consumers' attention when they are walking down the aisle of a retail store, so the package needs to "interrupt" their thinking and draw attention to itself. Add to this the size (dimensions of the package itself) and other retailer expectations, and the process becomes even more challenging. For instance, various retailers will have their own packaging preferences. After interviewing independent stores as well as big-box stores, like Wal-Mart, for my own product, I chose to adhere to Wal-Mart standards so my product would be accepted easily everywhere.

Your packaging should clearly communicate the name and function of your product. Every word counts, and you need to communicate the contents of the package and its features and benefits in the quickest way possible. Because if the consumer doesn't get it, she just won't buy it.

Once again you can learn from my own mistake. When I began developing my own packaging for the first time, I hired a marketing company. The graphic designer was very artistic and I loved his packaging design! And after launching the TP Saver, I found that people liked the package—

Designed by an artist rather than a retail packaging expert, my original TP Saver packaging was flawed. While it looked nice, the logo was not effectively placed to maximize brand recognition.

but had absolutely *no* idea what was inside. The package was not clearly communicating the contents or function of my product to consumers, and this was a potentially fatal mistake for sales. Even though the packaging was pretty, it just wasn't effective.

While a graphic designer is required to produce retail-ready packaging, not every person who calls himself or herself a graphic designer is an expert in this specialized area. Finding people with this skill can be challenging. When you interview graphic designers, request samples of product packaging that they have done. When I finally hired the right person to redesign my package, he explained a few fundamentals that you should keep in mind when developing your own packaging.

People read from left to right. The company's brand should appear at the top left, the name of the product in the center, and the function of the product beneath the title. The features and benefits should be communi-

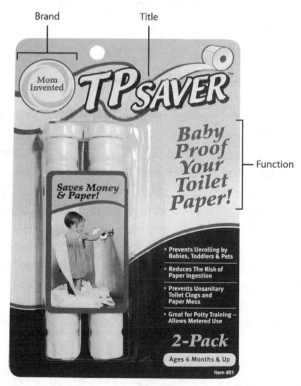

This is what my new TP Saver packaging looked like after being redesigned by a retail expert. Note that the Mom Invented logo was moved for better brand recognition.

cated in quick and easy-to-read bullets. With these key points in mind, the new designer was able to transform my package into something that both consumers and retailers understood and responded well to.

There are many options when it comes to packaging, and it all depends on your final product and how it will be displayed. Your packaging may consist of anything from a cardboard box that's displayed on a store shelf to a blister package that's displayed on a hanging rack—with countless options in between. This is a decision that will be made in collaboration with your expert team (designer, printer, and factory) and is based on several factors, including the shape of your product, its size and weight, how it will be shipped, and how it will be displayed.

Manufacturers (both in the United States and overseas) typically outsource the printing portion of the packaging. In other words, the packaging is often printed off-site and then returned to the manufacturer so that they may insert the product and finalize the packaging for delivery to the client. The packager will use the designs your graphic artist created when producing the final packaging.

Choosing Color for Your Business

The role and importance of color in conveying a message or meaning or in communicating a feeling about your business or product cannot be overstated. In his book, *Guerrilla Marketing*, Jay Conrad Levinson says, "The colors you use in your marketing weapons—stationery, signs, office décor, brochures, business cards—play an important role in motivating people. Colors speak loudly and clearly about your business. But they give forth mixed messages…colors speak louder than words. Colors stimulate emotions, excite, impress, entertain, persuade. They generate negative reactions if you don't understand them. Therefore, you must consider the meaning of color."

Here is a quick primer from Levinson's book on the emotional effects of color:

- Red evokes aggressiveness, passion, strength, vitality. In business, it is great for accents and boldness, it stimulates appetites, and is associated with debt.

- Pink evokes femininity, innocence, softness, health. In business, be sure you're aware of its feminine implications and associations.
- Orange evokes fun, cheeriness, warm exuberance. In business, it's good to use orange to highlight information in graphs and on charts.
- Yellow evokes positivity, sunshine, and also cowardice. In business, it appeals to intellectuals and is excellent for accenting things. Too much is unnerving.
- Green evokes tranquility, health, freshness. In business, its deep tones convey status and wealth; its pale tones are soothing.
- Blue evokes authority, dignity, security, faithfulness. In business, it implies fiscal responsibility and security. Blue is universally popular.
- Purple evokes sophistication, spirituality, costliness, royalty, and mystery. In business, it's right for upscale and artistic audiences.
- Brown evokes utility, earthiness, woodsiness, and subtle richness. In business, it signifies less important items in documents.
- White evokes purity, truthfulness, being contemporary and refined. In business, it enlivens dark colors and can be refreshing or sterile.
- Gray evokes somberness, authority, practicality, and a corporate mentality. In business, it is always right for conservative audiences.
- Black evokes seriousness, distinctiveness, boldness, and being classic. In business, it creates drama and is often a fine background color.

Shipping

Freight-forwarding companies offer domestic as well as overseas services. (See earlier section in this chapter for more details on freight-forwarding and shipping options.) Shipping domestically is understandably less complex than shipping product from overseas. You'll still need to choose a reputable company to ensure safe delivery of your product, so do some online research and ask for references before making a final decision. Going with a well-known brand name, such as UPS or FedEx, is almost always a safe bet, but can be a bit pricier than smaller companies.

Shipping Tip

For shipments under one pound, the U.S. Postal Service Priority Mail is about the best value a small business can find. You get two- to three-day delivery, a free box, and online tracking for $3.85 (with their box) anywhere in the continental United States. You can track all your packages at www.usps.gov/clicknship. Also, they will ship you as many free boxes as you want—at no charge—*and* preprinted labels with your company name. Call 800-222-1811 to order preprinted labels and boxes.

Filling Your Orders

Your next decision will be whether to stock and ship inventory to your customers from home, or to hire a fulfillment distribution and warehousing company. Many inventors start out doing the shipping themselves, as I did, packaging product on the kitchen table. However, when you grow, it is nearly impossible to keep up and it is critical to the success of your company to provide excellent customer service. The last thing you want to do is upset your retailers by sending out late shipments. Packing products is surprisingly time-consuming, as it also demands the proper shipping documents (discussed in more detail in Chapter 8). To find an appropriate fulfillment house, search the Internet or your telephone directory or ask other inventors whom they recommend. Eventually, we hired a fulfillment company to fill our orders. We now pay rent for warehousing our goods and additional charges for each box, label, and labor (handling fees). Make sure to find out exactly how much the services and warehousing will cost. One helpful resource is the Mailing & Fulfillment Service Association (www.mfsanet.org) which has a directory of fulfillment companies to meet your specific needs.

Warehousing

Unless the shipment is scheduled for delivery to your home, or you've already contracted with a fulfillment house, you'll need to make arrangements for the storage, or warehousing, of your products. Many shipping companies also offer warehousing options, which can simplify the process for you. Each service is a separate fee, so be sure to get a proper rundown of costs. Make sure you understand all of the steps you need to take to get your items from the manufacturer to your warehouse, and how much each of these steps will cost.

You may also choose to find your own warehousing options. Perhaps it's a monthly rental at an established self-storage facility. Or perhaps a friend or family member has an unused garage or storage capacity they'd loan you. Once again, your options will be largely dictated by the size and amount of your inventory. If it's 10 boxes, a homegrown solution may work, but if you're beginning to store thousands of units, you'd probably rather go with a commercial storage facility that can monitor shipment inventory and pickup. As I mentioned earlier, companies that specialize in warehousing and fulfillment can be found online. Another great option is to work with a manufacturer who has extra space and staff already in place.

Shipping and Warehousing in the United States

Shipping costs in the United States will vary based on the dimensions of your packages, weights, and distances traveled.

TIP: Some carriers are less expensive on some routes than others, so compare different carriers. If there are enough goods to ship on a pallet, this will often reduce the handling fees involved and also protect your goods.

Like shipping to your own warehouse, some carriers are less expensive on some routes than others. Similarly, some are more competitive for certain size boxes.

TIP: If you have two relatively small boxes going to the same address, it is often less expensive to tape them together so that they ship as a single box. This only works if when combined, they are within the carrier's minimum weight and dimension requirements.

Outsourcing the warehousing function gives you more time to spend on sales and marketing—and helps you avoid the challenge of storing boxes in the living room! Compare the costs of multiple vendors. The costs of line items vary from warehouse to warehouse. Some warehouses may simply charge a percentage of your order. Be prepared for the following potential costs:

- Setup fee
- Receiving-packages fee
- Storage fee by square/cubic foot or by pallet
- Stacking or shelving fee per box
- Fee for removing item from shelf to fulfill an order
- Packaging fee and box fee (if warehouse must break open an existing box)
- Shipping-label fee

   TIP: If you are starting small, partner with a company that's already doing fulfillment (warehousing and shipping products to customers).

Chapter Wrap-Up

You may be surprised about all the elements of manufacturing beyond the assembly line—factors like materials, labor, packaging, shipping, and warehousing. But with awareness of all these factors (and the potential costs associated with them), you'll be able to plan and budget more effectively in anticipation of receiving your final product. When you receive your first shipment, you'll have a sense of accomplishment that you never imagined. Now you're ready to take your product, and sell, sell, sell!

Taking Care of Business

Setting Up Shop

In previous chapters we've discussed how inventing a good product is just half of the equation—you must also turn your invention into a viable business to find success! Running a business requires that some business systems be put in place before you can sell your first widget. These steps may not be quite as exciting or fun as, say, developing your invention or testing it with friends and family. They are, nevertheless, necessary to get your business on solid ground to move ahead.

In this chapter you'll learn about the systems, documents, and structures you will need to put in place and how taking these steps early can save you money and create business efficiencies. When I launched my business, I had absolutely no idea what I needed and often found myself scrambling without critical systems in place. I found myself drowning in a sea of acronyms—C-Corp, ICANN, SKU, PO, UPC—that made sense to everyone, it seemed, but me. And because Mom Inventors, Inc. grew so quickly, I was under even greater pressure. I didn't know the first thing about how to ship orders, bill customers, or track inventory. Since then, however, we've streamlined our operation and put systems in place.

My objective here is to give you an overview of what I didn't know then to enable you to move your business forward on a solid footing. The key is knowing you don't have to do it all on your own; there are experts available in every field who you can find and ask for help.

Missy Cohen-Fyffe, inventor of Clean Shopper (www.cleanshopper.com), took full advantage of the resources and helping hands around her. She says, "I always laugh when I hear people say, 'You did this all by yourself?' No, I had a SCORE counselor [discussed later in this chapter] who helped me source a sewing contractor; I had a friend who watched my children so I could develop my product and company; I had friends and family who purchased my first units and used them frequently so they could spread the word; I had a local post office that gave me tons of tips and actually agreed to come to my house to pick up packages, so I didn't have to take time out of my day to drop them off; I had attorneys who didn't charge me an arm and a leg to answer my endless questions; an accountant who provided a detailed explanation of the different types of business structures available; a friend who agreed to handle my books early on; the list just goes on and on."

Missy Cohen-Fyffe, inventor of the Clean Shopper, runs her multimillion-dollar business from her cozy home office. She created a working environment that felt right for her.

In her book, *It Takes a Village*, Hillary Rodham Clinton talks about the need for community to share in raising a child. As you can see from Missy's statement, a "village" can also be helpful in "raising" a successful home business!

Whether your village is big or small, it's also helpful to be aware of some fundamentals before you begin organizing your day-to-day business. The first thing you'll need to do is to decide exactly where you'll run your operations.

Setting Up Your "Space"

It's essential to create a defined space that's devoted to your business. Don't expect to run it from the dining room table or the kitchen counter. Not only should you set aside physical space—probably somewhere separate and defined in your home, at first—it also means setting aside mental space in which you can conduct business freely. Finding both types of space can be a challenge, especially if you have children at home.

Mom Inventors, Inc. was launched from my second daughter's bedroom! I will never forget the moment NBC's *Today Show* called in May 2004 to consider having me as a guest for their segment on women entrepreneurs. My babysitter had called in sick that day, and I was caring for daughters Sophia (age two) and Kiara (a newborn), but because it was relatively quiet I took the chance to answer my business phone. The moment I began speaking to the producer, Sophia decided to have a "bring down the walls" tantrum. I offered to call right back, hung up the phone and began negotiating with my two-year-old. I promised a visit to her favorite park—and chocolate—if mommy could make just one quick phone call. When I thought the deal had been struck, I picked up the phone and dialed. The moment the call connected, Sophia reneged on our deal. I grabbed all the markers on my desk, fell to the floor with paper and began frantically coloring with Sophia as the producer commenced her interview. Though I was invited to be a part of the show, a smooth, businesslike interview is not the reason I was chosen.

Be Realistic about Running a Business

"Don't kid yourself that you can do it with your kids running at your feet. You'll make needless mistakes and it will be one step forward and two steps back."—Leianne Messina-Brown, inventor of the Gourmet Tote (www.gourmettote.com).

If you are responsible for child care, you should harbor no illusions that your children will quietly read books and color while you conduct business. While research, planning, and writing can be accomplished at night or during nap time, it is important to arrange some workday child care coverage—even if it is only two hours per week. If paid help isn't feasible, look to family members or community services for help. The key is to arrange the same two hours each week that you can use and depend upon to schedule important telephone calls or outside meetings. Expand your coverage when possible. You may not accomplish everything on your list during these fleeting time slots, but you can begin to tackle the most critical items on your list.

The Gourmet Tote, which is designed with special insulation and "shelves" that can carry multiple dishes, makes it easy to transport food to parties, tailgates, or family picnics. Leianne Messina-Brown, who's always on the go with her own family, invented the Gourmet Tote because she was tired of carrying party casseroles in the back of her car without a good way of securing them and keeping the food warm.

Tools and Technology

Nearly every mom inventor that I have interviewed for this book said there is one tool she can't do without: the Internet. And, of course, your key to accessing it is through a computer. This section details exactly what other technology will likely help you as you begin your business. While you may have some or all of the following resources, you may wish to upgrade or dedicate them solely for business use. You will need:

- *A computer.* A laptop with wireless capability which gives you the ability to work from anywhere in the house, and to access the Internet for free in areas that offer "Wi-Fi" links, like airports, coffeehouses, and some libraries is great for moms on the move. But, you can also buy a relatively powerful desktop computer for a surprisingly low investment so buy what your budget allows.
- *DSL or cable high-speed Internet access.* Though it costs more than traditional "dial-up" Internet access, I believe high-speed Internet access is absolutely critical for busy moms. When I first began my business, without any child care help, I felt like I had a kitchen timer ticking the minute Sophia fell asleep for her nap. Under this kind of time pressure, searching the Internet with a dial-up connection can feel excruciatingly slow. If this is all you have right now, plan to get DSL or cable when you are able. It's well worth the extra $20 to $30 per month investment.
- *A dedicated telephone line.* A line for business use only is essential. If you can't afford to put in an additional phone line when you first start your business, use your cell phone. Leave a professional message with your business name, and only answer the phone when you are able to speak (without the kids screaming in the background).
- *An 800 number.* This is also an inexpensive and effective tool for establishing credibility and can easily be set up by your long-distance provider. It gives the appearance of a professional operation. However, keep in mind that this means you pay for the 800 calls that come into your office. I tend to give our 800 number to customers or to those doing me a favor by returning my call. In addition to the cost of each call, we pay $10 per month for this service plus $.10 per minute for calls we receive on this line.
- *A professional answering service.* Fortunately, they're not as expensive as they used to be. For $40 per month, I was able to hire a local

24-hour answering service. I found an answering service helpful when I began making my first media appearances and didn't want to miss possible orders that might come in from calls after the show. With an answering service, a live human answers the telephone 24/7 in your business name. You can find a service in your local telephone directory or on the Internet by typing "answering service" into the Google search engine.

- *A fax machine.* This is also essential. I was surprised by how commonly retailers submit their purchase orders by fax. A new fax machine is available for approximately $200 dollars; however, I recommend an all-in-one fax, printer, and scanner, which costs around $350+ at your local office supply store or on the Internet. It takes up less space and is more cost-effective than purchasing separate machines for each function.

Giving Structure, Taking Shape

Before you go further in setting up your office operations or hiring staff, you first need to establish the identity of your company. This means deciding on how your company is structured, then naming your company and giving it a "public face." This section will tell you how to begin this process.

Choosing Your Business "Identity": Sole Proprietorship, C-Corp, S-Corp, or LLC

While you can save money by performing many of the steps in starting a business yourself, there are certain critical times when I highly recommend hiring an expert. Deciding how to "structure" your business is definitely one of them. Your business structure will define how your business runs financially and how it will be taxed. This will be how you are identified by the U.S. government, potential investors, and customers. As with patenting, an expert in this area can offer sound advice that will help you save money and protect your business and personal assets in the long run. Moreover, if you set up your company for growth from the beginning, you are less likely to spend extra time and money restructuring your business in the future.

A good accountant or corporate attorney can advise you. This expert should also inform you about what official documents you'll need to file with state, local, and federal agencies. Your local Small Business Administration (www.sba.gov) office can also assist you in making this decision. In the meantime, here's a basic overview of your possible business entities, provided by corporate attorney Ann Rankin (www .annrankin.com).

- *A sole proprietorship.* A sole proprietorship is the simplest type of business to start because it has few legal requirements. Basically, to form a sole proprietorship you need only a business license to begin operating. The owner of a sole proprietorship has complete control and receives all the income. It sounds wonderful....but if anything goes wrong, you will have unlimited personal liability. This means that all your assets and future assets—business *and* personal (house, car, furniture)—can be taken to satisfy the claims of your creditors, so it's pretty risky if you're investing money that you've borrowed and suddenly can't pay back. In addition, sole proprietors usually have great difficulty raising capital from investors. To save money in the beginning, you might consider starting as a sole pro- prietorship, then converting to another type of business entity at a later date.
- *A partnership.* This business entity has the same disadvantages as a sole proprietorship—unlimited personal liability. With a partner- ship, however, the liability is spread across the partners. "General" partners have unlimited liability, while "limited" partners are more protected. Every limited partnership must have at least one general partner, who has unlimited personal liability. Like sole proprietor- ships, partnerships also have difficulty raising money from outside investors.
- *A corporation.* There are two types:
  - Use a *C corporation* structure if you think you will be raising millions of dollars and having an initial public offering (IPO). This form of corporation protects you from unlimited personal liability. While you can lose the money you invest into the cor- poration, your personal assets are protected as long as you follow corporate formalities. One disadvantage of a C corporation is that it is subject to double taxation. When it makes a profit, those

profits are taxed at the corporate rate. Then, when it pays you a salary or gives you a dividend, the salary and the dividend are taxed again, at your individual income tax rate; so the money is taxed twice!

– An *S corporation* may prove to be a better option if you don't plan to make a public offering of securities. It has the same benefits of limiting your liability that a C corporation has, but it doesn't involve double taxation. With an S corp, profits and losses are taxed only at the shareholder level, not at the corporate level. You must follow certain corporate formalities with an S corp, such as avoiding the comingling of corporate funds with your personal funds. There are also some limits on the number and type of investors you may get.

- A *Limited Liability Company (LLC)*. This is often your best option if you don't plan to make a public offering. Its structure protects everybody, even the "managing member," from unlimited personal liability. It can be taxed either as a partnership or as a corporation; you choose. One obvious benefit is that you'll avoid double taxation if you choose to be taxed as a partnership. Also, there is no limit to the number or kind of members, and it is more flexible than an S corp.

For more information before meeting with a professional, the Small Business Administration (SBA) is a smart resource. Go to www.sba.gov and click on the link "Starting Your Business" on the right-hand side of the screen. Then go to the "Startup Topics" box and click on "Forms of Ownership." This will spell out each of the business entities mentioned above in greater detail.

Getting Your Ducks in a Row—Officially

After you've decided on a business entity, you'll have to make it official with your state and local governments. It may be necessary to meet requirements from city, county, state, and federal government agencies. For instance, I had to get a city business license, file my company name with the county and with the state, file articles of incorporation with the state, and apply for my Federal Employer Identification Number with the IRS. Most of these steps can be taken yourself, but you may also want to rely on the advice of an accountant or attorney.

To begin learning about the requirements in your region, visit the Website of each relevant government entity in your area. The Secretary of State's office in your state government is generally a good place to start. Another terrific resource for state and local agency information is www.statelocalgov.net. This directory lists all of the Websites in a given state, from the governor's office to the smallest of counties. Click on the "Business" link on your state's official Website. Most state Websites will describe the business and legal requirements necessary to establish your business entity.

No matter where you reside, you'll also need to register for a Federal Tax ID number, also known as Employer Identification Number (EIN), as mentioned above. (The only exception is if you're creating a sole proprietorship, in which your Social Security number will suffice.) But for a partnership or corporation, the IRS will need this number to identify your business for tax purposes. You'll soon find that large retailers will expect you to provide this number as well. (Often large retailers expect you to complete a detailed vendor application, which establishes you as a "real" entity.) To obtain an EIN you must complete IRS Form SS-4. You can apply online at http://www.irs.gov/businesses/small; click on the link "Employer ID Numbers (EINs)."

In addition, some states require a seller's permit. Information that pertains specifically to your state can typically be found on your state government's Website under the Board of Equalization. Aside from the hassle of more paperwork, the upside is that this permit, sometimes referred to as a resale permit, provides you with the opportunity to purchase items wholesale and then resell them. For example, I purchased T-shirts and baby bodysuits wholesale, printed our Mom Invented logo on them, and then sold them in our Mom Invented eBay Store. I am responsible for making sure that the sales tax on these items is charged to the customer and passed through to the state.

Special Start-Up Advantages

If your business is minority-owned, you may wish to be certified by the National Minority Suppliers Development Council (NMSDC) or one of its regional affiliates. If your business is woman-owned, you may wish to be certified by the Women's Business Enterprise National Council (WBENC). Such certification may provide an advantage with certain retailers; for example, some of the mass-market big-box stores have special departments that deal with these types of businesses. I found success with this in our own business. After some difficulty penetrating one major retailer through the "normal" route, I decided to contact the Director of the Minority/Women's Office, and I received an immediate response.

To be certified as a woman-owned or minority-owned business, a company must be at least 51 percent owned, controlled, and operated by a woman or minority.

For more information, contact:

National Minority Suppliers Development Council
15 West 39th Street, New York, NY 10018
212-944-2430 / www.nmsdc.org

Women's Business Enterprise National Council
1156 15th St. N.W., Suite 1015, Washington, DC 20005
202-862-4810 / www.wbenc.org

Dun & Bradstreet Registration

No matter who owns your business, you should register your company with Dun & Bradstreet. This is a common resource that businesses use to verify the legitimacy of companies and their history. In addition, certain large retailers such as Wal-Mart will ask you for your D&B number on their vendor application form. Even the smallest company can register with D & B. It is free to register and can be done quickly over the phone by calling 800-333-0505 or by visiting their Website at http://www.dunand bradstreet.com.

The Home Field Advantage

Having a home office offers tax advantages if your business is profitable. To take advantage of this, figure out what percentage of your home is dedicated to business use—say, 20 percent of your house—and then you can write off the interest, insurance, and taxes on that portion of the home. You can also write off incremental expenses such as an extra can for garbage, extra phone line, etc. But deductions are limited to income from your home office endeavor. You can't take a "loss" from a home office. In other words, if your business loses money, you will not be able to deduct expenses attributable to a home office.

There is a Web resource that I find useful called www.tanned-feet.com. It is a free business-oriented Website designed to help entrepreneurs. Here's a tidbit from the site about home offices:

> If you run your business out of your home...you do not have to own your abode to deduct a portion of the cost! Moreover, it does not have to be a house. Apartments, condominiums, boats, or anywhere else where you can sleep and eat can qualify for the home office deduction. In order to claim the home office deduction, you must meet the following criteria:
>
> 1. The home office is the principal place of business for your business.
> 2. There must be a separately identifiable place in your home for the business.
> 3. The space so set aside must be regularly and exclusively used for business.
>
> If all three requirements are satisfied, then you can deduct a portion of the cost of your home, before rent, mortgage payment, or otherwise.

Become a Website Wonder

Part of legitimizing your business and giving it an official "face" to the world is creating a Website—especially if you plan to manufacture and sell your product yourself (rather than licensing, which we discuss in Chapter 10). A Website imparts information about your business, displays your professionalism, and will help you to be taken more seriously. You can approach creating this Website yourself or hire a firm to do it for you. I advise tackling the job only if you're technically comfortable—and even if you are, don't underestimate how much time it will take. Earlier in my career, I created my own Website using computer software called Microsoft Frontpage. Many new computers are preloaded with Frontpage; if your computer does not have this program you can purchase it online (www.microsoft.com/frontpage) or in your local computer store. Even though I was comfortable with the program, it still took me approximately 100 hours to get the Website up and running.

Other options today include packages from Internet Service Providers (ISPs) that include e-mail, Website hosting, and basic Website templates that you can use to dramatically simplify the setup process. Hosting services that include Website templates can be found for as little as $10 to $30 per month. Keep in mind, however, that if you're planning to sell products directly through your Website, you'll require more sophisticated features like a "shopping cart" for your site. This type of service is also available for purchase on the Internet; one such service is www.quickcart.com.

Professional designers and Web techs can offer a level of professionalism that may be challenging to produce on your own. That's why when I launched Mom Inventors, Inc., I hired a professional. To find an expert in Web design, consult a general marketing and advertising company (more expensive) or an independent Website developer. Find them in your telephone directory or on the Internet. Or, even better, ask people you know for recommendations. Or, search the Web and look for sites you like; at the bottom of the home page you'll sometimes find the name of the Web design firm. Or you can e-mail the company and inquire who created the Website. Depending on the level of experience and skill, a design firm will typically charge from $25 to $150 per hour. If your project is a large one, you may prefer to get a quote based on the entire project rather than a per-hour arrangement.

When you do contact a Website developer, take the time to find examples of what you like visually and technically (i.e., if a site offers a shopping cart or "Paypal" service). This will help the developer to visually understand the look and feel you are trying to achieve. The more information you provide, the less time (and money) it will take for the developer to design a site that satisfies you.

Before you hire a Website developer, take time to review their portfolios. Once you determine if you like their design style, here are some additional questions to ask a potential Website developer:

- How long will it take you to build my Website?
- How do you charge? By the hour, by Web page, by project?
- How extensive is your technical knowledge? In other words, are you more of a designer (good at creating graphics) or more of a

technical/systems expert (shopping cart, e-mail capturing devices, etc.).

- Will it be designed so I can easily update it? If not, how much will it cost to have changes or updates made?
- Do you have a portfolio I can review?
- Do you have three references (name and telephone numbers) of clients that you have worked with in the past that I can call?
- When I send you revisions, how long does it take you to make them?

Of course, before you finalize your Website, you'll need to develop a formal name for your business. The ins and outs of choosing a name are covered in the next section.

The Name Game

What's in a name? A whole lot, especially when you're building relationships and an image with buyers, vendors, and customers. That's why choosing an effective name is a vital early step in developing your business.

That said, feel free to explore and brainstorm business names! One of the most common mistakes I see is when inventors name their company the same as their product. For example, if you invented a day-glo dog leash and you named your company "Day-Glo Dog Leashes, Inc." it would be tough to release any other pet product through the same company name. Naming your company the same as your product can inhibit growth, defining your company in terms that are too narrow.. You may think now that this is the only product you plan to ever develop and bring to market. However, if you truly have an inventor's mindset, you will continue to think of one product idea after another.

Julie Aigner-Clark, founder of the Baby Einstein Company, started her business as a single product company with her first video to stimulate and educate infants. Under the general name of Baby Einstein, she was able to go beyond that single video to add countless more videos and educational products. She turned her small home-based venture into a multimillion-dollar company that was eventually acquired by Disney. Similarly, take the time to think of a company name that's "big" enough and that feels right to you. Like naming a new baby, this can be a fun and creative experience!

Another error to avoid is naming your company something that's meaningful to you but meaningless to customers. Many mom inventors

I've observed combine their kids' names in some way. While it's cute, it can also result in names that are difficult to remember, hard to understand, or tough to pronounce (picture yourself answering the phone all day using this name as a test). Also, your name needs to convey the right image for the company. Ask friends and family for their suggestions and feedback. A word of caution here—like naming your baby, asking family can be touchy, especially if they really dislike the name you have chosen.

Once you have decided on your company name, search the Internet and purchase the domain name that you have selected. (See the section later in this chapter on consulting ICANN, a government-sponsored site that regulates facets of the Internet. This site will help show you how to obtain a domain name.) Hopefully, someone else will not already own the name you've chosen. Companies that sell domain names often offer packages with e-mail address accounts along with your domain name. These e-mail accounts can further legitimize your business and present a professional image, as opposed to using an e-mail account with a Hotmail, Yahoo, or AOL address. (I even know businesswomen who use e-mail with their husband's name. This implies they are not technically savvy, and it is highly unprofessional.) This is also a tip-off that you are a small (sometimes interpreted as "unstable") company. Presenting your company as a serious player from the beginning, by using an e-mail address with the name of your company, will allow you to prove yourself and the credibility of your company to others...retailers in particular.

Your company name and Website address are important company assets. They help present a sound, professional image and help increase the value of your company to prospective customers, partners, investors, or even acquirers in the future. Once the name of your company is finalized, I recommend trademarking the name. (See the discussion on trademarks in Chapter 5.) You can register a trademark yourself online by using the USPTO Website, or hire a professional (typically a patent attorney) to submit it for you.

Managing Your Business

Once you have the framework in place, it is necessary to start attending to the nuts and bolts of building your business. These are the systems and resources that will enable your business to run smoothly, such as staff, office processes (including invoicing and inventory systems), insurance, and customer service.

It's All about the People

Contrary to popular belief, you don't need to hire an employee to cover every respective area of your business. Hiring "virtual employees"—those who work for your business, but on a fee-for-hire basis—has become an effective alternative for small and growing businesses. For example, I do not employ a full-time attorney, package designer, Web developer, or product engineer. I hire their services when I need them. They don't come to my office to work and I haven't even met them all in person, but I do consider them part of my team. I get the benefit of their talent without having to oversee insurance, payroll, or other complexities associated with hiring employees and I only pay them when I have a specific need for their service.

As your company grows and the workload increases, you may find it necessary to hire part-time or full-time staff. There are definitely more complexities to doing so, including payroll management, insurance issues, and more. When you do reach the point where it's necessary to employ workers yourself, consult with an accountant to know what steps to take from an accounting perspective.

Office Operations

To run a successful business, you'll also need certain systems and processes in place that will allow you to perform transactions (make and receive payments), manage your inventory, make shipments, and serve customers. Running many facets of a business can become very complicated, so these systems and processes should help simplify and streamline your business. The following is an overview of the basic systems you'll need to put into place.

Getting paid: merchant accounts. If you're selling a product, you'll need an easy way for your customers to pay you. Credit cards and electronic payments are the most popular payment methods today for both end-users and retailers. A *merchant account* is a global payment-processing service that enables merchants to process secure transactions, 24 hours a day. The company that provides your merchant account will process credit cards and electronic checks and work with many business transaction modes including Internet, broadband, wireless, call centers, and retail. You can find merchant account companies through your industry association or bank, by searching online, or even through discount clubs such as Costco. In addition to signing up with a merchant account service, you will need to open a bank account with the capability to link to a global payment-processing service. Some banks may offer the entire package. A merchant account costs approximately $50 per month plus a per-transaction fee. Note that some banks charge initial setup fees.

You can't fight the (invoicing) system!   Not only will you need a conduit by which your customers can pay you (your merchant account), you'll need a system that tells you from whom—and when—all your payments are due. Unlike a store in which you pay for your goods before you walk out the door, you may be shipping goods and expecting payment later. So, when you send out an order, it will be accompanied by an *invoice*, basically a bill that details what products you've provided, how much is owed to you, and when it's due.

When I came back from my first trade show, I had about 50 new orders from retailers who wanted the TP Saver. I manually created all 50 orders as Microsoft Word documents. This was a good, low-cost way to start. However, it wasn't efficient and didn't allow us to scale with our business growth.

Once you begin to receive orders, a systematic method for shipping, invoicing, and tracking is essential. Fortunately, there are a number of options available. We use a computer software program from Intuit called Quick Books. It's available for purchase at www.quickbooks.com. Basic QB 2005 costs $199.95. Not only does it let you create shipping orders, invoices, and purchase orders, but it also lets you track inventory. These are the core components that you will need for your business.

So what are these four components, exactly? In your Quick Books (or similar accounting program), you'll be able to set up four template documents: Purchase orders, shipping orders, invoices, and an inventory-tracking report. Purchase orders are documents that detail the supplies or products that you order from vendors, manufacturers, or factories, giving them a record of what you've ordered and what you owe. Shipping orders give directions to your warehouse to ship a certain amount of product to a specific customer (say, Wal-Mart). Invoices bill customers for the product you're sending them. And your inventory-tracking report keeps track of all this movement of cash and supplies, in and out of your business.

The benefit of a program like Quick Books is that it automatically links all this information together for record-keeping purposes. For example, if I send out a shipping order requesting my warehouse to ship 100 units to one of my customers, that shipping order is linked to both my invoice and the inventory tracking system (deducting 100 units from the total number of units that I have in stock). Another advantage of a software program like Quick Books is the ability to generate reports that tell you exactly how much inventory has gone out, your income and expenses, outstanding invoices, etc., by week, by month, or by year, so you can perform business analysis. Plus, once you enter a customer's information into Quick Books, it retains that information, making it even faster the next time you need to invoice a recurring customer. To learn more, visit www.quickbooks.com. Also, consider asking your accountant or a bookkeeper to help set you up on a program like Quick Books initially. This may save you much time and frustration as you initially learn the program. Plus, it will save you money to have a smooth-running system from the beginning, rather than hiring a bookkeeper later to clean up any potential messes.

Plenty more on purchase orders. You'll encounter purchase orders in two ways in your business: when you create them and when you receive them. As a manufacturer, you will hire vendors to produce something for you. Therefore, you will need to provide them with purchase orders for their work. For example, each time I order TP Savers from my factory, I provide the factory with a purchase order. This official document should state specifically what you are ordering and how much you are expecting to pay (a fact you've already verbally agreed to with your vendor). Details include the date of the request, quantity ordered, item description, unit price, and the payment terms.

There is also a place on your purchase order for comments. In this area, I always spell out my expectations in detail. For example, I'll note the specific materials to be used (ABS plastic and elastic), the length of the elastic in inches, the expectations for the packaging (e.g., four-color printing with a gloss finish on the front side of the packaging and the Pantone color specifications), in order to ensure we are both on the same page. It is also important to spell out how the pieces should be packaged for shipping. For example, if I order 20,000 units, all 20,000 units cannot be thrown in a box together and shipped. In my last PO I wrote, "Of the 20,004 TP Saver packages, 12,000 pieces need to be packed individually in cartons of 6 units with 8 cartons per master box totaling 48 units per master box. Each box should then be put in sturdy bulk boxes for transport." Note: I figured this out through trial and error by asking our retailers (customers) how they would like the product delivered to them. (See Appendix B for a sample purchase order.)

Just as you send out purchase orders to buy your inventory or supplies, retailers will send you purchase orders to purchase your products. I usually receive these by fax, but may also receive them by e-mail and telephone. Make sure your fax machine is working and loaded with paper at all times!

Before you receive a purchase order, you will need to agree to payment terms. For example, we always ask our customers to pay Net 30 (this means within 30 days of receiving our invoice). However, some of the larger stores will say that they will only pay Net 45 days or Net 60 days. Another term that I had never seen prior to working in this business was "2% Net 60." This means that the retailer will get 2 percent off the total bill if they pay in full within 60 days.

Bringing in the Dough

Collecting payments from small retailers can be time-consuming and difficult. As a new product company, many will be reluctant to pay upfront. We decided that it was worth it to us to offer an additional 5 percent discount for prepaid orders (usually paid by credit card). This way we almost never fail to get paid, and our retailers appreciate the extra discount. Plus, we can use the cash right away!

Shipping orders.   A shipping order is a simple document that you use to request shipment of product from one location to another. If you store your products at an off-site warehouse, a shipping order provides an official request to the warehouse to ship to a given customer. This also provides a record and paper trail to follow if any problems arise.

As I mentioned before, a program like Quick Books keeps track of your shipments and manages inventory. When you create a shipping order in Quick Books, it will automatically deduct that inventory from the inventory-tracking portion of the program so you don't have to reenter that infomation into every facet of your program.

Beware of Shipping COD

Cash on delivery (COD) may seem like a safe bet—after all, the package won't be delivered until payment is exchanged—but in reality, it can be fraught with problems. At my first trade show, I learned this lesson firsthand, when one retailer asked if I would ship a case of TP Savers COD. To appease this new customer, I agreed without knowing much about it. After three delivery attempts, the United Parcel Service (UPS) was unsuccessful at delivering the case, and I was charged $20 anyway for shipping.

Tiffany Whitchurch of Simply Tiffany Taite, Inc. (www.simply tiffanytaite.com) learned this lesson a much more expensive way.

Tiffany Whitchurch, founder of Simply Tiffany Taite, Inc., always loved pearls and wanted her daughters to enjoy them too. When she had difficulty finding these special keepsakes for small children, she decided to create her own unique product line.

She reports, "A 'customer' placed a $1,050 order with my sales-person, acting as if I had an established relationship with her, and asked to have the order sent COD. The items were delivered, but when I went to cash her check I was told it was from a *closed* ac-count! A *felony*! Needless to say, this was how we learned to only accept money orders and cashier's checks!"

Customer Service Is Key

It's critical to take care of your customers, thereby creating loyalty and long, fruitful relationships. Depending on how your business is struc-tured, your customers may be end-users—those who buy your products and use them—or retailers—those who buy your products to sell to end-users. We sell our products wholesale to retailers and then they sell our products to their customers. When dealing with retailers, here are some strategies to ensure they remain satisfied (and to ensure they keep buying your products!).

- *Order confirmation.* When you receive an order, fax or e-mail a note that says something like: "Thank you for your order. We ap-preciate your business. Your shipment will be sent by _____ date." Then be sure to meet or beat this date.
- *Tracking notice.* Make sure to keep package tracking information in your customer files. Many times a store (the large stores in particu-lar, that have to manage lots of inventory) will say that they never re-ceived a shipment. In these instances, tracking proof is invaluable.
- *Follow-up.* Call after your product has been received to make sure your customer is satisfied.

Service Will Set You Apart

Positive customer service ratings can typically be earned by fo-cusing on two things:

- Setting expectations that you meet or exceed—underpromise and overdeliver. For instance, if I know my customer will be sat-isfied with a 72-hour shipping turnaround, I will tell the customer I'll meet that expectation, even though I know we can do it within 24 hours. Then, when they receive the shipment "early" they'll believe their expectations have been exceeded. This kind of reliability creates loyal customers.

- Communicate. In business, everyone has times when they fail to meet their commitments. The key to surviving these foibles is by communicating. Most customers will allow for a few mistakes if you proactively communicate and work to find a resolution. Contact and reassure customers about a problem before they have to contact you. They often have bosses too, and don't want to look like they are not on top of things.

Warehousing, Fulfillment, and Inventory Tracking

Warehousing is simply the storage of your inventory, and fulfillment is processing (i.e., mailing out product and tracking that product) the purchase orders that come in. And while you may want to perform this function initially from home, as I mentioned in Chapter 6, as your business grows you may seek out other options. Wading through the floor-to-ceiling stacks of boxes in your home or garage and shipping everything yourself may become inefficient, not to mention overwhelming!

As an entrepreneur who likes to control the process, your first instinct might be to find warehousing or storage space to rent and to continue managing it yourself. However, another option is to delegate this time-consuming and relatively straightforward task. Try partnering with a company that already does warehousing and fulfillment. For instance, early on I discovered that one of my online retailers had excess warehousing space, as well as regular staff that filled orders. Through them, we were able to arrange for our inventory to be stored and our orders to be fulfilled (for a fee, of course).

For such services, anticipate a setup cost ($750–$1,500), monthly storage fee, merchandise receiving fee, boxing fee, and fulfillment fee per order. Some companies will charge more for storage and less for fulfillment, while others will emphasize the opposite. There are also companies that specialize in warehousing and fulfillment. To find one in your area, visit the MFSA (Mailing, Fulfillment Service Association) at www.mfsanet.org. Click on the first button on the left-hand navigation bar to find a mailing or fulfillment company by state and service.

Understanding Insurance

One of the unexpected challenges and surprise costs for a small manufacturer is liability insurance coverage. This type of insurance will help protect you and your business in the event you are sued for problems or injuries that (allegedly) arise from your product. Unfortunately, in our litigious culture, insurance has become increasingly difficult to find; in some cases it's almost impossible, or prohibitively expensive. For instance, we have low-risk products, yet our premiums have ranged from $200 to $900 a month.

Here are some things to keep in mind when looking for product and general liability insurance. You'll deal with two "layers" when getting liability insurance—the carrier, which is the actual insurance company, and the broker, who sells you the policy. Some brokers work directly with a particular carrier, e.g., State Farm, while others are "independent" and represent many carriers. (This relationship is similar to travel agents who sell tickets on multiple cruise lines, airlines, and hotels.) There are advantages and disadvantages to dealing with both types. For instance, a broker that's associated with one carrier may have more leverage to convince the company to take you on; while an independent broker who really shops around may offer more competitive rates and options.

Industry associations often have insurance programs for their members. They can also usually advise as to which carriers insure in your particular industry. This way, when you contact an insurance broker, you can ask if they have relationships with those carriers. The telephone directory will also provide a large number of brokers you can contact. Or you can start with your home or car insurance broker for leads. Your local chamber of commerce can also point you in the right direction.

When you settle on a broker, be sure to communicate with that person when filling out the forms. While you cannot and should not mislead the insurer, there are often different ways to state the same thing on application forms that will increase your chances of acceptance. Your broker can advise you on how to state something to your greatest advantage.

What Will It Cost?—Money-Saving Tips

- The fees to establish your corporate entity will vary by state. To save money, get the professional guidance necessary and then find free or low-cost help to complete the documentation your-self. Your local SBA office, chamber of commerce, or state gov-ernment office will likely offer this kind of assistance.

- To save money on Website design, start with a template, often included in your Web hosting package, rather than building a Website from scratch or hiring an outside firm.

The UPC

Here's something else that may not immediately pop into your mind when launching your business—getting a Univeral Product Code (UPC). This is the bar code symbol, that oh-so-familiar pattern you see on just about every prod-uct you buy—a series of black bars and white spaces with numbers below. The numbers, which are encoded in the symbol, uniquely identify the prod-uct. This group of numbers, referred to as a Global Trade Item Number (GTIN), is captured by in-store scanners, which help track sales and product orders via computer. The GTIN in a UPC is always 12 digits in length.

Much like every individual has his or her own Social Security number, every company is assigned a unique bar code. The bar code can be used on up to 100 products, which means there is no need to apply for additional bar codes if your first product spins off into multiple offerings.

Your UPC is obtained from the Uniform Code Council (UCC) and uniquely identifies your company within the UPC system. Once your ap-plication is accepted by the council, you'll receive the number on the UCC membership certificate which will be included in your membership kit.

Most good-sized retailers will expect you to have a bar code on your product, to adapt to their in-store computer system. While not essential for small boutiques or independent retailers, it is to your advantage to purchase a bar code and incorporate it into your packaging design from the start. Then, once an opportunity from a major retailer arises, you'll be ready to go.

To get the ball rolling, go to the Uniform Code Council, Inc. (www. uc-council.org) and on the right-hand side of the screen, click on the link that says, "I need a UPC bar code." Or, to become a member, call the UCC's Partner Connections team Monday through Friday, 8 a.m. to 6 p.m. EST, at 937-435-3870. You can also contact them via e-mail at info@ uc-council.org. I have found the staff to be enormously responsive and help-ful. The membership fee is determined by the number of unique products you need to identify, as well as your company's gross sales revenue. You will need to complete the online membership application to find out what your company's membership fee will be. Since I began with a single product at the very beginning of my business, my fee was the very lowest—$800. It was still, however, another one of those unexpected and unplanned costs!

What's a SKU?

When a retail buyer is interested in purchasing your product, they'll ask, "What's the SKU (pronounced "skew") number?" SKU stands for stock-keeping unit. According to the Uniform Code Council, each product in a store "requires a separate identification number to distinguish it from other items. In inventory control and identification systems, it represents the smallest unit for which sales and stock records are maintained." Essentially, within the 12-unit bar code, digits 10 and 11 are your internal SKU numbers. In the bar code example below, the SKU is "01."

When a retailer scans a bar code, the first nine digits are the numbers assigned to you by the Uniform Code Council. This sequence will always remain the same, and can be used on up to 100 products produced by your company. The next two numbers are of your choosing, to differentiate your products from one another.

As part of the bar code, there are digits that you, as the business owner, have the freedom to change. These digits are called SKU numbers. As you add new products to your company, the bar code stays the same but the SKU numbers change. You assign the SKU numbers yourself. For example, the TP Saver SKU digits are "01" and another of my products Good Bites has the SKU digits "40." This allows us to better track our different products.

For example, the UPC for TP Saver (baby version) is 8-92458000-01-1. To the right of the SKU is a final number on the outside of the bar code lines, which is a "check digit" that verifies to a retailer that all your product and company information is correct. For the pet version, the TP Saver UPC is 8-92458000-02-1. Notice that only the two digits changed before the final "check digit." These are the digits we assigned to the products.

The Best Things in Business Are (Sometimes) Free!

Certainly, there is no one book or resource that can answer every question and challenge that arises when launching your business. Fortunately, there are some excellent free and low-cost resources that can help you get your business off the ground.

Service Corps of Retired Executives (SCORE)

I am dazzled by the impact of the Service Corps of Retired Executives, or SCORE. Almost daily, inventors tell me about the great experiences they've had with their SCORE counselors, retired executives who volunteer their time to help small business owners. Not only do they provide knowledgeable advice for entrepreneurs, but they often have contacts and resources that can be equally useful. The best part? The services they offer are free and confidential, and they can help you build your business from idea to start-up to success.

The SCORE Association, headquartered in Washington, D.C., is a nonprofit group dedicated to entrepreneurial education and the formation, growth, and success of small businesses nationwide. SCORE offers advice online via e-mail as well as face-to-face small business counseling and low-cost workshops at 389 chapter offices nationwide. For information on this organization, visit www.score.org.

Small Business Administration

Every state has at least one Small Business Administration (SBA) district office, with multiple resource partners to support the needs of the small business community. In addition, many districts have an office specifically dedicated to women called *Women's Business Centers*. Women's Business Centers (WBCs) are a national network of more than 80 educational centers designed to assist women in starting and growing small businesses. The mission of the WBCs is to level the playing field for women entrepreneurs.

According to the U.S. Small Business Administration, "Women business owners are critically important to the American economy. America's 9.1 million women-owned businesses employ 27.5 million people and contribute $3.6 trillion to the economy. However, women continue to face unique obstacles in the world of business."

WBCs offer free services that you can use to your advantage, such as comprehensive small business training and support services for businesses in all stages of development and all industries. Classes cover topics like "Start Your Own Business" or "Business Action Planning," and they also offer a Financial Resource Center that provides loan packaging, consultation, and more.

To find a Women's Business Center in your area, visit www.sba.gov/wbc.html and click on the link "Find Your Local WBC." If for some reason the link doesn't work, you can go directly to the state locator at www.onlinewbc.gov/wbc.pdf. Each Women's Business Center is listed by state.

There are also independent microenterprise programs offering a variety of training and support throughout the country. To find those in your state visit www.microenterpriseworks.org. On the left-hand side of the screen, click "Microenterprise Organizations Near You" and then click on "Member Programs by State/Provinces." In addition, many community colleges offer programs to support local entrepreneurs. And, also check with local chambers of commerce and community organizations to find out about special support programs.

ICANN

Internet Corporation for Assigned Names and Numbers (ICANN) is a nonprofit corporation that is assuming responsibility from the U.S. Government for coordinating certain Internet technical functions, including the management of the Internet domain name system (Website addresses). More information about ICANN can be found at http://www.icann.org.

So how can this organization help you? Inevitably, you'll purchase a domain name for your own Website, as we discussed earlier in the chapter. When purchasing this company domain name (e.g., www.mominventors.com), it is important to buy from a company that is registered with ICANN, so you know it is legitimate. To locate the registry of qualified companies selling domain names, visit http://www.internic.net/alpha.html.

Financial Challenges of a Start-Up Business

Unless you are one of the few lucky ones who hit it big from the beginning, financing a start-up can be grueling. There have been many occasions in which we have found ourselves overdrawn at the bank, behind in payments, and lying awake at night not knowing whether we were going to make it through the month. In fact, there are times we've had less than a dollar in our bank account! Take solace in knowing that this is often the initial experience of many successful companies.

In the meantime, there are some financing strategies that can help you move forward with your business. These strategies will help ensure you don't overextend yourself and that you can tap into additional resources when you need them.

Cut corners in your everyday life. Most likely, profits will not be rolling in a month after you launch your business. So, think of what you can do without. I cancelled our daily newspaper and magazine subscriptions to save money each month. I also curtailed grabbing fast food for the

Account History
Business and Personal Accounts

Balance Detail

BUSINESS CHECKING 263-XXX	Amount
Ending balance as of last business day	$0.16
Available balance (Learn what this means)	$0.16
Enroll for Online Statements	

This is an actual Mom Inventors, Inc. bank statement showing 16 cents in our account early on in the business. We know from personal experience that this journey is not easy!

kids during the day, bringing along lunch and healthy snacks in a cooler in the car. Consider the little things that you can do without—that daily $4 coffee, the weekly manicure, the dinner at a restaurant—and cut them from your budget until you start bringing in profits.

Keep working.   Don't give up your day job too soon. Many successful inventors work on their project at night and on weekends, and take the process as far as possible before leaving their paying jobs. If you have a supportive spouse or partner, involve them in the planning. When you reach a point where your business becomes a full-time venture, perhaps you can negotiate with your partner, whereby he or she agrees to support the family needs while you build your business.

Spread it out over time.   I encourage you to spread this process out over time so you don't incur large expenses all at once.

Work with your vendors.   One of the best ways to finance your project is to find vendors who will share your financial strain. While you can't ask them to work for free, you can ask them to give you their absolute bargain price now. Let them know that with success, their support will be rewarded by your loyalty. You may also request to pay via a scheduled payment plan. Time your payments for when you know you will have available funds, such as on payday.

In addition, be sure to communicate! If you're going to be late with a payment, don't avoid your vendors—let them know upfront. This way you can work on a solution together, such as incremental payments, etc. The quickest way to sour a relationship is to ignore their inquiries.

Lose Your Pride

Entrepreneurship inevitably brings difficult financial times. Be prepared to swallow your pride to ask for help and money. When you need a discount, ask for it. When you need to borrow money, ask anyone you can. Better to borrow low-interest money from friends and family than from a high-interest credit card.

Look into microloans and special programs.   There may be grant or loan programs offered through professional organizations such as your local chamber of commerce or women's groups in your community. For a site that lists microloan programs in your region, visit www.microenterpriseworks.org. Click on "Organizations Near You." Other programs include www.accionusa.org and www.count-me-in.org.

Develop a relationship with a local bank.   Some mom inventors have found that local community banks are often more flexible than large global banks for helping small businesses.

Investigate small business loans.   The U.S. government's Small Business Administration (www.sba.gov) offers a program that guarantees loans made by banks to small businesses. The benefit is that they may help you get a loan if traditional banks see your venture as too risky. This is an option worth pursuing if you don't have access to a home equity loan (see next section). There is also an SBA-backed loan program called the "Community Express Loan." To apply for an SBA loan, go through local banks in your community (typically smaller business banks). For a list by state, visit http://www.sba.gov/financing/basics/lenders.html. One provider with offices in every state—and recommended by one mom inventor I know—is Business Loan Express. Contact them via www.blx.net or at 1-800-722-LOAN. The Innovative Bank is another resource that makes SBA-backed loans to woman-owned small businesses. Their loan maximum is $16,000. For more info, go to www.innovativebank.com, click on "Loan Products" and then click "SOHO Loans." The requirements are spelled out and the application can be downloaded from their site.

Apply for a government grant.   While difficult to find and often burdensome to apply for, you may be eligible for a city, county, state, or federal grant. For a list of federal grant programs, visit http://www.sba.gov/financing/basics/grants.html. Check with your own state and local governments for programs there, as well.

Get a home equity loan.   If you are a homeowner and have equity (i.e., you owe less on the house than it is worth) in your home, this is probably the best source of additional funds. The interest rate will be competitive and, assuming your payments have been timely, your bank will be inclined to lend you the money.

Use your credit cards.   Though it's not your best option—the interest rates are higher than most other lending options—countless small businesses end up relying on personal credit cards to access funds. In a pinch, a credit card can provide the required capital needed to overcome a hurdle.

Find investors.   Using other people's money to launch your invention can be a good way to finance a new product business, but there are definite drawbacks. First, few investors have a high enough risk profile to put money into an unproven idea and an unproven business person (you). So in reality, many times your "investor" is actually someone who is willing to "give" you money with the outside chance he will ever see it again. If you do find someone truly willing to invest in your venture, the downside is the control you give up. An investor at the beginning stages will probably expect to share in the decision-making process, as well as a share of the future profits. That's something you may not want.

However, once you actually have a product, you've invested your own money on the business, you've demonstrated some success, and you can show growth potential for your company with new capital, bringing on an investor may be more feasible. I would resist venture capital investment as long as possible, because venture capitalists tend to drive a very hard bargain (they want to own more of your company than you may be willing to give up). Your best bet is your family and friends. Also, consider members of your community or professional groups with which you may be involved. Before you start selling a percentage of your company (and future earnings), however, spend time working with a professional like an SBA counselor or a microloan support person so you're sure to understand the financial implications.

One strategy that can work with varying degrees of success is to pay your service providers (such as your patent attorney, engineer, etc.) in the form of ownership in the company. As a last resort, this may make sense. We have resisted this approach because it can really complicate your business relationships. Plus you might see the level of service from this vendor decline. Think about it this way: If your attorney is doing your work as an investor in a high-risk endeavor (he sees it practically as pro-bono work) and he has another high-paying client, who do you think will get priority treatment?

Strategies for Getting a Loan or Investment

People tend to cringe when asked for money. Especially when the request seems casual or not well thought out. Even when you have carefully considered this option, your request can seem hasty to your prospective investors.

However, almost everyone appreciates being asked for advice. And in fact, people often want to "put their money where their mouth is," supporting their ideas with money. Therefore, if you want to ask someone for money, I suggest asking them for advice first. (Conversely, if you want unsolicited advice, just ask for money.) One of the most effective ways to achieve this is to develop a formal team of advisers. Many companies have benefited tremendously from forming a "Board of Advisers," a group of people who can offer information of value to your business, who agree to provide advice on a regular basis. Some may be chosen for their unwavering support. Others may be experienced in certain areas, and others may have access to financial resources. Even if none of them have financial resources, they may be able to introduce you to people who do. And overall, they can demonstrate a coalition of support for you and your business.

Chapter Wrap-Up

The key to launching your business is to be as organized and forward-thinking as possible. By structuring your company from the outset, registering with the appropriate government agencies, and setting up efficient systems, you'll be well-prepared to handle all the sales sure to come your way. See the next chapter for how to get started selling!

8

Making the Sale

Getting Your Product on Store Shelves

You may already have preconceived notions about sales. On one hand, you may think selling is relatively simple and straightforward—you have a product, and the end user buys it from you. On the other hand, you may believe that "sales" is simply "not your thing." The reality lies somewhere between these viewpoints.

It's important to note that most people are initially uncomfortable with the idea of selling, so if you feel that way, you're not alone. But, just like ballroom dancing, playing bridge, or typing, with practice, you can learn to do it. I believe you are the most qualified person to sell your product.

The process of selling a product is relatively basic. However, achieving sales of a significant level, especially in a competitive market, is easier if you understand the way a market adopts a product as well as the most effective way to develop a sales plan.

In his book *Turn Your Idea or Invention into Millions*, expert inventor and author Don Kracke says, "An idea is *one* thing. Distribution is *everything*." In this chapter we will provide an overview of how a market opens up as a new product is introduced. Next, we will cover the steps in creating a basic sales plan and describe the different types of customers, ranging from end users to small and large retailers. Finally, we will provide basic sales techniques and discuss pricing and how to calculate markups and profit margins.

Putting Sales into Perspective

I frequently ask mom inventors about their goals or dreams for their inventions. Often they say they want their products on the market for the purpose of helping others, and occasionally they'll mention the gratification of seeing their product on store shelves. Surprisingly rare is the mom inventor who simply says she wants to make money. And even more rare is the woman who says she wants to make a lot of money.

While I believe in the gratification of improving peoples' lives, I also feel that many women answer this way because they're simply uncomfortable saying they want to make money. Some think it's not ladylike to admit that their motive is to make money. However, I think it's important to get over that misperception. Earning money is about creating choices for you, your family, and perhaps your community. And in order to make that money, you must successfully sell your product.

Creating Demand for Your Product

Unless you're very lucky or very connected, you probably won't launch your product directly into mass-market retail stores like Target or Wal-Mart immediately. Instead, there's a product sales life cycle you should follow that basically takes you from the ground up and allows you to build sales in a smart, methodical fashion. In addition, you'll need to put some thought into defining your market, positioning your product, and creating targeted packaging that reaches the proper audience.

Envisioning Your Sales Life Cycle

Picture a funnel lying on its side. Next, envision pushing enough units of your product through the bottom of this funnel to fill it up as you move

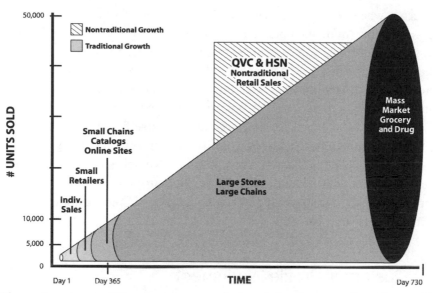

Shown here is a traditional market growth funnel. Begin your sales efforts with smaller markets, and move on from there.

from the narrow end to the wide end. The distance from the small end to the large end represents time. You will need more units to fill the expanding funnel the closer you get to the top of the wide end. The narrow tip of the funnel represents the very beginning of your sales effort and the top of the funnel represents the point in time when you have achieved the peak of your distribution goal. The market growth funnel image visually illustrates how you'll go about creating demand for your product.

Before you even think of selling your product, it's vital to be armed with the proper information. Market positioning is the discipline that allows you to examine the marketplace, analyze it for opportunity, and discover where your product fits in and how it can benefit this market. This information is critical in helping you decide who to sell to and how to position your product as unique and worthy of a buyer's attention. While market positioning is a huge and complex discipline, here are a few basic elements that will serve your purposes as you begin.

Defining Your Target Market

Your first step in positioning your product should be to clarify and define your target market. This effort will dramatically improve your chances of success when you hit the road (or phone) selling. To the greatest extent possible, determine the potential for your sales efforts. Clearly understand if your product fits a narrow niche market or if it has more of a mass-market appeal. For instance, a scrapbook designed for brides fits a niche market—women planning their weddings. A scrapbook designed for women in general fits a mass market. To define your own target market, identify who sells similar products and familiarize yourself with any competing products. You will have gathered some of this information during the steps you took in Chapters 2 and 4. Then, once you've defined your largest potential market, you'll need to determine your customer profile in order to properly position your product. Use the questions in the Customer Profile Worksheet to help you define who your customers are.

Customer Profile Worksheet

- How old are they?
- Are they male or female?
- What is their income range?
- What is their level of education?
- Are they married or single?
- Do they have children?
- Do they have specific ethnic or other characteristics?
- What are their lifestyle priorities?
- Where do they live?
- Where do they shop?

An in-depth understanding of your target market and their motivations and behaviors can help you better focus your sales efforts. This information will enable you to speak confidently about your product in a way that appeals directly to the things your customer cares most about.

Positioning Your Product

You know exactly how your product can help people. But your potential customers don't. To sell your product effectively, your customers must feel that your product provides them with a benefit that is worth the money you are asking for it. *Product positioning* is the process of describing these benefits and features verbally and in writing. Depending on the market, your positioning may also illustrate how your product differs from others in the marketplace.

Your product's *benefits* explain how, in the long run, the product will enhance the end-user's life. For example, a specialized cleaning product may cut down the time it takes to clean the kitchen. Your product's *features* are the specific characteristics that describe your product. In the cleaning solution example, features might be "antibacterial formula," "easy to apply," and "fresh, clean scent."

Truly knowing your customers and the benefits they value is essential because a great product that is positioned incorrectly will not sell. For example, one of our products, Shoe Clues, are durable stickers that are inserted inside the heel of a child's shoes to help the child learn how to put the correct shoe on the correct foot. This sticker was produced at a high cost (and retailed at a high cost) relative to other stickers because they had to be much more durable than typical stickers. Thinking we understood our customers, we designed our initial version emphasizing the educational benefit of the stickers. The packaging showed a photo of a proud girl and described features that were education-focused. We later learned that our customers were accustomed to buying cheap stickers that wore out, so they felt our stickers, too, might not last and could not justify paying our price for them.

Ultimately, we redesigned our package with a strong emphasis on the stickers' durability, supported by a strong differentiation statement: "Most durable stickers ever made." While the benefit of empowering the kids was still evident, the durability feature was critical. We knew that if the price didn't seem exorbitant, the new packaging would improve sales. This lesson cost us several thousand dollars but it worked. The initial response from our retailers has been positive. We still make mistakes, but I assure you that we now spend more time understanding what motivates our customers to purchase a product *before* we position them.

Product Packaging

There are a number of other issues that need to be addressed prior to launching your sales campaign. Packaging design was discussed at length in Chapter 5, but equally as important is the type of packaging and its size. According to Cathy Downey, president of Downey Associates, a manufacturers' representative firm, packaging is the "silent salesman"—both in design and presentation. Some products lend themselves to clip-strips (those items hanging between shelves in the grocery store) or peg hooks, while others are better off merchandised on store shelves. To determine your best option, research similar products and how they're currently sold.

Also important is the size of the outer and inner cartons in which your products are packed and shipped. If your target retailer is accustomed to receiving shipments in cartons of 12 units, it will be important to have them shipped to your warehouse in this configuration so they can be easily reshipped without the cost of repacking. (This can add up!) Some retailers will also expect you to keep a certain number of units available in your warehouse, so they can replenish their own inventory quickly.

Okay, now that you're equipped with your market knowledge and well-positioned and properly packaged product, you need a sales plan.

Smart Sales Planning

A sales plan should not be perceived as a complex hurdle. Instead, view it as a written document that helps you think through and organize your approach to sales. Unless you are crafting your plan for another audience such as investors, only you will see it, so design it in a way that works best for you. Typical elements of a sales plan are your sales goals, sales activities, target accounts, tools required, and time lines.

Set Goals

Goals should be specific and measurable. You should base these goals on the specific nature of your product, and they should consist of realistic, attainable steps. For instance, "selling a million units" when you first begin is more a dream than an attainable goal. Goals must be both volume and time-based and broken down into manageable parts: e.g., sell 5 units to end customers within 60 days and sell 100 units in 6 months to independent retailers in my state.

Sales activity is what drives results, so a rule of thumb is that if you wish to increase sales results, you must increase activity. While this is nearly always true, keep in mind that some types of activity will be more effective than other types, and that you should evaluate the effectiveness of different activities on a regular basis. For example, you may find that calling on local retailers personally is much more effective than calling them on the phone. Your tactics and activities will also change as your targeted customers change.

For most new companies, the initial target customers are actual end users rather than retailers. So, an activity associated with this sale that you can write in your sales plan might be "Set up a Website" or "Rent a booth at a local event." Similarly, activities associated with targeting independent retailers would likely involve goals like "mail introductory letters with follow-up calls" or "drop off samples" or "attend an industry trade show."

Develop a Timeline

In addition, an essential element to a useful plan is a time line. By basing your activity and results on a realistic time line, you give yourself clear steps to take within defined time lines. Plus you are able to measure your own progress on a regular basis.

Your plan, however, should also be fluid. If you are underachieving your goals, you will need to take corrective steps: increase your activity, change your activity, recruit (or pay for) help, or adjust your goals. The most important point is to be kind to yourself without being critical—simply make adjustments and move forward.

Follow a Proven Process

In most sectors, your plan should follow a process for creating a market. Start with selling directly to your end users. This will give you confidence in selling. Create "reference-able customers," customers you can contact. This gives you an opportunity to get feedback on your product and packaging that can improve your chances as you expand to retailers.

Once you've achieved some success and worked out some wrinkles, your next target customer group would be local independent specialty stores and online stores. For instance, if you've designed a line of greeting cards, approach your local gift shops. Note that retail buyers are risk averse. They have to be because they have little influence on their customers' preferences. Developing a successful case study proving sales of your product in smaller local stores will give larger regional chains and catalogs the kind of justification they need to feel comfortable in trying your product. Such local sales are a good way to build a case study with little or no risk to either the retailer or to you. I have commonly offered new products to local retailers on the basis that they pay me *nothing* unless they sell. The caveat is that they agree to share customer feedback and to place a regular order if the product moves; either way you gain knowledge.

Success locally and online will then give you leverage to get placement of your product with larger, regional independent stores and with catalogs. As you generate success with this group and continue to expand your roster of independent and online retailers, you have begun to "create demand for your product."

Generally, it is at this point that the opportunity and decision to enter sales channels considered to be "mass market" open up. For traditional retail, these include national stores like Sears, Target, Wal-Mart, and Kmart.

Of course, you'll need to choose the sales channel appropriate for your product, and it may not be immediately obvious. Some products will find tremendous success in niche areas you may not automatically consider. In the children's industry, for instance, there is an entire market for products sold for school or extracurricular fund-raisers (e.g., Girl Scout Cookies). Also realize that some products will never be appropriate for a mass audience and will do better as a specialty item. So, use the process of creating a market outlined here as a guide, not an absolute. Talk to people who are in your target market to discover more about where they shop. Keep your communication with your retailers, reps, and other contacts in your industry open. Plus, be cautious but seriously consider any shortcuts that appear (i.e., a mass retailer who is interested in your product right away, before you have to "funnel" your way upward). It is important to trust your judgment and intuition as well as your brain. Emo Phillips said, "I used to think the brain was the most wonderful organ in my body, and then I realized who was telling me this."

Knowing Your Niche

While specialty stores usually won't reach as large an audience as a big-box store, there are still benefits. One of these is that the profit margin is usually stronger. Customers who tend to shop in these stores aren't there to seek the lowest price, but to find quality products and better service. The challenge is to generate enough volume to be lucrative. Try specialty chains, buying groups, and trade shows to reach these stores more efficiently (covered later in this chapter), rather than trying to sell to each small store directly.

Sample Plan

Tools Required

- Product sheets
- Website
- Price list
- Business line
- Voice mail
- Testimonial letters

Sales Goals

	Monthly	Quarterly	Yearly
No. Units 1st year			

Date	Activity	Results
1st Month	Establish Website, create product sheets	Sell 2 units to end users
2nd Month	Attend 1 event and e-mail friends and family a coupon and ask for referrals	Sell 4 units to end users
3rd Month	Make appointment with 3 local retailers and contact 10 online stores	Sell 24 units to retailers
2nd quarter	Contact 20 retailers within region and 1 catalog	24 units to end users 36 units to retailers 24 units to online retailers
2nd half of year	Contact more regional and national independent retailers Contact 5 catalogs Contact buying groups Contact small chain-store buyers	24 units to end users 48 units to online retailers 192 units to independents 48 units to catalogs

Putting Your Plan into Action: Sales 101

Once you've thought out your plan and put it on paper, there's nothing left to do but sell, sell, sell! Here's a step-by-step guide to making sales and increasing the size of your sales distribution over time.

Step One—Sell Directly to Customers

When you sell directly to end-user customers, there is no middleman. You inform potential customers about the product, and they decide to purchase it from you. The advantage is that you don't need to convince a retailer to take a risk by buying your product, and you don't have to share the profit. Plus, it's the simplest way to start selling. The disadvantages are that you're not utilizing an established channel to reach a larger number of consumers, as a storefront or catalog would provide. Nonetheless, selling direct is likely to be your first line of attack in creating your market.

There are a number of ways to get in front of your customer, and I recommend utilizing as many as possible. First, a Website presence is essential. The growth in shopping online continues, and even if a final purchase isn't made, many sites are still instrumental in influencing a consumer to buy a product at a later date. In addition to establishing your own Website, it can be even easier to sell your item online by using sites like eBay or Yahoo. Community groups you're affiliated with represent another great opportunity to sell. I know some moms who launched their products through the mommy group associated with the hospital where they gave birth.

Also, appreciate the value of selling to your friends and family. And, when you find someone who loves your product, ask her where she would envision purchasing it. This will help you form a "hit list" of retailers to eventually contact.

Satisfied customers lead to more customers; especially for a new company. In addition, your success with them will give you confidence for your next sale. I remember feeling more nervous selling our first 12 units to a small retail store than I now feel when meeting with buyers from national supermarket chains.

Using eBay to your advantage.   Even if you are not one of the 100 million registered eBay.com members, you have likely heard about the site. And as someone considering the many potential channels of distribution for your product, you should at least consider eBay or another auction site, such as Yahoo Auctions, as a way to sell your product directly to customers.

eBay is a massive online entity with two sides: the Auction side and the Stores side. More high profile is eBay's auction side, often referred to as the eBay "core," where items for sale are "won" by the highest online bidder. The eBay Stores section, on the other hand, offers vendors the ability to set up online stores in minutes with almost no investment. Items here are sold at a fixed price, just as they are on most other e-commerce sites such as Amazon.com. Ebay's fixed pricing structure is referred to as "Buy It Now."

We use both sides of eBay. We have a Mom Invented eBay store, where we post all our products as well as many other mom inventors' products. The upside is that eBay gives us a quick-and-easy portal to sell our products over the Internet. The downside is that unless we have auctions running in the other side of eBay, our products won't come up in searches made by those 100 million members everyone talks about. Therefore, we always have auctions running on the core side of eBay with the principal goal of luring core eBay visitors to our store.

eBay is designed for the beginner. Since eBay makes money based on the success and volume of transactions, they have a strong incentive to make selling and transacting business easy. Anyone can register to become an eBay seller—all it takes is a simple three-step registration process. Once a seller, eBay has a series of rankings to publicly rank sellers based on their level of success, and a rating system where buyers rate the seller after each transaction. This way, eBay's users also do most of its policing.

For a small company, generating online traffic like eBay's would be nearly impossible, so it can be lucrative if you maximize its advantages. We recommend starting out small on the auction site to get a feel for it. Listing is simple so start slowly. In fact, your first listing can be anything you feel like selling. You may wish to test the process with a low-risk item to get comfortable with the process. Then, once you understand it, expand your offerings.

Once you become established on the eBay auction side, the Stores can be helpful. For a very small monthly fee ($15.95 per month at the time of this writing), you can have a basic store with your own online address (URL) operational in minutes. Note, however, that there are some drawbacks. In addition to your monthly fee, eBay will take a commission on every transaction made using the store. (The percentages vary depending on the size of transaction.) In addition, you'll be charged a fee (which also varies) each time you list a new item. And there are restrictions as to how you are permitted to list items. For example, if you sell shoes, and you sell style A in red in sizes 3 through 9, you aren't allowed to simply list your style and the various sizes. You must actually post the same red shoe photo for size 3, another for size 4, another for size 5, and so on. Add an additional color, and you double the number of listings you must make. Finally, as of this writing, eBay does not offer a "shopping cart" feature like you find on nearly any standard e-commerce Website.

To register or open an account on eBay, click on the "Register" box on the left-hand side of the homepage. They offer an audio tutorial that will walk you through the process. To open an eBay Store, look on the homepage underneath the search box. There is a link called "Specialty Sites: eBay Stores". After you click on that link, look to the far right side of the screen. There is a button called "Open a Store." I recommend that you browse other eBay stores for ideas before setting up your own. If you feel that you need additional help, there are many books available at the library, bookstores, or online that will offer more guidance.

Note: as a customer, eBay can provide great values for a start-up business. You can buy virtually anything on eBay, including the core elements to running a business—ranging from office products to technology equipment to closeout merchandise. Take advantage!

Step Two—Selling Wholesale

Once you've obtained feedback directly from your customers, you can refine the packaging and price point to be well prepared in approaching your next market—wholesale outlets, the small, independently owned retailers, "mom and pop" shops, in your town and other locations. At this point you can also use customer references and testimonials to help make the sale.

There are a number of reasons to start with these smaller retailers rather than chain stores. First, since they lack the volume or financial muscle to compete with the major chains in their area, they often need to differentiate themselves by offering new and unique, hard-to-find items. Second, the owner is often working in the store, so you can speak directly to the decision maker. Finally, these people are typically local and will be inclined to help another local entrepreneur.

To sell to independent retailers, you will need a minimum of five basic tools:

1. *A business card.* It should have your company name and contact information.
2. *A product "sell sheet."* This is a simple document with pictures or illustrations of your product, a list of features and benefits, pricing and shipping requirements, and your contact information (see the sample sell sheet in Appendix B).
3. *Quality product photos.* These should be available in high-resolution format for print catalogs and media opportunities (300 dpi), and low resolution for online stores (72 dpi).
4. *A succinct introductory letter.* Write it with your customer in mind. For example, a retailer is not particularly interested in why you came up with your idea or how many kids you have. However, they are interested in specific product features and benefits, real customer testimonials, other retailers' experiences with your product, and their potential profit margin. Most important, keep it brief. While you will undoubtedly modify it for different people and purposes, a template to start with can be useful (see the example cover letter later in this chapter).
5. *Product samples.* These will illustrate firsthand the quality, features, and benefits of your product.

When approaching storeowners and managers to make your sale (techniques are covered further along in the chapter) always be professional, no matter how they act toward you. Keep in mind that this retailer knows others through their community and that they do speak to each other. Once you've created a good relationship, ask for their help—and offer yours in return. For example, after including my first retailer in a press release I wrote, she offered to show my TP Saver to all her peers at the upcoming industry trade show.

You've Got to Lose Some to Win Some

Many new companies expect to make good profits from their first sales. But sometimes it's more beneficial to reduce your price and think of these initial sales as a marketing investment rather than as profit-making sales. Though these strategies may cut into your initial profits, over the long term you'll more than make up for it.

For example, offer the retailer a few free units as a trial. Also, consider offering low minimum unit purchase quantities; instead of requiring them to buy a minimum of 20 pieces, make it 10. Also, refer your direct customers to this retailer instead of selling them product yourself. It will pay off in the long run. For example, we sell our products direct to consumers on our Mom Invented eBay store; however, we make sure to price them above our suggested retail price so as not to undercut our retailers. In addition, when consumers ask us where they can purchase our products, we always refer them to our retailers rather than take the sales ourselves. You may lose a few dollars profit, but you'll gain critical points that lead to long-term relationships with your retailers.

Step Three—Selling to the Big Guns, the Mass-Market Outlets

It's common for new inventors to think that if they just got their product into Wal-Mart, they'd make millions. (Myself included!) While this surely has been the case for many companies, it's not a realistic goal for most products. That's why you should approach the mass retailers only after you've created a proven market through the sales channels described previously. This is not just because of the difficulty of getting them to buy into your product, but also to allow you to get yourself set up well enough to support this type of sale. When dealing with these major accounts, the sale is just the beginning of the deal. Handling fulfillment, returns, rollbacks (forced price concessions), slotting fees, advertising, and other mass-market specific issues will require infrastructure and proper resources to handle successfully.

Dealing with Fear

Selling your product for the first time may not only feel intimidating—it may even feel like what you are saying is false. I remember the first time I called a buyer in a big-box retail chain. I was terrified. I couldn't help but think, "I made up this company, it doesn't really exist. Who needs my invention, anyway? And, how is she going to believe me when I say I am the company President? I also worried she might ask me questions I didn't have answers to, or use terms I didn't yet understand. Worst of all, what if she didn't like my product?

I now recognize that most of my fear had to do with the potential of revealing my inexperience, and the fear of the unknown. As it turned out this buyer didn't want the TP Saver until there were proven sales elsewhere. Therefore, I ended the conversation with, "Once I have a proven track record, may I call you back?" She agreed. Once I got over my initial fear of calling, I was able to end with a question that left me with an open invitation to call back. I have since built my sales by "creating demand for my product" and I now work with this buyer. The point is, don't be afraid of what you don't know. Do your best, and turn lemons into lemonade. Every experience, pleasant, unpleasant, or in-between, is a chance to gather the tools you need to successfully sell your product.

Once you are ready to approach the mass-market retailer, it's necessary to be prepared. While there's no magic formula to knowing the perfect time in your product's life cycle to approach a mass retailer, there are some practical things to keep in mind when you do decide to do so.

1. *Get to the correct buyer.* Finding the proper person in a large organization can be one of your biggest challenges. Be sure to do your homework, or if you find it's too daunting, hire a distributor or manufacturers' representative (these options are covered later in the chapter). Often these third parties have established relationships with buyers, which makes it easier to open doors. Plus, mass retailers are often wary of working with unproven companies that could potentially burn or disappoint them.

2. *Take advantage of special programs.* For example, Wal-Mart has a "local purchase" program that gives the store manager and district manager some authority to try a local item. You'll need to navigate some red tape, but it can be done. Contact the mass retailer you're interested in and ask a manager if they offer this type of local-purchase opportunity. If they take a chance on you and your product sells well locally, it might encourage the store to take on your

product regionally or nationally. This is a powerful back-door method to launch your product into the stores as opposed to calling the corporate office yourself. Other options worth looking into include special programs, like minority business offices.

3. *No matter how you plan to approach a mass-market outlet*, realize that the time line is going to be long; it could be a year or more before you get a decision or see your product on store shelves. And, you could still hear the answer "No."

What Buyers Want

It's rare to get insider information from an experienced buyer. But Cathy Downey, a former buyer with more than 20 years' experience purchasing products for companies like Sears, Spiegel catalog, and One Step Ahead catalog, generously shared her views and experiences. She's now president of her own manufacturers' representative firm, Downey & Associates, based in the midwest, representing products in the infant and juvenile industry. The following is a Q&A between Cathy and me:

TM: What is a professional retail buyer?
CD: A retail buyer is responsible for the procurement and placement of product in a retail store, catalog, or Website that fits within sales, margin, and profit goals.

TM: What is the buying process like?
CD: Buying a new item from a new vendor is a more involved process which the buyer views as risky. While established vendors have a history of providing a quality product in adequate quantities and meeting retailer requirements, a new vendor represents the unknown. Does this company have the resources to supply the retailer? Can they react if demand exceeds expectations? Do they have adequate product liability insurance? Are they compliant with other legal requirements like flammable fabrics or hazardous materials? Are they in compliance with fair labor practices?

TM: How many times per year do you consider new items and when do the products get introduced?
CD: Most retailers change out their floor twice a year, in February and July. Presentation of product is made to management in September and February.

New products are reviewed continually, but the process intensifies in July and August and early December and January. Trade shows are critical for new or small vendors. This is where buyers will scout for new items.

TM: When presented with a new product what key things do you need to consider?
CD: Does the product have application to my customers? Does it solve a problem? Is it easy to understand? Is it safe? Is it priced well? Where has it been placed? Is it innovative? Is it unique?

TM: When you examine a new product, how do you determine if it will be successful?
CD: Experience plays a large role in determining if an item will be successful. Is it an improvement on an existing item? Is it truly unique and does it satisfy a need? Does it have broad appeal? If it is targeted at a narrow group or unique need, sales will be small because the customer base is small.

TM: What do inventors need to learn or understand prior to approaching you?
CD: Before approaching a buyer, know the retailer. Shop their store. Know what they carry. Do they carry a product similar to yours? How is yours better? Is the product suitable for the customer base?

TM: What are common errors people make or misperceptions they have?
CD: (1) Not knowing the retailer or the market—do your homework! (2) Not being ready for prime time. Is the packaging finished? Product finished? Sell sheets complete? Presentation professional? (3) Confusing a retailer with a manufacturer. Retailers are not going to produce your product. (4) Hounding a buyer. After your first call, wait 48 to 72 hours before calling again.

TM: How can an inventor (vendor) improve their chances of having a buyer consider their products?
CD: The biggest way to improve your chances with a buyer is to be prepared and to use a sales rep. The rep will have a relationship with a retailer and is aware of their paperwork needs. When a rep picks up a new product, it gives it a cachet. The buyer knows that a rep must see merit and potential in the item to add it to the line that he or she carries.

TM: Do you prefer items to be packaged in a certain way?
CD: Does it communicate the product? Is it attractive yet sturdy enough to withstand shipping? Is it bilingual or in some cases trilingual? If models are shown on the package, are they ethnically diverse?

TM: If the inventor (vendor) is a single-product company, what can she do differently to stand out from the rest?
CD: Single-product companies need to be so new and different that a retailer can't live without the product. For example, Diaper Genie fit this description. Retailers did everything possible to put it on their shelves.

TM: What can a vendor do to make the buyer's life easier?
CD: The biggest thing a vendor can do is follow through: ship on time, ship complete (full amount of product requested in the purchase order), and most important, communicate. If there is a problem, let the buyer know up front. Late shipping? Perhaps you can be moved to the next catalog, etc. If you don't communicate, you are dead in the water.

TM: What questions should a new vendor ask you?
CD: Do you have legal requirements? Product liability, etc. Do you require EDI (electronic ordering system)? What are your margin requirements? When are you looking to add new products?

TM: What questions should a new vendor expect to answer?
CD: Where is item placed? [Who else is selling it?] What is your production capacity? What is your turnaround time? Does it meet safety standards?

TM: What materials should a new vendor have ready for you?
CD: (1) product sell sheet, (2) finished product, (3) finished packaging, and (4) company information.

TM: What is the most common mistake that prospective vendors make?
CD: The most common mistake is to come unprepared. A vendor called on me once with unfinished samples in a black garbage bag and packaging roughed out on a piece of paper. The senior buyer was also in the meeting…we told him to come back when all of the things we outlined were accomplished. This is a rare occurrence [that the vendor was invited back and it was only because the senior buyer could see the merit in the prod-

uct]. Normally, the buyer is polite, quickly finishes the appointment and you are done!

TM: If you were the founder of a company, with a product that you developed, how would you approach you?
CD: You have to have a unique story. Sell yourself as the entrepreneur!

TM: Thank you so much!

Seeking Out Shortcuts

While a steady, progressive approach to creating demand for your product, as described in this chapter up until now, should be the rule for burgeoning entrepreneurs, there are certainly exceptions that can help you get big sales in a much shorter time line. One such outlet is TV shopping networks like QVC or HSN. Though this is a young phenomenon, only about 15 years old, these programs have a regular and loyal audience similar to a successful catalog or Website. The difference is in their size and the way in which they communicate with the customer.

By some measures, QVC is the third largest television network in the country with millions of regular viewers. Plus, when you sell through QVC, you or your designee speaks directly to the customer. This is a great way to reach a mass customer audience while skipping the trade show, sales rep, distributor, online, and retailer intermediaries (all these outlets are discussed later in the chapter). And even if someone doesn't buy over the phone, you're still reaching a mass audience with advertising that can translate into retail store sales on the local level.

Amy Bergin of the Couponizer is scheduled to launch her product on QVC in the fall of 2005. To initially present her idea to them, she responded to the 2004 product search in Atlanta by filling out a Website application. Shortly thereafter she got an e-mail inviting her to make a five-minute presentation, and a month later she received their decision to be included on the show.

The lesson? It's relatively easy to submit your product to QVC, and they are eager to find new, innovative products and are supportive of entrepreneurs. To determine if your product is a fit for QVC, ask yourself these questions:

- Does it demonstrate well?

- Does it solve a problem or make life easier?
- Does it have unique features and benefits?
- Does it appeal to a mass audience?
- Is it topical or timely?

Then, if you've answered yes to these questions, tap into QVC's product search program at www.qvcproductsearch.com. Even if you cannot attend one of their local events, you can still submit your product. The paperwork is simple and can be submitted online.

There are additional ways to approach QVC and HSN. One of these is through their new-product review sessions, or "cattle calls." Early on, I submitted the TP Saver to one of QVC's product searches in West Chester, Pennsylvania (where QVC is located). When I received an e-mail confirming that QVC was interested in my product and invited me to participate, I was elated. Due to my naiveté as a new inventor, I arrived thinking I was "special" only to find that I had to wait in line with over 2,800 other special inventors!

Once I overcame my initial surprise, I was completely mesmerized by QVC. It is one of the most well-run, efficient organizations I have ever seen. I thought the cattle-call experience was going to be frustrating, but the staff managed and treated each of us as if we were the only one in the room. Like the other hopeful inventors, I had my opportunity to present the TP Saver to a buyer. Although the buyer thought that the product was novel, the price points didn't work. The minimum unit price QVC will take is $15, and the suggested retail for the TP Saver is $5.99. However, all was not lost. QVC offered us a variety of free seminars to attend to thank us for participating. I attended every seminar and learned a great deal about branding, product presentation, packaging, and speaking to my target customers. This in itself was worth the trip.

Another inroad to TV shopping networks is to approach the category buyer for your product directly. Also, begin following their programming. Like regular television, they are always looking for new ways to keep their presentation fresh. To do this they create special program themes, like "beauty" or "kitchen essentials." Watch for special programs in which your product would fit, and jump at any opportunities that come up. Finally, there are some manufacturers' reps who base their business on selling to QVC. This may provide another avenue for success.

Note that though the process may be relatively simple, it is still very competitive to get a product accepted by QVC. The products they take on must truly appeal to a mass audience. Also, the product must fit within an interest area of their core demographic—91 percent of their buyers are women. The product must demonstrate well or be easy to show on TV. No matter how fantastic, it would be hard to demonstrate the excitement of a software program or a novel. And, be prepared for their "guaranteed purchase" clause. QVC will place a purchase order and hold inventory but they don't pay you until your product is sold. And, if your products don't sell, they return them. Not only is it costly to produce and deliver the inventory required in case of a tremendous success, there are costs associated with taking back unsold merchandise. While QVC measures success based on many extremely intricate mathematic and programming factors, their base target sales rate is *$6,000 per minute in sales*. Definitely worth the effort!

Doing It Yourself—Sales Techniques and Tips

When it comes to reaching your customers, you have options: selling to customers and retailers yourself or hiring someone to sell your product for you. Obviously, the advantage to doing it yourself is more profits for you: You won't have to give a salesperson or distributor (covered later in the chapter) a cut of the sales. In addition, because you're creating demand for your product, it makes sense to perform initial sales yourself. When you do, it's important to follow a few strategies and understand some key tactics to closing the sale, all of which are covered in this section.

Warming Up the Cold Call

Once you have a target list of retailers you want to contact, you'll need to prepare before picking up that phone. A proven strategy is to draft a letter introducing yourself and send it to the retailer before contacting him or her. With your letter, include your product sheet and if possible a referral from a customer. The goal of this letter is not to sell them product but to open the retailer up to your call. This is known as "warming a cold call." (Note: depending on the size and cost of your product, it may make sense to also send a product sample.)

Sample Introductory Letter

Dear _____:

I recently learned about your store from _____. From what I have learned, I would be honored to sell my Unique Thing in your store.

My Unique Thing is the only product ever made that does _____. Stores such as _____ have found it to be a solid addition to their offerings.

This product retails for ____ and garners 50 to 60 percent gross margin with minimum orders as low as _____ units. To first-time buyers, I am offering the following added bonus (free shipping, extra unit, free display, extra discount...).

I have enclosed a product sheet with our Website and contact information. I will follow up by phone next _____. In the meantime, please feel free to contact me with questions.

Yours truly,

Your name

Once you've sent your letter, give it a week and be sure to make the call. Making calls, even when they have been "warmed," can be difficult and nerve-racking. As I said before, selling is a learned skill. If you haven't done it before, the fear is rational. But, it is a skill you can learn, just as you can learn to swim, salsa, write poetry, or become a parent for the first time. It requires preparation, rehearsal, and practice. Plus some tried-and-true strategies, like the following:

1. *Get the decision maker on the telephone.* Knowing this person by name is critical. When possible, get that information prior to this call, rather than asking for the "buyer" or the "owner." The latter is a sure way to have your call filtered. Instead, look them up on the Internet and find out who the owner is, or call another time and say, "I want to send some free product information to the owner, can you give me the correct spelling of his or her name?" Warning: also be prepared for the owner to

answer the phone. If this happens, be ready to jump in with your pitch.

2. *Plan your call.* Your script should be brief, informative, and rehearsed. It should close with a question or call to action (see Cold Calling Tips for suggestions). During business hours, storeowners are juggling everything from landlords to personnel to advertising to customers. They seldom have time for phone discussions. That said, mornings are typically better for cold calls than afternoons. And often the best time to reach the owners is before or after hours.

3. *Understand that rejection is an essential part of sales.* "Sales" is a numbers game. The more prospects you have in your sales pipeline, the more chances you have for a yes. (The more prospects also means you will receive more nos.) So if you make a mental shift where you equate a no answer as one step closer to your next yes, it can actually become gratifying to hear a no. That is why we consider no to be the second best answer! We have a clear decision, don't waste additional time on that prospect, and are now one step closer to our next yes. And never take it personally. The worst thing you can do is respond to a retailer in an unprofessional manner. Use a rejection, instead, as an opportunity to start a relationship with this buyer. I've even had buyers who didn't buy my product, but who referred me to stores who did.

4. *Remind yourself that no may just mean "no, for now."* Always graciously ask a buyer why she didn't like the product. You will be amazed by what you learn. She might like the product, but it's bad timing—the big-box stores (Target, Wal-Mart, Babies R Us), for example, may have already set their planograms for the quarter or year (a planogram is a map of the product selection for the entire store). Or they may not like one aspect of the product, which can be easily changed. No matter what, it's important to listen and to understand that your product just may not be a good fit for the store. Being disrespectful and annoying to a buyer is the kiss of death!

Cold Calling Tips

- Whenever possible, warm up for your call in advance with a letter or some "reason" to call.

- When you call, have your prospect's name in front of you as well as a pencil and pad for notes.
- Use a familiar tone, like you would have when calling a friend. Also, smile...it can be heard.
- Speak slowly. If you rush, your voice goes up and you sound immature.
- Be important. Without sounding arrogant, you must come off as someone of substance. Speaking slowly helps.
- Understand the challenges and be prepared for them.
  - Getting through the "gatekeeper," the person whose job is to screen calls for your target prospect, is the first step. The gatekeeper is never your ally, so don't be fooled that your many calls are establishing a rapport with that person. The challenge is to get past the gatekeeper without sounding rude or disrespectful. While the gatekeeper is not going to help you make a sale, he or she can irreparably harm your chances at selling to your prospect.
  - The second challenge is to control the conversation discreetly, yet effectively. Whenever you come up against a difficult gatekeeper or buyer, phrasing your request as a question enables you to remain discreetly in control of the conversation (e.g., "This is Jane Doe for John, is he in? Okay, would it be better to call him in the morning or afternoon?").
  - The third challenge is to close. Some people feel that even though a conversation has gone well, asking for the order right away is pushy. Remember that these people are taking customers' money all day long. They represent the epitome of closers, and they understand the way business works.
- Hang up. Once you get a sale, don't continue to chat. Say thank-you and hang up.

Secret Techniques from Sales Stars

- If you are calling a larger company and hitting a gatekeeper wall, simply call back and ask for human resources. Even gatekeepers know that they need to be wary of asking too much about why someone might be calling this particular department. Once you get someone in human resources, explain that you meant to speak with Joe Smith and would they mind forwarding your call. As long as you have them on the phone, ask for his extension "in case you get disconnected."

- If you are calling a company with an automatic calling system ("...please dial the four-digit extension of the person you are trying to reach, or for a company directory press 411") but your contact is conspicuously missing from the directory, try pressing zero and see if the operator puts you through. However, if your target is missing from the list, you will not likely get passed through. Simply call back. Once you do, press any other person's extension. When they pick up, simply say, "I'm sorry, I must have entered the wrong extension, I was trying to reach John Smith, would you mind transferring me? Also, I wonder if I have his extension down wrong, what do you have?" Most people in a company, other than a gatekeeper, don't care to gate keep and will simply forward your call.
- If you need to get your contact's name but the gatekeeper decides to play FBI with you, simply thank her and hang up. Call back a day or two later, or better yet, have someone else make the call. Then simply say, "Hi, my name is Jane Doe. I am working on an event and wish to send an invitation to your owner. Can you please spell his or her name?" This usually works!
- Try calling using an extremely casual tone, using the owner's first name and your first name. "Oh hi, it's Jill, is John there? Huh, oh, it's Jill Johnson, can you tell him I'm on the line?" Few gatekeepers are willing to insult someone who appears to be a close buddy with their boss.

Sample Call Script

The following is an example of language to use when making cold calls to give you a starting point. Feel free to modify it so it feels natural to you. Note that you are "Jane Doe" in the following examples:

First, the easy example:

JD: Hi, this is Jane Doe, is John in?
Gatekeeper (GK): Who is calling?

JD: Sure, it's Jane Doe with XYZ, is he there?

GK: One moment please.

John: This is John.

JD: John, this is Jane Doe, I recently sent you some information on my Unique Thing. I am following up to ask you to give it a try. Did you have any questions about Unique Thing?

John: Oh yeah, I saw that but I didn't really have time to look at it.

JD: I completely understand. I can go over it with you now briefly…first, it is important to know the most compelling thing about Unique Thing. (*Tell him this compelling thing.*) Do you carry anything that does this now?

This, hopefully, will lead into a conversation about your item and a request for the sale.

JD: John, this sounds like a great fit. If I am willing to start you with just X units and offer you _____, can we go ahead and give it a try?

John: That sounds fine.

JD: I look forward to our working together. I will ship those right away.

Now the difficult example:

Hi, this is Jane Doe, is John in?

GK: Who's calling?

JD: Sure, it's Jane Doe from XYZ company; is he in today?

GK: What is this about?

JD: I am following up on some recent correspondence; is there a better time to call?

GK: That depends; where are you from as he is really busy?

JD: I understand; all my clients are busy. I am from (Home Town). I was told by a friend that he is someone I should talk to. Is he generally around in the morning or afternoon?

GK: He is here all the time.

JD: I understand, just so I know when to try back, when does someone start answering the switchboard?

GK: 8:30 to 5:00. He is always here early.

JD: OK, I will try back later. Please tell him I called. Thank you for your help.

Note: Now you know to try calling before 8:30 a.m. or after 5 p.m. next time. Owners often answer the company phone after hours, and calling then is a great way to avoid a talented gatekeeper like this one. In addition, calling on holidays and weekends can also be effective. You will be amazed at how many presidents of companies answer their business telephones during off hours or when employees are on vacation.

Be aware that any time you feel yourself extremely concerned or intent on the decision of any one prospect, you need to step back and get more prospects in the funnel. Nobody should base the success of their business on one customer's decision.

Closing the Sale

If you are going to succeed, you must close sales. One of the biggest mistakes made by new salespeople is simply failing to ask for an order. Looking back on my first trade show, I remember making this mistake many times. The scene looks like this: A buyer arrives at the booth; I greet her warmly, invite her to view our product, give a quick demonstration of my TP Saver, talk about the features and benefits, and mention our great show discount and then smile as she nods and says, "We'll come back later."

What I should have done is asked for the sale directly by saying something like, "Can I put that order together for you now?" Because closing the sale is nothing more complicated than asking for an order. In fact, the more you can minimize the magnitude of this simple step, the better. If you feel momentarily disappointed or undone by this process, often taking a break will renew your memory that stamina is the name of the game. Be good to yourself.

Understanding the mindset of the buyer, especially the small retailer, is important. They are among the biggest sales targets in the world. They have a large sign, they are open to the public, and they are always in the store. From the time she arrives at her store to the time she leaves, the store owner is asked to buy everything from Girl Scout cookies to advertising. With good reason, this person has learned to say no. In fact, she has become more comfortable saying no than using almost any other word. Therefore, the more you can help her make the decision without actually saying yes, the better. After you have gone through the features and benefits and answered questions, building rapport, you are ready to close. Try different methods and stick with the one that works best for your situation and that you are comfortable with.

Sample Closes

- Should we start with 12 units or do you want the extra discount at the 48-unit level?
- Would you like those shipped to the store or the warehouse?
- OK. Would you like to pay up front and get the extra discount, or be invoiced?

My husband compares one of my favorite closes to the martial arts technique of using an opponent's own weight against him. This is the "no that means yes" close. Remember how much buyers like to say no. Try this statement on for size:

- Is there any reason you wouldn't want to give this a try?

Strategies to pin down objections.   While getting the order is clearly your number-one objective, the second is to find out a buyer's true objections. If you have demonstrated your product, covered the features and benefits, probed and answered questions, then gone in for a close and they still say no, use this as an opportunity. What do they see that you don't? When they object, you need to pin down the issue so you can address it. But first, understand that what they say is not always the real issue. By restating their objection to them and *listening*, you can often learn the true objection. Once you do that, come up with a way to address their concern.

Tip: There can be an awkward silence after delivering a close. Avoid the temptation of "stepping on your close." That is what you do when you try to fill the silence by talking. Give your prospect the opportunity to make a decision.

After the Close

Again, once you have closed the deal, be sure to stop talking. Say "thank-you" and move on to fulfillment! More deals have been lost that were first won by a proud salesperson who decided to open up a new conversation with his prospect, giving her time to rethink her decision. Now that you have the sale, you need to deliver.

Something to keep in mind: The graceful art (and value) of a simple thank-you note has somehow been lost in our culture. Think about how

Handling Objections

Objection	Real issue	Conversational response	Tactical response
This costs too much.	You need to reestablish or reassert value	"I understand that your store has a reputation for offering value. What do you think your customer would think about this product?"	Offer discounts; tell success stories
I don't think this is the right quality.	This may be a result of negative press given by competitors	"I understand that you have a level of quality you require. Do you have specific concerns?"	Then talk about steps in creating quality and the materials used. If necessary, compare with lesser products or materials on the market.
I need to compare with some other companies.	She fears making the wrong decision.	"I understand that you need to be confident that this is the right decision."	Give her confidence that she won't regret working with you. Offer money-back guarantees, trial deals, testimonials from other new customers.
Fear of getting burned.	Help her overcome the fear of dealing with a	"Dealing with a new company is always a concern. I have that	Talk about your background, your company values, and your

continued

Handling Objections (continued)

Objection	Real issue	Conversational response	Tactical response
	new, small, and unproven company.	issue in my business every day. How have you dealt with new companies before?"	personal values. References should also be volunteered.
I am not in a rush. I will think about it.	She doesn't like making snap decisions. Or, maybe she isn't the real decision maker.	"I understand that you need time to make this kind of decision. Is there anyone else you will need to discuss it with?"	Provide bullets of the reasons to buy, and then give a reason to buy now: e.g., "This offer is only for this month."
Not interested.	This person sounds clear. What else can you get from her?	"I see that this isn't a fit for your store. Is there anything I can do to make it a fit?" Or, "Can you recommend anyone else who would do well with this?"	Focus on building a relationship that you can leverage in other ways.

many thank-you notes you have received this year. You will realize two things: There have been very few, and most important, you remember who sent them. Use the fact that nobody does this anymore to your advantage. If you send a simple thank-you note (not ornate flowers but a simple, clean note) you will dramatically stand out with your new customer. Even when someone has said no, thank them for their time. E-mail does *not* suffice. It must be handwritten, on a simple piece of stationery or card simply saying "thank-you" and don't use preprinted "thank you" stationery. Resist the urge to mix messages and incorporate follow-up sales information. That can be done in a separate letter. I am still surprised by how many people thank me for my thank-you notes.

Leveraging Prior Sales

As you close more and more deals and your customer base expands, it will make sense to leverage prior customers to penetrate larger groups. Some independent retailers are part of larger buying groups. These are central committees or actual distribution centers that work to leverage larger group purchasing power to garner better pricing and other marketing advantages. Once you have some of the members of these groups as your customers, it may make sense to approach the buying group directly. (Ask your customer for the name of the group.)

Catalogs and online stores in your industry are commonly good outlets for newer products as well. They offer an added benefit of helping advertise your product. One factor to consider here are lead-time requirements. Where online stores can often get products posted quickly, catalogs have lead times as long as 12 months.

More Ways to Make the Sale

In addition to contacting consumers, retailers, buying groups, or other sales channels by phone or via individual meetings, there are other options for reaching a large volume of potential buyers in a very efficient way. The first option, trade shows, provides another way to do-it-yourself by meeting with potential consumers or retailers that are interested in your product, showing them the product, and making the sale firsthand. Another option, hiring a distributor or manufacturers' representative, will provide you with third-party intermediaries who can help put your product into the right hands and who may be in a better position to convince retailers to buy. These options—along with strategies for success—are covered in this section.

Taking on Trade Shows

Virtually every industry in this country has a member-based trade association. These organizations serve two main functions. First, they represent the industry as a united front to government policy makers, and second, they help facilitate business for their members. To support the second function, they often organize and host trade shows, creating a venue for their members to display products to industry buyers. These trade shows can provide a great opportunity for you to promote your products to interested buyers.

Trade shows are typically held in a single location (usually a convention center) within a concentrated time; normally two to three days. There are also trade shows organized by private trade show companies. While it will cost money to rent a space, set up a booth, and travel to the show, exhibiting at a trade show is an incredibly efficient way to meet many buyers at one time, as opposed to visiting these retailers individually throughout the country.

Your first challenge when it comes to trade shows is deciding which ones are worth your time and investment. To help you decide, ask some of your best customers which trade shows they attend. They can give you insights as to which shows their peers attend and the perception in the industry of various shows. Another deciding factor will be cost. Space at smaller, regional shows will cost less to rent than at the larger national shows. Finally, be sure to consider the nature of the attendees closely. While some shows will cater to independent retailers, others will be dominated by buyers from mass merchants. Still others will be oriented toward grocery and drug outlets.

The cost of exhibiting at trade shows can vary widely based on the industry, the size of the show, and its popularity. A standard 10 by 10 booth will run from a few hundred dollars to $10,000. We pay about $1,000 per 100 square feet at our shows. To locate a trade show in your industry, visit www.tsnn.com. There is a search box where you can search by industry, show name, date, or state. Once you identify the specific trade show you are interested in attending, the exhibitor costs should be spelled out.

While trade shows are a good way to make sales, be sure to set realistic expectations. If you have a quality product, which fits the industry, you should expect some sales, but keep it in perspective. A trade show should be just one component of your sales plan. If you expect to make your entire investment back at your first show, you are not being realistic. Also, sales should not be your only goal for the show. Use your attendance there as an opportunity to gain industry knowledge, make contacts, get feedback on your product, and to build your product and brand awareness.

If you do decide to exhibit at a given trade show, there are some proven strategies that will maximize your time.

Make the best of your booth.   Your booth space at the trade show doesn't need to be elaborate. However, it's good to make the most of what you're working with to present a professional image. Your basic beginning package will probably include a table with a skirt and some chairs. As long as your booth is clean and conveys your product to the buyer, it is adequate. To add to your booth without spending thousands on high-end panel displays, be creative. Find stands or shelves at a discount store. Bring pretty tablecloths to cover inexpensive tables. Create a sign or banner to communicate the name of your company.

To save money at our first trade show, we bought white wooden folding closet doors with shutters from Home Depot for $79. We attached shelf brackets to the bottom so they'd stand up on their own. I got free clip-strips from my local grocery store, and also used "S hooks," which I painted white, to display my product. I focused the bulk of our budget on graphics. By blowing up our product images with high-resolution photos, we created a sharp memorable image in a homey setting. It worked great.

Your Booth's Location

Location is the most critical element of securing your trade show booth. Get a map of the show layout to determine your preferred locations. Most vendors jockey to be as much in the line of the main entry way as possible. Keep in mind that people tend to veer right after entering rooms. Also, the corners of rows benefit from traffic in multiple directions, so they are preferred. Some shows also permit you to indicate whom you'd prefer to be placed near.

Avoid being next to any vendors who will clearly dwarf you by their booth size. Also, avoid being placed next to any direct competitors.

Get some preshow attention.   Before the show, send a letter or postcard to key customers with an overview of your product, your booth number, and an invitation to visit your booth. Also mention any promotions such as free gifts or prize drawings to convince them to visit. While you don't have to break the bank on your mailer, an unusually designed direct-mail piece can serve to really get their attention before they've even met you.

To further reach media, as well as target customers, another preshow strategy is to draft and send out a press release prior to a show. Even if the media doesn't write about it, send the release to your target customers. They may come by to see what is going on with your company.

Work it, work it!   While you are at the show, be sure to welcome buyers into your space. As they pass, engage with them. They have come to the show to buy product (despite some of their efforts to convey the contrary), so give them a quick product demonstration then tell them about your great "show specials." You may wish to offer free shipping or additional discounts for placing orders at the show. At your early shows, your sales goal should be to open new accounts and establish new relationships—not necessarily sell millions of units at top price.

Things You Will Need at a Trade Show

- Receipt book
- Order forms
- Stapler
- Folder for orders
- Product sheets/handouts
- Business cards
- A bowl of candy for visitors
- A promotional giveaway (optional) such as pens with your logo on them
- Product samples
- Manual sweeper
- Extra packing tape
- Scissors
- Pens
- If possible, a dolly

Trade Show Tips
- Wear comfortable shoes. You will be on your feet a lot. The appeal of your high heels is quickly undermined by the anguish on your face.

- Don't leave your booth unattended.
- Don't eat in your booth.
- While tempting, try not to chat with your booth neighbors, especially when they are speaking with potential buyers.
- Have at least two people work the booth. Every so often take turns leaving the booth to keep your energy up.
- Use the chance to meet others in your industry and learn all you can from them. We still have friends we met at our first show.
- Look into preset rates, negotiated by the trade show, for hotels, car rentals, and airlines. Then investigate on your own for better rates. You'll often find great rates and discounts on airlines like Southwest, JetBlue, or ATA, or by using Websites like www.sidestep.com, www.priceline.com, or www.expedia.com. Another creative way to save money is to look at time-share companies when booking your lodging. Your stay for a trade show can often be long, especially when you add on the days before and after for setting up and dismantling your booth. In our case, we often bring our children and a babysitter, which requires a large and expensive room or suite. However, we were recently able to secure a three-bedroom, five-star suite with a kitchen for $99 per night, just for agreeing to attend a 90-minute seminar.

Sales Representatives

Another way to increase the efficiency of your sales efforts is to duplicate yourself. Hiring salespeople is one way to do this. However, unless you have a large cash reserve, hiring direct staff is typically difficult to justify financially at this stage of your start-up. Independent manufacturer's representatives represent a solution to this challenge.

Manufacturers' representatives are professional sales individuals who have struck out on their own "repping" various manufacturers' products. They are typically experienced in their industry. These manufacturers' representatives, often called sales reps, will normally carry a handful of products from different manufacturers within the same industry. They generally have exclusive rights to present and sell that manufacturer's line to the customers in their territory, and they are paid predominantly on commission from the sales they generate. Territories can be defined in a number of ways, including geographic region (e.g., the Pacific northwest), account type (e.g., all drug and grocery stores), or even by specific account name (e.g., Wal-Mart and Kmart). A manufacturers' representative carries samples of your product but does not take ownership of your product. When a rep gets an order for you, he or she will send you the purchase order and you will ship to the customer and invoice the customer directly.

You will usually need more than one rep to cover the entire country. You can also adopt a mix-and-match strategy; for example, we have reps who sell our products in some regions, and my husband and I handle other territories ourselves.

While developing a network of manufacturers' representatives sounds like the ideal solution, it is not without challenges. First, it is difficult for a new, unproven company to attract reputable sales reps in the first place. Because these people live on the commissions of their product sales, they cannot afford to spend much time "pioneering" new products or taking on too much risk. Therefore, they prefer products that have a strong likelihood of substantial revenues, such as products from well-established brands or new versions of high-volume items. When they do "try" your item, they tend not to push a buyer beyond some initial resistance, as they want to move quickly to the next product, which might make for an easier sale.

Second, manufacturer's reps are difficult to find. Since they are independent entrepreneurs who often base their business relationships on their personal network, they can be tough to identify. One place to look for them is through your industry trade association. Your association may have a database of representatives who have registered to attend their trade shows. Probably the best place to find them is through your retailers in various territories. Ask them about the reps who call on them and who their favorites are, and who they think might be the best fit for your product. While you're at it, ask for a referral. A call from a retailer who says they are about to order your product is a great way to convince a rep to take on your product. This leads to the third challenge: recruiting a rep.

Prior to our first trade show, I sent letters to 300 registered manufacturers' reps inviting them to visit our booth, in the hopes that we would be able to quickly establish a national network of sales pros selling our product. We had exactly zero reps visit our booth. In fact, those we saw at the show seemed to quicken their pace as they walked past our booth. However, by our third show, they began seeking us out without any coaxing. The key was that in the interim, we developed some accounts in their territories. This is the most effective strategy I know to lure them in. If you can, tell prospective reps that if they rep you, and bring in new accounts, you'll give them your already existing accounts in their region. This can provide a good incentive to join your team. Don't worry about the commission you'll give up; in the long run, this is a small cost for a quality rep. Plus they will assume the burden of supporting the accounts you pass along to them.

The last challenge is monitoring the rep's performance. It is common to hear manufacturers complain about their reps' productivity. But, if you have an unproven product, it's difficult to motivate them with your limited leverage. To counteract this problem, continue to push for accounts yourself, even in their territory. Eventually they'll realize you may stop passing accounts to them if they can't prove their worth.

Sales representative compensation varies widely depending on your individual agreement. If you keep in mind that they must be able to survive on the income they derive from your product in combination with their other product lines, a fair commission rate will become evident. Commissions are often commensurate with the accounts that reps secure. For mass stores, including grocery and retail, an average commission is about 5 percent. For specialty and niche retailers, which may take more legwork and are more about "pioneering" versus simple "order-taking," commissions average 10 to 15 percent. Different reps will have different expectations, but I prefer to pay them on collections rather than on orders. This way, they have a vested interest in making sales to customers who will be likely to pay.

Distributors

Another option to duplicate yourself, and thus your sales efforts, is to work with a distributor. A distributor buys product from you (the manufacturer) and resells to its retailer customers. Dealing with a distributor is more like dealing directly with a large retailer. The distributor takes ownership of inventory and assumes responsibility for selling, shipping, invoicing, and supporting its accounts. In many cases, a distributor will have its own network of sales reps and staff.

A distributor is often necessary if your goal is to sell to major mass-type distribution channels such as drug and grocery stores and big-box discount stores. While it is not impossible to sell to these mass-oriented retailers directly, it is a challenge. Large retailers tend to avoid working with small companies that have just one or two SKUs (products). A distributor, on the other hand, will combine your item with his list of multiple SKUs and assume the handling issues associated with dealing with small companies.

Unfortunately, recruiting a distributor is even more difficult than recruiting a sales rep. Since the distributor is going to be dealing with you, the small "risky" company, as well as take on responsibility for inventory management, merchandising, and collecting payment from the retailer, they are highly selective as to whose products they'll represent. In fact, they can often even be more difficult to penetrate than a large retailer! One strategy for securing a relationship with a distributor is to get your target retailer to say they want your item, and to have them refer you to one of their distributors. Even though you will have to give up a large amount of your profit margin to deal with them, it will be more than worth it. In addition to their shipping and warehousing services, they are responsible for ensuring that the mass retailer has your product displayed properly and keeps inventory on the shelves—an impossibility for a small company.

Dollars and Sense

Of course, before you sell anything you'll need to know how to price it. While initially this may seem overwhelming and difficult to figure out, fortunately there's a formula that can help ensure you're recouping your investment, making enough profit to stay in business, and making some money in the process. The key to pricing your product is to understand the concepts of gross margins and markups, and how to use these concepts to work out a winning formula.

Understanding Profit Margins

The entire process of bringing a product to market is driven by profit margins. If the gap between what customers are willing to pay for a product and what you can earn distributing it to them (i.e., the profit margin) is not large enough to justify producing the product, the product should not be pursued. In earlier chapters we covered the costs associated with planning and producing (manufacturing) the product. Here we will cover some basics about margins as they apply to distribution of your product.

I will begin by defining four terms that are often confused. First, *retail sales* are the sales of a product to an end user. For example, when you buy cookies at the grocery store, it's a retail sale. Second, *wholesale sales* are the sales, by a manufacturer or distributor, to a retailer who will in turn sell to end-users. Using the same example, this would be Nabisco selling its cookies to your grocery store chain. The third term to understand is markup. *Markup* is the difference, reflected in both dollars and percentage, between what a retailer will pay you for a product and its retail price (i.e., what the end user will pay). So, if Nabisco sells a bag of cookies to the grocery store for $2, and the store sells it to you for $5, the markup is $3. Fourth is *gross margin*. The gross margin, which is often confused with markup, is the percentage of profit derived on the transaction. The best way to convey these meanings is through more examples:

Demystifying Markup

If I, the manufacturer, make a product we'll call Unique Thing for $1.00, and I sell it wholesale (to a retailer) for $3.00, my markup was $2.00 ($3.00 − $1.00 = $2.00), or 200% (2 divided by 1 = 2.00). If the same retailer, in turn, sells Unique Thing for $8.00, her markup is $5.00 ($8.00 − $3.00 = $5.00), or 166% (5 divided by 3 = 1.66).

Getting to Know Your Gross Margins

Gross margin is calculated by dividing the markup by the cost to acquire it. Again, my Unique Thing markup is $2.00 ($3.00 − 1.00 = $2.00). To figure out the gross margin, simply divide the amount of this markup ($2.00) by the amount I sold it to the retailer for ($3.00). The manufacturer's (my) gross margin in this example is $2.00 divided by $3.00 = 0.67, or 67% gross margin. So in this case a 200% markup resulted in a gross margin of 67%.

The retailer gross margin for Unique Thing would be calculated the same way, just using her markup and costs: $5.00 divided by $8.00 = 0.625, or 62.5%. The retailer's 166% markup resulted in a 62.5% gross margin.

There are great free tools available on the Web that can be used to automatically calculate these numbers. One such margin calculation tool, among many other business calculator tools, can be found at www.mominventors.com under Resources. This calculator can help you

Basic Mark-Up Calculations Example for Unique Thing

Assumptions:
Production Cost = $1.00, Wholesale Price = $3.00, Retail Price = $8.00

Manufactures Mark-Up Calculation in $			
Wholesale Price (sold to retailer)		$3.00	
Manufacturing/Production Cost	–	$1.00	
Manufacturer's Mark-Up		$2.00	
Manufacturer's Mark-Up Calculation in %			
Manufacturer's Mark-Up		$2.00	
Manufacturing/Production Cost	÷	$1.00	
Manufacturer's Mark-Up %		2.00 →	200%
Retailer's Markup Calculation in $			
Retail Price to Customer		$8.00	
Retailer's Wholesale Cost	–	$3.00	
Retailer's Mark-Up		$5.00	
Retailer's Markup Calculation in %			
Retail's Mark-Up		$5.00	
Retailer's Wholesale Cost	÷	$3.00	
Retailer's Mark-Up %		1.67 →	167%

Basic Gross Margin Calculations Example for Unique Thing

Assumptions:
Production Cost = $1.00, Wholesale Price = $3.00, Retail Price = $8.00

Manufacturer's Gross Margin Calculation			
Manufacturer's Mark-Up		$2.00	
Manufacturer's Wholesale Price	÷	$3.00	
Manufacturer's Gross Margin		.67 →	67%
Retailer's Gross Margin Calculation			
Retailer's Mark-Up		$5.00	
Retailer's Retail Sale Price	÷	$8.00	
Retailer's Gross Margin		.625 →	62.5%

→ Note: Remember some of your basic math. The number two, usually written simply as "2" is mathematically the same as writing "2.00." Notice there are two decimal places to the right of the number "2." Most simply stated, when you convert a regular number such as "2," into a percentage, you are moving the decimal point two places to the right and adding a % symbol 2.00 → 200%. (Technically speaking, you are multiplying by 100 and adding the % sign which gives you the percentage representation to which this number is equivalent.)

2005 Mom Inventors, Inc.

Demystifying the margin and markup. This simple chart will walk you through the process of calculating the wholesale and retail pricing for your product and associated profit margin percentages.

determine the selling price for your products to achieve a desired profit margin. By entering the wholesale cost, and either the markup or gross margin percentage, we calculate the required selling price and gross margin. Enter up to 10 products and press the "view report" button for a printable version of the results.

To know what your pricing should be, it is important to ask your prospective retailers their margin requirements. This will vary widely, especially between specialty/catalog/online retailers and distributors and mass-market retailers.

It is not uncommon for retailers to request a minimum gross margin of 50 percent, often referred to as a *keystone markup*. An easy way to figure out this number is to double your wholesale price to the retailer. (Example: If you sell your product wholesale to a retailer for $5.00, a keystone markup means they'll sell that product at retail for $10.00, which equals a 50 percent gross margin for the retailer.) When you need to work backwards to come up with a price that gives your retailer his or her desired margin, it is helpful to use this as a starting point. High-end specialty retailers will often require an even higher gross margin.

In case the retailer doesn't mention how much margin they expect or "need" to make on your product, please do not be shy about asking them. You may feel that you are asking them to reveal their private financial information, but this is not true. This is how retailers think and how business works!

Distributor margins vary by industry and segment, but a margin of 25 to 40 percent is not uncommon. Keep in mind that a distributor will be selling to a mass retailer who will also want a 25 to 50 percent gross margin above what they will pay the distributor for the product.

For example, the margins and markups for a product sold through a distributor might look something like the following (assume a $10.00 retail price, 50 percent retailer gross margin and a 30 percent distributor gross margin).

$10.00 retail price
$5.00 wholesale price (to retailer from distributor)
$3.50 distribution price (from manufacturer to distributor)
If the manufacturer's cost is $2.00, her gross margin is 43 percent.

Make sure that there is something left for you! You may have to get your production costs down in order to make money and meet the margin requirements of both your distributors and retailers. This is possible to achieve because going through a distributor normally means that sales volume will be higher and the distributor incurs much of the cost of delivery.

What's an Adequate Gross Margin?

Unfortunately, there is no simple answer to this question. Gross margins vary dramatically by industry and product type. And even within an industry, they will vary. For example, recently the CEO of Procter & Gamble said that his company has a 19 to 21 percent gross margin. Of course, their massive volume enables them to be profitable at this rate. On the other hand, many small businesspeople I know have a 50 to 70 percent margin. Since you must figure out where you should fall, I will try to give you some ways to think about it so you can decide what the right gross margin is for your company.

Temper Your Early Profits

The topic of tempering your early profits was touched on earlier in this chapter, but warrants further discussion. When you first begin selling, it's natural to be eager to recapture your initial investment. But keep in mind that this is a long-term venture, especially when it comes to pricing.

While you want to make an adequate gross margin, you don't want to price yourself out of the market, thus forfeiting valuable relationships with retail accounts. Because early manufacturing runs are often small, your costs are often high, and therefore, you're tempted to pass on the higher price to the retailer. But remember that you need to create demand for your product and it's often difficult to create substantial sales traction early on.

Therefore, it is often necessary to forgo large profits in the beginning to get some sense of what the sales and profits could be at a "customer friendly" price point. Ideally you'll conduct market tests to arrive at an approximate price point to start with.

On the high end, your gross margin should be "as much as you can get." As illustrated above, the factors affecting this outcome are your production costs, your retailer's margin expectations, and the market price at which your product will sell; this last one being the most important. If your production cost is so low and your product is in such demand that you can sell enough of them for a 1,000 percent gross margin, go for it!

That takes me to the low end. When is the gross margin too low? Obviously, you can't have margins so small that they won't sustain your cost of doing business. The answer to this rests in knowing your goals and your expenses. If simply creating some part-time income satisfies you, and your labor is your only major expense, then you can tolerate a rather small gross margin. For instance, if you're making jewelry to sell locally, and your main "cost" is the time you take to produce each piece, you can get away with a low gross margin percentage. On the other hand, if your expenses are high and growing, and you are trying to generate a substantial return for yourself and other shareholders (investors, if you have them) you need a larger return. Remember that all of your company costs, such as your salary, phone, staff wages, marketing, rent, and other operating costs, must be covered by the gross margin earned on your sales. In fact, there's a term for the percentage of money that's left after paying for all these expenses— it's called your *net profit margin*. And only you can decide what net profit margin is acceptable; unless of course you have investors who have a specific expectation for their return.

Here's another example to illustrate. When investing money in the stock and bond market, you don't need to incur much risk to garner an 8 to 10 percent return. Therefore, you might conclude that you need to outperform this return on any output of capital (e.g., investment in your business). In other words, if you can make 8 percent relatively easily in the stock market, you definitely want to make more on a business venture into which you're pouring tremendous effort.

Of course, your own gross margin target should be specific to your product and goals and enough to cover your operating costs. For me, a gross margin below 35 percent would raise the question of whether the product should be pursued (unless I was doing millions of dollars a year out of the gate). I would tend to target 40 to 60 percent as a reasonable gross margin and again, on the high end, get as much as possible. You will know that your gross margins are too low if you find that you are unable to meet the costs you regularly incur to operate your business.

What Will It Cost?

At first, you'll incur most of your sales costs by making presentations and sales calls. Therefore, be smart about your expenses with the following strategies:

- Look into discount telephone services. With so much competition today, phone service should be inexpensive. Many companies offer all-inclusive flat-rate calling plans that include local and long-distance services for under $25 per month. Others offer flat-rate pricing as low as 4 or 5 cents per minute.
- To create a professional image without breaking the bank, get voice mail service through your phone company or another discount company. Most phone providers offer discount voice mail. Other special "virtual office" offerings can be found online or through companies like Costco or your local office supply store. One company we've used is www.call24.com, which offers live operator service with your company name for as little as $40 per month. For an additional charge, they'll also use any script you provide.
- Be conservative about print quantities for sell sheets or sales brochures. While printers offer a per-unit break when printing higher quantities, your sales approach will inevitably change, making current materials obsolete before you can use them all up. Also, avoid listing prices directly in brochures. Instead, include them on an insert printed on inexpensive paper that can be easily changed.

Chapter Wrap-Up

Creating demand for your product is a methodical process that helps build your sales from the ground up. As you find success in each phase of the process, you should then move on to the next bigger sales outlet. Once you understand your customer and have positioned your product, create a plan. Start by selling direct to consumers, then to small independent stores, and finally to larger mass retailers (if it's appropriate to your product). Remember, consumers are not rushing out to buy a product that they do not know exists. Also note that while understanding theory and process is important, there's no substitute for sweat equity—making the calls and doing the selling! "Sales" is a skill anyone can learn, and you are your product's best salesperson!

In the next chapter we will discuss advertising and publicity and how these disciplines can enhance your sales, build your brand, and create credibility with your wholesale customers (retailers).

9

Blowing Your Horn

Marketing That Works!

A good invention is certainly essential to your business success. However, if no one knows your great idea exists, or where to find it, your business (and your product) will go nowhere. The reality is that our society, in particular, is driven by media and marketing. To make money inventing, you must acknowledge and leverage this fact. Like almost every other subject in this book, marketing is a discipline that could take years to learn. However, there are certain key strategies that can help you succeed in promoting your product, many of which we've used ourselves to get our company Mom Inventors, Inc. and our brand Mom Invented™ in front of millions of people in America and Europe.

Learning the Lingo

When I first began this adventure, I didn't understand the differences between public relations, marketing, advertising, and branding. In fact, I often used the terms interchangeably. I have come to understand that they are quite different from each other

213

and serve different purposes. This chapter will define these differences, provide some basics, and share the steps you need to get
yourself on the map!

Before adopting specific tactics to increase awareness of your product
and your business, you should understand the lingo as it applies to marketing, public relations, advertising, and branding. The following provides
a quick overview for each of these concepts:

- *Marketing*. Marketing is a broad term, often used loosely, that includes branding, public relations, publicity, advertising (we'll define these more precisely later), and product positioning, as
  discussed in Chapter 8. The term can also be stretched to include
  everything from market research to Website promotion to direct
  sales. "Marketing" firms across the country offer a broad scope of
  services, most of which work toward a common goal: making the
  public aware of your product. So, marketing, in its broadest terms,
  is simply the practice of researching your market, positioning your
  product to fit, and letting people know it is available.
- *Branding*. Your brand is a distinctive name or symbol that commu-
  nicates a message and position directly to your target customers.
  More than a simple logo, a brand identity, which involves every
  communication medium from product packaging to product flyers
  to TV advertising to Website, gives your company or product a con-
  sistent personality. Examples of successful and highly developed
  brands include companies like Ben & Jerry's ice cream, Apple, and
  the Gap. The mere mention of each of these companies brings to
  mind a separate set of attributes. With each of these companies, you
  immediately identify a specific feeling, attitude, and personality
  that defines the brand.

  The goal is to create a brand that makes an impression and
  lasts. Designing your brand is one of the most critical business steps
  that you will take. Your brand will be the core of your business regardless of the products that you sell.
- *Public Relations*. Public relations is the process of communicating
  your message, usually through the unpaid media, to your target customers. Your public relations efforts should promote a positive
  image of your business, so that customers will have a good feeling

about purchasing goods or services from you. Your public relations strategy can involve everything from getting "free" editorial coverage in media like TV, newspapers, and magazines, to sponsoring seminars that support your product, to backing social causes that will help generate goodwill for your company. For example, company sponsorships of breast cancer walks are part of a larger public relations strategy.

- *Advertising*. Advertising differs from public relations in that it is a paid form of messaging. You see or hear hundreds to thousands of ad messages a day, through TV commercials, newspaper and magazine ads, radio advertising, billboards, bus "wraps" and ads, direct-mail, and the list goes on. The advantage of advertising is that you control the message completely, as opposed to public relations opportunities in which reporters often craft the message.

Let the Games Begin

There's a famous saying that goes "any publicity is good publicity." This means that even a bad review or other negative mention of your product is still getting your product's name in front of the customer. In today's forgiving society, in which so many people are vying to get their own 10 minutes of fame for just about any reason, this seems truer than ever. Nevertheless, it's best to approach your own public relations, branding, and advertising in a methodical and somewhat scientific way. The key to promoting your product and building your business is communicating your message consistently and frequently, to create top-of-mind awareness and to differentiate your products from the competition's. Also key is crafting and controlling the messages being communicated about your product.

Begin with Branding

Do not underestimate the importance of taking time to think about your brand. Inventors are often so eager to move forward that they rush through, or ignore completely, this portion of the product development process.

However, it's important to think deeply, early on, about the message and feeling that you are trying to convey. For instance, do you want your packaging and logo to say "cost-effective" or "upscale?" Do you want it to say "urban chic" or "suburban mom?" Obviously your logo, advertising, Website, and packaging, which add up to your brand, would vary significantly depending on which choice you made in these examples.

When I began branding my own company, I looked inward. What was I trying to create? The words that came to mind were *innovation, connection, motion, action, community, warmth,* and *moms helping moms.* The result is the Mom Invented logo, which is the basis for the brand:

My own Mom Invented logo was designed to represent a brand that symbolizes the dynamic creativity of moms everywhere, as well as our potential connection to each other.

The circle symbolizes community. The swirls around the circle show motion, movement, and action. After some study into color, I learned the power that color can convey, and chose warm hues not necessarily obvious for business: yellow and red. Though these colors wouldn't necessarily be appropriate for selling computer software, they felt right for my own business. And while I carefully considered all the advice I received, I also heeded my heart and followed my intuition. Make sure that the colors you choose will speak to your target customer.

Branding Exercise

Here are some specific activities you can use to begin thinking in terms of your own branding.

- Write down words to describe your company. For example: cutting-edge, family-friendly, exclusive, upscale, community-oriented.

- Write down associated images that fit with the descriptive words you listed. (For me, it was a circular motion image that illustrated community and fit the words *mom invented*). Is your company high tech, homey, fun? IBM makes me think conservative and stable, eBay and Yahoo create a sense of fun. The Pottery Barn brand connotes homey and earthy yet high quality.
- Write down who your customers are. What images do you think would encourage your customers to buy from you? Why?
- Think of names for your brand that your customers can relate to. Should it be the owner's name as seen with many local car dealerships? Or, should it describe a concept, e.g., natural or organic.
- Test your name and your initial brand messaging through either informal focus groups or via an e-mail blast (see Chapter 4 to learn how to do this). This way you can get direct feedback from your target customers. Make sure to ask what they like, dislike, what they would change, and what suggestions they have.
- Make sure to listen to this critical feedback. It is easy to get attached to your brand in the same way as you do to your product idea. Remember to listen to what people are telling you. In the end you will benefit from hearing and listening to the honest reactions people have shared with you.
- Listen also to what your heart is saying. After you have listened carefully and incorporated the useful feedback from others, it is important to also consider what you are feeling…as I did with the colors I chose.

Do-It-Yourself Marketing Strategies

Although there are advantages to hiring a marketing company, I believe there's a lot you can do first, on your own, when it comes to getting your message out (especially if you're working on a shoestring budget). These efforts are focused on helping you get editorial coverage rather than advertising coverage. Editorial coverage ranges from being asked to appear as a guest on a TV or radio talk show, seeing your product featured in a newspaper or magazine article, or providing expert insight to a reporter working on an article for a topic related to your industry. The one thing all these have in common is the ability to create awareness about your product to potential end users without having to pay for the exposure.

Crafting Your Press Release

Your first step in garnering editorial coverage for yourself or your product is to write a press release. This is usually a one- or two-page document that tells a story about your product. Most important, this story needs to be compelling and exciting—it needs to have a fresh angle so that reporters will feel drawn deeper into your story. Your first step would be to define your message.

Defining Your Message

Not only will your message and story be included in your press releases, you'll also use it to "stay on point" when speaking publicly to consumers, retailers, and the media. Make sure that you can tell your story in a concise and compelling way. This takes preparation. Ask yourself the following questions to get started shaping your story:

1. What's the story behind your business, or how did you think of your business or product? How has the decision to go into business changed your life? In what way? Was there some dramatic event that occurred that changed the direction of your life? What is unique about your story?
2. What is special or different about your business? What inspired you to create it?
3. What is the compelling angle to your story (your product or service)? For example, did your product help save a life, does it help kids learn a new skill, is it the next rave in the kitchen or garden, does it make life a little easier for harried mothers? Is there any element of drama that can be added? If not, create one!

In other words, add drama to your story. Realize that reporters are constantly looking for interesting new stories, so give them one. Perhaps you are an expert in a particular area, so write "The Five Tips for ____." Get creative, but, of course, not carried away...and never lie. This isn't just a matter of personal integrity; you also risk getting caught when the media does its fact checking. You cannot afford to harm your credibility with them. If you need help spicing up your story, ask others to offer their perspective, and listen to what they say. Your friends, family, customers, and colleagues may surprise you and view you in a way that you never even imagined.

Putting Pen to Paper

Once you've really thought through your story, you'll be prepared to begin the actual writing process. Keep in mind you can write multiple press releases; in fact, it's advisable to do so. Whenever you have a new angle about your product to offer the media, consider drafting a press release to let them know about it. Just be sure that angle is fresh and interesting enough to warrant a press release.

While it may seem tough to find new angles on saving toilet paper, for instance, we've found that thinking creatively can help us develop new reasons for the press to be interested. For instance, one idea for my own product would be to host a "Toilet Paper Olympics" in the parking lot of a major retailer. Parents could bring their little toilet paper bandits to this event, where we could also give away free Mom Invented products and ice cream. This type of event would interest a reporter more than a press release that simply spoke about product features.

Other goals might be to establish credibility or show company growth. Here are the headlines of three press releases we crafted to meet our objectives. The full releases can be viewed in the appendix.

May 26, 2004
TP Saver™ awarded the coveted iParenting Media Award for one of 2004's Hottest Safety Products

July 14, 2004
Senior Executive of Rapid-Growth Software Firm Joins Mom Inventors, Inc.

July 26, 2004
Mom Invented™ Brand is recognized by America's Largest Retailers

You may also consider tying your product into "bigger picture" issues to generate coverage. For instance, we considered sending the TP Saver to the Governor of Florida (along with press releases letting the media know our activities) when new legislation was proposed to charge a tax on toilet paper to pay for wastewater treatment. These are examples of how we brainstorm different angles to entice reporters.

In addition to offering a compelling story, your press release should also look professional. While drafting a simple Word document on your letterhead is just fine, be sure there are no typos, grammatical errors, smudges, or misspellings (especially a reporter's name!) There's no surer way to get your press release in the "circular file"—the garbage can. Reporters will not take your story seriously if it's not professionally presented. Tips on drafting and formatting a release can be found at http://www.prweb.com (in the left margin click on "press release tips and template").

Award Programs

Nominating yourself for award programs is another way to generate press! There is no shame in doing this. In a recent article in *Entrepreneur Magazine* ("Getting Props: Awards can boost your self-esteem—and your business," March 2005), Aliza Pilar Sherman discussed the many local, regional and national awards available for female entrepreneurs. Joining local chapters of organizations such as the National Association of Women Business Owners (NAWBO) and the National Association of Female Executives (NAFE) is a "surefire way to gain access to well-established annual awards," wrote Pilar.

To find out if there are any award programs in your area, contact your local chamber of commerce. Other award programs include: Athena Award (www.athenafoundation.org), NAWBO/Wells Fargo Trailblazer Award (www.wellsfargo.com/biz/intentions/women_bus_svcs), and The Stevies – For Women Entrepreneurs (www.stevieawards.com/women). To find other award programs, search the Internet. I typed "Award Programs Women Entrepreneurs" into Google and it brought up a variety of additional award opportunities.

Getting Help from the Experts

Even when you're "doing it yourself," you don't have to be on your own completely. A terrific and cost-effective resource to help you spice up your press releases and get reporters to actually read your e-mail story pitches is provided by publicity expert Bill Stoller at www.publicityinsider.com.

You can receive his free eZine and subscribe to "The Newsletter for PR-Hungry Businesses" for $97. It's worth the investment! Every newsletter is packed with actionable items, including tactics you can put into practice immediately without spending thousands of dollars.

Another useful resource is www.mediabistro.com. This Website is intended for media professionals such as producers, writers and editors, but you can use it to your advantage as well. On Media Bistro you can educate yourself about pitching your stories to television and print media, such as newspapers and magazines. Although the advice is intended for people whose profession is writing for these media outlets, there is no reason why you can't adopt some of their strategics. The key is to learn how to do this appropriately and effectively. Media Bistro offers courses online that will teach you how to write compelling proposals and how to pitch your own stories to the media. You can subscribe to this Website for $49 a year and have access to all of its content.

Piggybacking on an Established Event

As you're writing your press release, it can also be valuable to tie your story into existing events that the media may already be zeroed in on. You'd be surprised to learn how many days and months have been "adopted" by various causes. For example, if you're launching lingerie, why not send a press release out in time for National Underwear Day (August 13)? Or, if it's a health product, time a release for American Heart Month (February). You can find more than 12,000 dates and events like these in *Chase's Calendar of Events*. It's one of those resources that the people in the industry know about but hesitate to share, and can be purchased at http://books.mcgraw-hill.com for $64.95. This is a must-have resource for broadcasters, journalists, advertising and PR agencies, event planners, activity directors, and speakers. It's revised annually and the new edition is always published in the fall.

Many professionals in the public relations field also rely on a resource called *Bacon's Media Source* (www.bacons.com). Bacon's offers a variety of services, including TV and radio directories, updated daily, plus a Media Calendar Directory and an Internet Media Directory. Each directory can be purchased for $395. If you really want to target the media on your own, this is a valuable tool.

Bacon's also offers access to Editorial Calendars (known as EdCals). An editorial calendar is a publication's schedule of upcoming articles and special sections on a particular topic or focus. Typically, publications like magazines and newspapers develop editorial calendars a year in advance to define topics they plan to cover (while also keeping room for news or breaking stories). According to an article titled "Editorial Calendars: Map or Puzzle?" on Bacon's Website by media experts Linda Lyon and Roberta Silverstein, "Editorial calendars (EdCals) are the most overlooked gadget in the public relations toolbox. When used effectively, EdCals are a boon to any company's public relations program; applied badly or ignored, it's a missed advantage for your company. There are over 160,000 stories every year scheduled around EdCals—that's a lot of opportunity."

To use an editorial calendar, first narrow down the publications that are appropriate for your product (for example, *Parenting* or *American Baby* for children's products). Then examine the editorial calendar for each. When you make your story pitch, you can then tell the editor or reporter that your story might be appropriate for a specific month, such as, say, September's month on baby safety or January's month on educational toys. In these issues reporters will show readers new and innovative products that relate to the topic.

One more tip: Be sure to think ahead. Find out the lead time for stories—for example, do they need the story three or six months in advance? Also find out who the reporter will likely be for a particular topic. Look at past issues online and send an e-mail directly to the reporter of the story if you can't seem to get the information you need from the magazine. Surprisingly, each time I have written directly to reporters, they have written me back. When you write to the reporter, don't tell them your life story and don't attach photos of your product. If they are interested, they will ask you for more information. Simply say that you've invented and launched a safety gadget and were wondering how you might be considered in the next article on new safety gadgets or during baby safety month. This may trigger the reporter's curiosity. However, if the reporter does not respond, move on. Don't hound her or send repeat messages. The key is to send your release out to as many relevant reporters as possible. If your story is compelling, someone will likely pick it up. Similar to sales, garnering publicity is a numbers game.

Announcing the News

Once you draft a release, getting it out there is key! One resource I use regularly is www.prweb.com. This is a free Internet-based wire service that gives you the option of sending your press release "over the wire" where the media has access to it. You also have the option of paying a "contribution" to get higher placement in the PR Web news feeds. I was extremely lucky in that the Today Show picked up one of my stories from PR Web. Though I've since discovered this kind of pickup is extremely rare, it still can happen.

Now, I typically pay the extra $40 so I can have the option of including an image with my press release. So, when I write a story about a "hot" new product, I add a product photo. When I write about the Mom Invented brand, I attach an image of the logo. When I wrote about a senior executive joining the company (who happened to be my husband), I attached his photo and landed a story in our local newspaper. People are visual and in my view, it is worth the investment to add a picture. In addition to putting these on the wire, I always forward the release directly to target reporters as well as key customer prospects.

Other newswire services can help send out press releases, including PR Newswire (www.prnewswire.com), PR Leap (www.prleap.com), PR Web (www.prweb.com). A software program Press Blaster (www.pressblaster.net) is also available to help you distribute your own press releases. Some of the services require payment, but these do come with assurance that your press release will be sent through specific distribution channels (note that this isn't a guarantee you'll get press coverage!). Read their offerings and figure out which service fits your needs.

At this point, you may be thinking "Wow, this 'free' do-it-yourself stuff is sure adding up!" However, I believe that investing a few hundred dollars in yourself and your education, as well as using some of these proven distribution methods, is being a smart businessperson. You will ultimately increase your knowledge, and attain skills that can directly impact your business. I am frequently amazed at how much money inventors are willing to spend on "experts" and on expensive ads, when they are hesitant to spend $20 on a book or $50 for a half day of childcare so they can attend a valuable seminar.

Keep in mind that if you hire an expert consultant, PR firm, or publicist, you will be paying much more. While I'm not negating the value they may bring—in fact, I've found much success with my own publicist—there's a lot you can do on your own first. The key is to get serious, take action, and get the word out yourself about what you are creating.

Publicity Quick Tips

1. Remember that reporters are constantly looking for stories. The key is to make your press releases compelling. They should tell a story.
2. Think of reporters as customers. They need to see your name a number of times before it will register. They need to "buy" your story. Build your press release program in a way that lets them become customers.
3. Start with the local media and then approach the national press. This will build credibility, helping you eventually get coverage in the more competitive national market. Plus, sometimes the national press will come across your story on their own when they scour wire services for stories.
4. Plan your press releases in a series—for example, three announcements written in different press releases, released in three subsequent weeks. Design this series of information so that it ties together and tells a bigger overall story about your company.
5. Send your press release out via a free newswire service on the Internet.
6. Identify specific reporters you would like to target and snail-mail your press release to them directly. Then follow up with a telephone call or e-mail.

Sweet Success!

So, you've crafted a great release, sent it out on the wire or through the mail, and voila! you've received interest from some of your target media. Great job! Once you get past the initial excitement, the news will begin settling in and you'll realize that you'll soon be under the hot lights. And whether it's the literal hot lights—you've been asked to be on TV—or the figurative type—a magazine reporter wants to interview you—it's natural to feel some nervousness or apprehension about what you'll say, how you'll look, and how you can best get your message out.

Relax. You'll do fine! If you've gotten this far, you've already demonstrated your publicity savvy. Now's the fun part—getting the word out about your awesome new product to hundreds or even thousands of people.

Stay on Point

Your reason for courting the media is to sell product and grow your business. It is fun to be interviewed but be sure to think about the message(s) you want to convey. I usually think of some main points (not more than three) that I want to convey, and I rehearse sound bites that convey them (I even practice saying them out loud).

During your own interview, look for opportunities to get your message out. One mom inventor I know recently got a "big break" to feature her product on television. She demonstrated her product beautifully on TV, but she was so excited that she forgot to say where people could buy it. It was a fun segment but ended up having little business value.

As Seen on TV

This section focuses on TV appearances because, by far, they're the most demanding and stressful of all your media appearances—if only because you'll be seen and heard, often on a live broadcast.

Since launching my business, I have been fortunate to appear on over 20 local and national television programs including all three traditional broadcast networks (NBC, ABC, and CBS) as well as on Warner Brothers cable network. Programs I've appeared on have included NBC's *Today* show, *NBC Nightly News with Tom Brokaw, Inside Edition, CNN Live*, and ABC's *Good Morning America*. In addition, I have been interviewed by reporters from *Time, Newsweek, The New Yorker, People, The Wall Street Journal, The London Times, Fortune Small Business, Contra Costa Times, Dallas Morning News*, and CNN radio, as well as a number of international, national, and local radio stations. Each experience has been entirely different, and it would have been great to know what to expect in advance. To help reduce some of your own preshow jitters, here are some good strategies:

You are what you wear. Though this doesn't mean that you need to spend a lot of money on wardrobe, you do need to think closely about what you'll wear. I've worn my own clothes, borrowed outfits from family members, and even bought one jacket for $18 that I wore on KTLA *Los Angeles Morning News*. What they all had in common, though, is they conveyed the right look, with the right colors. Colors that work well on TV include red, blue, and black; white is never a good idea. In addition, learn about the viewing audience in advance, and be sure to look the part in order to best "connect" with them. For example, dress like an executive to appear on a business news show, and tone it down for a "sophisticated mom" look to appear on a soft news show targeting women. When I appeared on *CNN Financial News*, for instance, I wore a bright red, yet conservative suit. The viewers of this program are primarily men and I wanted to make sure that I was taken seriously. You also never know when prospective investors may be observing you and may approach your company. Therefore it is important to look and speak like a professional.

Also be mindful of the region you are in. Fashion do's in Southern California may be fashion don'ts in Indiana. And, when in doubt, look professional. If you want to be taken seriously as a businesswoman, wear something that will drive attention to your face, which will focus attention on what you're saying, not what you're wearing. In addition, I always think it's a bad idea to wear something low cut when representing your business, especially on TV. Even spitfire Erin Brockovich eventually toned down her look!

Makeup matters.   While you may be a makeup expert dating from your teenage years, for some reason I missed Makeup 101. (Going to an all girl's school with nuns, and no boys in sight for four years, may have been the reason!) This fact became extremely apparent after seeing myself on my first television appearance. The pallor I seemingly shared with Herman Munster alarmed me.

I knew I needed help, so I visited one of the makeup counters at my local mall. I asked specifically for a makeup artist who was knowledgeable in makeup for television, which is entirely different than for everyday wear. Two hours later one of their top artists had taught me how to apply shocking amounts of makeup without scaring my kids!

Jen Fleece of Fleece Baby had a makeup experience of another kind. For her first TV appearance, on ABC *News Now*, Jen had a half-hour drive to the studio in Atlanta. She left two hours early so that she could dress and do her makeup when she arrived. She couldn't have anticipated a rainstorm and traffic jam that brought her to the doorsteps of ABC one minute before show time. As she ran in, they said, "You're on the air now!" Jen had to go on national television for the first time with no makeup and hair that

Jennifer Fleece with her daughters Killan, 4 and Eloise, 2, shortly after she launched her product Fleece Sheets to the market.

was wet from the rain. Lesson learned: Never leave your house for a television broadcast without being fully prepared to walk on the set, even if it means that you have to wake up at 4:00 a.m!

Expect the unexpected.   It's also important to note that each time you make a media appearance, your experience can differ wildly. That's because different shows have different formats. I wish I had understood this prior to going on camera for the first (or second, or third) time.

My first experience was with Katie Couric on the *Today Show*. Katie is lovely and although I felt nervous, she put me at ease. I found that if I focused on her completely and listened and responded to her questions, I was

Me with daughter Kiara (six months) and Katie Couric of the *Today Show* in May 2004. I brought Kiara with me to New York City and nursed her minutes before my national television debut. Multitasking at its best!

just fine. After reviewing the tape, I also learned that there were times that I was on camera and didn't realize it. Lesson learned: Smile and look focused even if you think the camera is not on you.

In my next appearance, on *CNN Live*, not only was it 4:00 a.m., but I was seated in a room with an automated camera. The only human contact I had was with the anchorman, across the country, through my earpiece. There was not even a monitor on which to see him. It was pretty surreal. With my earpiece in my ear, looking into the void of a camera, I did my best to listen carefully and respond with an animated face. It wasn't easy but it worked.

On some shows I have been instructed to speak directly to the on-air host, while on others I have been told to speak directly to the viewers through the camera. For example, Gayle Anderson, morning news reporter for *KTLA Los Angeles Morning News*, warned me to expect a nonconventional "Jerry Springer–style show but with clothes and no fighting," which I definitely now understand. She expects her guests to connect directly with their viewers by looking straight into the camera. The point is that it is important to ask the producer of the show about the format beforehand, so you can be prepared. Also, make sure to put the earpiece in the ear that feels most comfortable and the least distracting. Even though I am right-handed, I like to have my earpiece in my left ear. One last point about earpieces: You may hear a voice other than the anchor speaking in your ear. This is the producer. While you should listen and respond to the anchors, you must *not* respond to the producer while the segment is in progress.

Tough questions.   Business reporters often feel obliged, as part of the nature of their job, to ask you financial questions about your company. Be prepared! This is not the right time to have that "deer-in-the-headlights" look on your face; especially on television. You also don't want to skirt around this or look skittish because it calls your credibility and legitimacy into question. Here are three suggestions for how to handle financial questions: (1) Share the information if you are comfortable. They may or may not use it and your financials, good or bad, may be what makes them want to write about you. (2) Avoid sharing by saying, "my company is private and we do not disclose our financial information." (3) Skirt the issue by using future projections

I invited three mom inventors to join me for a live television segment on *KTLA Los Angeles Morning News* with reporter Gayle Anderson. Each mom had the opportunity to show her products to over three million viewers. From left to right are Jenny Lee, myself, Gayle Anderson, Jennifer Hughes, and Corrita Concon.

rather than historical figures. For example, "Our projections for next year are $500,000." If you feel uncomfortable talking about financials, practice your preferred answer until you can say it without pause.

Other Media

Newspapers, magazines, and radio outlets may, of course, also call you. If you're being interviewed by any of these media, being prepared is equally important. Before the interview, mentally review the messages you'd like to communicate. During the interview, listen carefully and respond directly to the reporter's questions. On the radio, try not to go on too long, and speak with a smile on your face. Listeners are more apt to respond to upbeat-sounding individuals!

The Momentum of Magazines

While television is an enormously powerful medium, the viewer has to be watching at that one moment in time when you are on air. The power of magazines is that they last longer than a brief television appearance. Don't underestimate their power in the media hierarchy!

Consumers tend to read magazines in short bits and pieces, keeping them around the house longer in order to steal time here and there to read stories. In addition, magazines sit in doctors' offices for weeks or even months, with thousands of people viewing them over the long run. For example, *People* magazine is distributed to three million subscribers, but its estimated "impressions" are six million per week. This is why magazines often have such a phenomenal impact. The challenge of working with magazines is the lead time they require. Some magazines require up to six months lead time for story ideas or information.

Beyond Press Releases—Getting Creative with Promotions

Of course, there are countless additional ways to get your message out to the public, beyond press releases. The key is to get creative and think outside the box. If you can think up the idea, you can probably make it happen. The only limit is your imagination and your budget!

Product Placement—Celebrity Gifting

Another interesting approach to marketing your products is through celebrities. There is a thriving industry whose objective is to get products in front of celebrities, in the hope that they'll promote them or give permission to use their names for product endorsements. You may have heard that it's becoming big business to get your product included in the celebrity bags at award shows like the Oscars. According to news reports, the retail value of one such group of bags at the Oscars exceeded $110,000 each! Certain products, (like mine, the TP Saver) are not particularly appropriate for inclusion in a celebrity gift bag, and it would be a waste of time for me to pursue such an outlet. However, I have included the Mom Invented baby bodysuits in bags given to both Julia Roberts and Soledad O'Brien after the birth of their new babies. Our effort was rudimentary and the benefit is still to be determined. However, you never know when you might hit the "celebrity jackpot," so to speak.

For example, Lisa Carvajal, inventor of Take-Out Time-Out, an aid to help discipline children when away from home, had just launched her terrific new product over her Website. One day, she watched Kelly Ripa of ABC's *Regis & Kelly* talking about a strategy used on the TV show *Super Nanny*—the importance of using a "naughty spot" when disciplining your kids. Lisa sent Kelly a personal, yet professional, cover letter with a reference to Kelly's discussion on the show along with a sample of her product. Lisa's product, a mat that looks like a target, where kids have time-outs, no matter where they are, fit in exactly with what Kelly had been talking about. As it turned out, Kelly *loved* the product and actually showed and endorsed it on the air, saying that she had tested it out and it worked. Now that's publicity!

Because it's so tough to get celebrity endorsements like this one, or to even have your product included in celebrity gift bags, you can be creative in other ways...and still tap into the celebrity mystique. For example, when Jonathan Holiff of The HollywoodMadison Group (a marketing company with a focus on celebs) was asked to generate celebrity interest in a major U.S. chewing gum company, he knew it might be a challenge to do so directly. So, he devised a more circuitous opportunity. He created a tele-

Lisa Carvajal invented the Take-Out Time-Out, a discipline mat for moms on the go. Lisa took a chance and sent a sample to Kelly Ripa, who ended up personally endorsing the product on her show!

phone poll campaign of 1,500 participants, in which consumers were asked which celebrity had the best smile. He then used the results—"the top five celebrity smiles," as voted by the U.S. public—to create a press release and generate press coverage, giving his gum client that elusive celebrity connection.

In addition, there are also companies that allow you to personally "introduce" your product to celebrities at television award shows and specials, assuring that the celebrity will actually receive your gift. One such company is Backstage Creations, a specialty marketing firm that caters solely to this niche. Of course, you can expect to pay thousands of dollars for the privilege. However, the results may be worth it if your product fits the right criteria. See the firm's Website www.backstagecreations.com for success stories.

Blogging

A blog (short for "Web log") is your own personal Website. Basically, your blog allows you to vent to the world. And whether you're blogging about politics, weddings, or the price of tea in China, there are no real rules. The use of blogs has grown in recent years (there are millions) as an unrivaled form of self-expression. Also, people can comment on what you say, link to your blog, or e-mail you in response.

While many people use blogs for their own personal reasons, blogs can also be a smart business tool. For instance, professional and amateur journalists use blogs to publish breaking news, and some blogs even command thousands of hits per day. Blogs provide a format to connect with people around the world, and you can allow them to post feedback directly on your blog. You can also delete anything you don't like.

I had heard about blogging from several people but couldn't conceptualize how it worked so I decided to try it myself. I wanted to see if I could use a blog as a unique way to connect with more mom inventors, share information, and get feedback on products. To get started, I used www.blogger.com and found this site to be professional and informative. It took three quick steps (less than five minutes) to sign up for a free account including a template for my blog Website page. My blog is http://mominventors.blogspot.com.

My first question was how to lead people to my blog. I found this information at http://help.blogger.com , in the "Beyond Blogging" section, where I clicked on "Promoting Your Blog." The document taught me how to set blogger application settings as well as other strategic ways to get blogs on lists and linked to other blog sites.

I encourage you to set up a blog of your own and use it as a marketing tool. Allow yourself to get creative and use this as yet another interesting way to seek information from consumers and elicit feedback from prospective consumers.

Amanda C. Kooser wrote about the growing influence of blogs in her article "Who Let the Blogs Out?" in the October 2002 issue of *Entrepreneur Magazine*. She talked about blogging expert Peter Scott, who created a Weblogs Compendium (www.lights.com/weblogs)—a premium resource for entrepreneurs seeking an introduction to blogs. "For a small business, the beauty of using a Web log (a.k.a. Blog) is that you can promote your business and you can also get other people to work with you on your business," said Scott, in the article. The elements of interactivity, community and collaboration will be key as growing businesses adopt blogs for customer relations, advertising, promotion, and even internal communications. Scott sees blogs becoming a mainstream feature of business Websites in the future. They are far less restrictive than message boards. With message broads you have to tread carefully when trying to promote your business or product as well as listing Web links so as not to offend the participants. Whereas with blogs, linking to other resources, businesses, Websites, and other blogs is a core component, adding value to the information.

If you'd feel more comfortable reading other blogs before creating one yourself, they are easy to find. There are blogs covering every topic imaginable. You can do an Internet search by typing in your area of interest like "parenting" and "blog" in the Google search engine. Lists and lists will appear that you can peruse.

Even celebrities are blogging: http://weblogs.about.com/od/celebrity-blogs. Why is this important? If one angle in your marketing strategy is to introduce your product to a celebrity, this may be an interesting way to let her know about it. Do this wisely. Read and get to know the celebrity and her interests before just blatantly trying to sell them something. Recall Lisa Carvajal's tactic. She tied directly into something that was of particular interest to Kelly Ripa.

The Four Seasons of Publicity

by Bill Stoller (www.publicityinsider.com)

First Quarter: January–March

What the Media's Covering: Early in the year, the media is looking ahead. It's a great time to pitch trend stories, marketplace predictions, and previews of things to expect in the year ahead. The media also likes to run this time of year "get your personal house in order" sorts of pieces...home organizing, weight loss, etc. Anything that's geared toward helping people keep their New Year's resolutions can work here.

Key Dates and Events: Superbowl, NCAA Tournament, Easter, the Academy Awards.

Second Quarter: April–June

What the Media's Covering: An "anything goes" time of year. With no major holidays or huge events, April is a good time to try some of your general stories (business features, new product stuff, etc.). Light, fun stories work here...As May rolls around, thoughts turn to summer. Now they're looking for summer vacation pieces, outdoor toys and gadgets, stories about safety (whether automotive or recreational), leisure activities, and things to do for kids.

Key Dates and Events: Baseball opening day, tax day (April 15), spring gardening season, Memorial Day, end of school, summer vacation.

Third Quarter: July–September

What the Media's Covering: Folks at PR firms are on vacation, marketing budgets are being conserved for the holidays and reporters are suddenly accessible and open to all sorts of things. Get to work here, with creative, fun angles. Entertainment-themed pieces do well in the summer, anything with celebrities work, lighter business stories, new products, trend pieces, technology, news, back to school education-themed articles....Reporters are about to get deluged once again come September, so use this window of opportunity wisely.

Key Dates and Events: July Fourth, summer movies, summer travel, back to school.

Fourth Quarter: October–December

What the Media's Covering: The busiest time of the media calendar, the fourth quarter is when the business media turns serious and the lifestyle media thinks holidays....Business angles need to be hard news. Fluffy trend pieces won't cut it, as business editors begin to take stock of the state of the economy and the market. It's a tough time to put out a new-product release. For the nonbusiness media, think Christmas. Christmas travel, Christmas gifts, Christmas cooking....If you have a product or service that can be given as a holiday gift, get on the stick early.

Nail down lead times for the publications you're targeting, call to find out who's handling the holiday gift review article and get your product in the right person's hands in plenty of time—along with a pitch letter or release that makes a strong case about what a novel, unusual, or essential gift your product makes.

Key Dates and Events: Labor Day, World Series, Thanksgiving, Hanukkah, Christmas, and New Year's Eve.

Hiring a Marketing Expert

There comes a time in almost every facet of business when you need to weigh what you have time for, and what you can do well, versus the value of outsourcing to an expert. While doing it yourself is a great way to start generating publicity, as your business grows you may find it makes more sense to hire someone to help.

The e-mail from Ann Noder, president of public relations firm Orca Communications, came after I had received coverage in local newspapers and television, and then booked myself on the *Today Show*. Given my early success, I wasn't certain that an investment in a publicist was prudent when I seemed to be fine on my own. In fact, after my one-minute appearance on the *Today Show*, my Website received over a quarter million hits, my telephone was ringing off the hook, and suddenly, I was really in *business*—even though I had been in business for the prior 18 months.

The power of the media had become obvious, but because I was so busy with day-to-day operations, I soon realized I didn't have time to research the calendar of events properly, pitch my stories to reporters, and keep track of follow-up calls. Plus, I didn't have the budget necessary to buy the appropriate advertising. I realized then that I needed a professional publicist, after all. Despite my own early success, this turned out to be one of the best decisions I have made. This allowed me to focus on my primary business: new-product development, sales, and crafting the future of the company.

While I was lucky that Ann contacted me, and that we ended up working well together, finding that "right fit" isn't always so easy. Here Ann offers tips on finding and deciding on a public relations agency that is appropriate for you:

- Personal references and word of mouth are often the best methods to find a reputable PR agency. Ask around or search for agencies through the Public Relations Society of America (PRSA, www.prsa.org). Although this is a professional organization, membership doesn't guarantee credibility. Search for firms that have a track record. Interview their clients.
- A good public relations professional will only take on companies or products for which they feel they can generate media coverage. For example, Ann's firm looks for items that are new, innovative, solve a problem, are highly visual, and issue-oriented.
- There are basic materials you should already have prepared when hiring a publicist:
  - Company/product background information
  - Sample of the product (if possible)
  - High resolution photos (300 dpi)
  - List of goals—(where do you see the company in 1 year, 5 years, 10 years)?
- The most common mistake that prospective clients make is asking specific questions about sales and how public relations will affect sales. Any public relations agency that guarantees specific coverage should not be trusted.
- The most common mistake a new client makes is expecting too much too soon. Public relations is a long, hard process. It takes a lot of pitching and follow-up to secure news coverage.
- Put a "press room" on your Website. This is a section on your site that has information for the press and tells them whom to contact.
- A publicist or public relations contract will cost from a few hundred dollars to thousands of dollars. While results cannot be guaranteed, the strategy and plan should be made perfectly clear.
- One way to limit the expense no matter which firm you go with is to start with a shorter contract or campaign (sign up for three

months instead of six). This saves you money and allows you to re-assess the agency after that term. Also, consider narrowing a campaign to include just print or just broadcast coverage. This will lower the fee from what it would cost for a full, national campaign to include all types of media outlets.

Advertising

Advertising can also be an extremely effective tool in creating awareness about your product. The advantage of advertising is that you control the message, and you don't have to rely on the whim of reporters or producers to pick up your story. If you pay for advertising space, it's yours. Which leads to its biggest disadvantage—advertising can be extremely costly, especially when it's not effective.

Irrespective of the type of media used, there are generally two types of ads: direct-response ads and brand-building ads. A direct-response ad might say, "Come in today and save 70 percent on closeout shoes." This one-time ad can be effective, if the offer is compelling enough. This is particularly true if it has been preceded by a brand-building campaign.

Brand-building ads tend to focus on a clear message delivered consistently. In my opinion, this is only effective if you can narrow your advertising focus enough to be able to afford to "own" a particular target. For example, choose one particular magazine, appear in it regularly in the same place, so you'll be sure to be seen multiple times by the publication's readers. If you use radio, choose one station and run your ad on a particular day of the week during the same time slot. Better yet, choose two complimentary publications and refer to each other in the ads to cross promote your message.

Choosing Your Ad Vehicles

When it comes to advertising, it may appear that TV is the only way to advertise, and preferably on a major network. That is, until you learn just how expensive it is to run one 30-second spot. Even during TV's slowest hours, like the wee hours of the morning, commercial spots are very expensive. And while it can be a good investment if you have the resources (obviously, there's a reason Pepsi, Coke, and McDonald's advertise on TV as much as they do), TV may be cost-prohibitive to the nascent entrepreneur. In addition, unless you have a product that truly appeals to a mass audience, TV advertising can be wasteful and ineffective.

A few of the mom inventors I know have learned this lesson the hard way. When Wendy Tuey, inventor of Proud Body (www.proudbody.com), a pregnancy belly cast kit, tried her hand at advertising, things didn't work as well as she had hoped. After spending about $10,000 producing a TV spot and hiring a call center for the anticipated sales volume, she found the TV ad wasn't effective at all. She got no more orders than usual.

However, she had better luck with print advertising. Perhaps it's because her advertising was much more targeted; she placed ads in publications like *Fit Pregnancy, Pregnancy,* and *ePregnancy,* a captive audience for the unique product she was selling. While she had different results (at different price points) with each of the publications, in general these efforts were much more successful than her TV advertising.

It's best to approach any type of advertising carefully. That's because if you don't do it right, you might as well be flushing your dollars down the toilet. When deciding whether or not to advertise, here are some key things to keep in mind:

Wendy Tuey created Proudbody, Inc., a company that creates plaster belly casts to capture an expecting mom's beautiful pregnant form.

- *Choose your media carefully.* If you have a niche product, it simply doesn't make sense to advertise to a mass audience on TV, even if you do have unlimited resources. Choose targeted outlets, such as specialty publications, radio stations with targeted demographics, and Internet sites that appeal to your audience.
- *Stretch your dollars.* Once you've chosen your media, it's also important to make as many "impressions" as possible. *Impressions* are the number of times you reach your target audience. It's not nearly as effective to run an ad one time, in one publication, as it would be to run the same ad six times per year. With increased frequency, consumers will begin to recognize and remember your brand or product. In addition, it may be more effective to run your ad six times in the same magazine, rather than one time each in six different magazines.
- *The larger the ad, the better the recognition.* Of course, not everyone can afford a full-page ad in *People* magazine. But you may be able to afford a full-page ad in a targeted publication like, say, *Dog Fancy* if your product is for pet owners. Advertising is one sure place where bigger is definitely better. A tiny eighth of a page ad in the back of a magazine may not be worth the investment if few people see it.
- *Color is better than black and white.* Another general rule is that a color ad is usually much more powerful than a black-and-white ad. That goes especially for newspapers, when you're staring at a sea of black and white. Of course, color will also generally add to the cost of your advertisement.
- *Make sure it looks good.* It never ceases to amaze me when someone lays out major cash for a media buy (the amount it costs to purchase ad space) and then runs a shoddy-looking, ill-designed ad. Once again, you might as well throw your money out the window. If you're going to invest in advertising, make sure your ad reflects your product or company in the proper light and that it's effectively conveying your message. That means good design, good writing, and a strategic message. It doesn't matter how many times a consumer sees your ad if they don't understand it or it doesn't cut through the clutter—or worst of all, leaves a negative impression.
- *Don't overlook the power of radio.* It can be an extremely effective medium and is often quite cost-effective, especially when compared to TV. And as with TV and magazines, choose your station carefully.

The Power of the Web—Banner Ads, Search Engines, and Keyword Advertising

If you have a Website, you are also in a position to take advantage of another important advertising medium—the Web. There are at least two ways to advertise on the Web—banner advertising and keyword advertising.

Banner Advertising. Banner advertisements are like small display advertisements in a magazine, except that they are interactive and can include not only moving/changing elements, but also a clickable link to your Website. Unfortunately, banner ads are not particularly effective, unless placed in great quantity or at very selective locations such as niche Websites that are obvious destinations for people who are likely to be interested in your product. If there are particular Websites that are especially appropriate destinations for your advertising, it's worth contacting such sites to determine what their advertising policies are. For most budding entrepreneurs, banner advertising is not likely to be very effective, and probably shouldn't be the first use of your critical advertising dollars.

Search Engines and Keyword Advertising

Search engines. Of the hundreds of millions of users of the Internet, virtually all of them at one time or another use a search engine to find what they want on the web. The most popular search engines are Google (www.google.com), Yahoo! (www.yahoo.com), MSN Search (http://search.msn.com), and AOL Search.

The search engines use different mechanisms for finding Websites in which their searchers might be interested. These search engines catalog all of the words on the Websites they "spider" (i.e., look through electronically). Some search engines also catalog images, photos, and other elements in addition to text. To make sure that the search engines have at least spidered your Website, you can actually "submit" your site to those engines. See http://submit.search.yahoo.com/free/request where you can submit your site to Yahoo!, essentially asking Yahoo! to include your site in its searches.

There are a large number of services that you can employ to submit your Website to the various search engines for you. To find them, just go to one of these engines and search on the terms "submit website." When a user types in key words into the search field, the search engine compares those words with all the words it has cataloged and returns a list of all the Websites it can find that includes those words.

So if you have a Website that includes the words "car seat," in theory your Website would turn up on a search of the words "car" and "seat." Unfortunately, that search on Google yields almost 20,000,000 results! Even if you use parentheses around the words (which limits the search to those sites that include those two words together in that exact order), Google still returns over 1,000,000 results. Where do you think your small website that sells car seats would appear in that list of a million? That's right; probably so far down that no one would ever search the results thoroughly enough to find it.

There are businesses that can help you "optimize" your website so that it is more likely to be found by the search engines, but for most sites that's likely to be a waste of money. Go to a search engine and type in "website optimization" to see the hundreds of companies offering this service

So what good are the search engines to you, if your website is likely to show up as the 900,000th result? It doesn't have to be that way. First of all, if you come up with a unique product name, someone can find your site simply by typing in the name of the product. Typing in "shoe clues" in Google turned up only 410 results, and 7 of the first 10 results were about the Mom Inventors, Inc. product of that name (including www.mominventors.com itself). Also, if the key words that you use to describe your product are unusual, or are presented in a unique combination, then a key word search is more likely to find your website. For example, another Mom Inventors, Inc. product is "Good Bites—Crustless Sandwich Cutter." If someone were to type in "crustless" and "sandwich," even without quotes, the Mom Inventors, Inc. product shows up high in the results.

Keyword advertising. If you are fortunate enough to have gotten sufficient publicity so that Web surfers are typing your product name into search engines, then you will benefit from this form of free marketing. But, if the name isn't known, or the description of your product is fairly generic, then you might want to consider buying keyword advertising. When you do a search in one of the search engines, you will see in most search engines either above or to the right of the results "Sponsored Links" or something similar. These are essentially advertisements purchased by companies both large and small. These advertisements include just a few words you want to say about your site (or product) and a link to your website. Google's program, for example, is called AdWords, and a purchase through the AdWords program can get your ad shown not only on Google, but Earthlink, AOL and AskJeeves, as well. Yahoo! has a similar expanded network.

What makes these advertisements special? A few things: first, they are tied to key words. They only appear when a user types in the particular key words that you, the advertiser have chosen. So, by choosing your keywords very carefully, you can manage to have your ad appear just when someone who is most likely to be interested in your product might see your ad. Second, you only pay for the display of your ad when someone actually clicks on it. Third, you actually bid for positioning of your ad relative to the ads of the other advertisers who have selected your same key words.

The cost of buying these keywords depends on a wide variety of factors, including which words you select. There is a lot of flexibility in setting up these advertising programs, and you can use them for a surprisingly small amount of money. But the rules can seem quite complex. See for Google:

> http://adwords.google.com/select/?hl=en_US&sourceid=awo&subid=
> WW-ET-adsenseland&clickid=en_US

and for Yahoo!:

> http://searchmarketing.yahoo.com/arp/srch.php?o=US1447&cmp=
> Yahoo_SponsorResults&ctv=Sponsored_Search&s=Y&s2=S&s3=

One interesting approach to using keywords is to select keywords that don't necessarily relate to your product, but rather to your target customers. For example, one small business, a personal financial planning consultancy, purchased as keywords the title of a popular book on family finances. The ad campaign proved to be a very inexpensive mechanism for driving new clients to the consultant. If you're convinced you want to participate in these programs, but don't have the time or aren't sure you have the expertise to do it all yourself, there are companies in the business of advising on, and managing keyword ad buying programs.

You should be using search engines early on in your efforts to bring your idea to life, both to determine whether someone else is already marketing your idea, as well as to see what potential competitors (and perhaps partners) you might have. Because if there are competitors (or partners) out there, there's a good chance that they are purchasing keyword ads!

Hiring an Ad Agency

When it comes to advertising, it's definitely challenging to do it yourself. That's because most of us don't have the design or writing skills to maximize our ad dollars. And while many media outlets offer their own in-house ad design, often these ads are rudimentary and cheaply produced. Although hiring a traditional ad agency can be an investment, it's better than doing a haphazard job of advertising and wasting those precious dollars completely.

An ad agency can help you strategize your message, advise you as to which media to use, and negotiate prices on your behalf. In return you'll pay a fee or a markup on services rendered. To choose an appropriate agency, follow the strategies outlined earlier in the chapter on choosing a PR agency. Many of the tenets remain the same: relying on references, reputation, and prior work.

There are agencies of all sizes, and I don't recommend you go with the heavy hitters—those agencies that Pepsi and Coke use—from the outset. While it would be great to have the best in the biz working on your account, it's simply not financially feasible. There are doubtless many local agencies in your region to investigate. Also, consider using a smaller graphic design house or a talented freelance designer to craft your ad. Once again, professionalism is key.

In addition to creating ads, agencies can help you craft an entire advertising and promotional strategy. Finding a good agency is like adding to your team of experts. Most full-service agencies can help you do everything from your initial branding, including positioning, message development, and logo design, to focus group testing, ad design, and final media placement. While you may pay more to work with an agency, it may save you bundles in the long term by helping you avoid costly mistakes.

Chapter Wrap-Up

Marketing is essential to the success of your product. Without it, no one will know about your product, much less where they can find it! When you first begin, try to generate media coverage yourself. Also remember to think creatively about different promotional opportunities that may be specific to your product. And if you're not having luck or you're overwhelmed with other business tasks, consider hiring a public relations or advertising firm. Their expertise can often mean the difference between success and failure.

Finding a Partner

Licensing 101

You've learned in the previous chapters that developing your invention and setting up your own business is a doable undertaking, but certainly not a minor one. Taking a product from concept to market is an enormous commitment of time, energy, and money. Of course, if successful, the financial rewards and personal gratification can be well worth the effort.

However, perhaps you don't have the time or inclination to set up a full-fledged business that addresses everything from manufacturing to marketing. Perhaps you love the process of developing your idea, but not necessarily the prospect of running your own business. Or maybe you just don't have the financial resources to get a business off the ground. If this is the case, there is another option for launching your idea into the marketplace: licensing your invention or product.

So what is licensing, anyway? A *licensing agreement* is a contract between an inventor of a product (you) and another person or company, usually a manufacturer, who will develop and sell your product in the marketplace. In this agreement, the inventor (licensor) licenses the rights to her idea or patents, copyrights, or trademarks to a manufacturer (licensee). (Here's a quick memory device to get the two terms straight: remember the endings of the words *inventor* and *licensor* go together.) Typically, in return for the idea, the inventor/licensor will get a percentage of the sales revenue.

There are two points I should mention before continuing in this chapter: First, my company, Mom Inventors, Inc., licenses, manufactures, and sells products. That means that we have inventions submitted to us regularly and make the difficult decision of which products we will license. So in the interest of full disclosure, note that my perspective is that of a manufacturer, or licensee. In this capacity, I feel I can give you valuable tips about how to approach a manufacturer to maximize your chances for licensing success. In addition to licensing products ourselves, we have also assisted inventors in finding other partners and negotiating their licensing agreements, so I have witnessed how other licensees operate as well.

Your Licensing Partner

Because your relationship with your licensee—the manufacturer—should not be adversarial, I tend to refer to the licensee as your licensing "partner." The deal you negotiate must work for both parties to be truly successful. And, by thinking of the company as your partner, you can help foster a good relationship, which may lead to other product licensing agreements in the future.

Why Should You License?

You may wonder, "If I'll only end up with a small percentage of the profits, why should I license my product in the first place?" Well, there are definitely benefits to being a licensor, especially if running your own long-term business isn't something that interests you. Some of the benefits are as follows:

1. By licensing to a manufacturer with established distribution channels, an inventor's product can quickly be integrated into the product mix and get rapid market penetration. This likely achieves a much broader distribution than a new, sole inventor can achieve.
2. The licensee assumes all the costs in producing, marketing, and distributing the product; thus taking the financial burden off you.

3. The licensee assumes all the risk associated with the product. This applies to a number of areas, including possible market rejection of the product, product liability issues, and other unforeseen market conditions.
4. The licensee is the majority stakeholder and therefore has a vested interest in pursuing legal or costly patent enforcement issues in the face of competitive knock-off threats.
5. You, as the licensor receive a royalty payment, usually based on a percentage of product net sales, as compensation for assigning rights to the licensee.

Why Do Manufacturers Want to License?

There are benefits to manufacturers when they license your product, too. Especially during negotiations, it's valuable to understand how licensing your product can benefit the licensee:

1. For manufacturers, licensing inventions from outside inventors is a great way to save money on in-house research and development (R&D). It is basically a way to outsource product development. In fact, many companies have recently reduced their in-house product development budgets with the hope of taking advantage of the availability of outside intelligence.

    For example, Procter & Gamble recently launched a "Connect and Develop" program, which aims to access outside intelligence and inventions to develop successful new products. One of their success stories is the Spin Brush, an electric toothbrush created by outside inventor, John Osher, which has become a $200 million dollar business for P&G. At Mom Inventors, Inc., we have also found that innovation often means looking outside our company walls, because there is so little time available to develop new product ideas after managing the day-to-day business.
2. Outside inventors often have a unique hands-on approach to inventing. An independent inventor typically creates her invention based on her own experience in wrestling with a problem and developing solutions that work, which is less common in the corporate lab.

3. Independent inventors tend to devote tremendous thought and effort to their products, whereas at a large company, many ideas are competing for mind share.

4. Outside inventors are not shackled by the internal rules and restrictions that tend to develop in large organizations. They are more likely to offer products and ideas that fall "outside the box" of existing thought at the company. This is a great way to bring "fresh" ideas into the company without incurring the expense of new personnel, mind-expanding consulting approaches, or off-site group exercises.

The Squirrel-Proof Birdfeeder

One story that's become part of business folklore illustrates how the most motivated individual is often the one to develop the best solution:

A store advertised a new product called a squirrel-proof birdfeeder. After having wrestled with vandal squirrels for months with his own birdfeeder, "Joe" went to the store, eagerly grabbed one of the new birdfeeders, bought it, and took it home to set up. Over the next few days he noted with excitement that the squirrels circled it, yet were apparently stumped, and the birds enjoyed the full benefits. But one morning, about a week later, he was shocked when he found his birdfeeder empty of seed when it had been full the day before! He refilled the feeder and spent the rest of the day observing the squirrels as they made repeated visits to the birdfeeder, helping themselves to his bird seed.

Outraged, he went back to the hardware store and began to protest to the storekeeper.

"How can you advertise this as a squirrel-proof birdfeeder"? he asked.

The storekeeper said that it was the manufacturer making that claim, not he. But he added, "I will be happy to give you back your money. We shouldn't even sell a product making such a claim, because anybody knows there's no such thing as a squirrel-proof birdfeeder."

Joe asked how the storekeeper knew.

The storekeeper answered with two questions: "How many minutes do you spend per week thinking about how to keep squirrels out of the bird feeder?"

"At least 30 minutes *every* day," Joe responded.

To that, the storekeeper asked, "How many minutes a week do you think your squirrel thinks about how to get into that bird feeder?"

In other words, the more motivated the individual, the more likely she'll come up with a solution to solve her problem. Inventors seeking out a solution to their own challenges—rather than someone else's—can offer creative and inspired insights borne of personal experience.

Step into the Manufacturer's Shoes

Before you even begin the process of approaching manufacturers to license your product, it's valuable to think about your product from their perspective first. Manufacturers are juggling dozens of tasks and challenges daily. They also have many opportunities and possible directions in which to take the business. Your product is only one of many possibilities, so it is critical to understand their viewpoint.

While the manufacturer may be impressed with the cleverness, uniqueness, or downright brilliance of your invention, they will consider it, most of all, as a potential business opportunity. That means no matter how terrific the idea, they will pass on your offer if it doesn't make business sense or is too complicated to take on. For most companies, taking on a new product is a big deal. It consumes a tremendous amount of internal resources. Most companies can launch, and therefore license, only a few new products each year.

This means that you'll need to present the business case for your product in the best, most professional way possible. The more you research, uncovering the potential challenges and providing solutions, the more likely you will fulfill the need of the manufacturer. At Mom Inventors, we receive many terrific idea submissions, but we tend to consider more closely the prospects who've researched and answered most of the business-related questions ahead of time. And the stand-alone statement, "Millions of people will buy this; I just know it…" does not meet this criterion.

Making Your Case

So how do you know what the manufacturer will need to know? Just as you would if you were developing your own business plan, try to anticipate all the possible questions. Your first step should be researching and compiling knowledge through market research. As discussed in Chapter 4, first collect secondary market information on the overall size of the potential market. Then drill down using primary research to validate your claims about customer interest, price points, and real demand. We love to see submissions from inventors who have conducted focus groups (not with people they know). This saves us a lot of work and often helps inform our decision to move forward.

Your next step should be compiling data on competing or similar products, as discussed in Chapter 2. Further, you should do as much research as possible to determine if the invention is patentable or can be produced without infringing on other filed patents (also covered in Chapter 2).

The next step can be challenging, but providing information on the production process can also prove to be extremely helpful. This is particularly true if there are unique materials or unusual challenges the product might pose in production (see Chapter 6).

Finally, the more an inventor can research and bring real information about regulatory issues or steps that need to be taken for legal protection, the better (Chapter 5).

Preparing Your Presentation

Once you've gathered all your data, you should present it in the most effective way possible to your target licensing partners (we'll discuss how to find them in the next section). A prototype is often the most effective and attention-getting way of presenting your idea (see Chapter 3). We receive hundreds of product submissions from inventors, and submissions with prototypes are often the first ones we look at; intentionally or not, they just grab our attention. Of course, in some cases it may not be feasible for you to develop a prototype. In fact, some manufacturers won't even accept them. In these cases, use clear, understandable three-dimensional drawings. These can be prepared by either a graphic designer or an engineer.

Note that it's critical to present supporting information in a clear, concise format. I recommend developing a simple sell sheet, which is a one- or two-page document that clearly states the problem or need, a description of the product, the product benefits and features, summary of the market opportunity, and the legal status (e.g., patent No.123…, patent-pending, copyrights, trademarks). See Appendix B for an example of a sell sheet.

Also prepare a simple introductory letter to accompany the sell sheet. This letter should briefly introduce yourself, explain your interest in contacting the licensee, and set a time line for follow-up.

So Many Fish in the Sea

Once you've prepared your prototype or sales materials, your next big question is, "To whom do I offer this great business opportunity?" I recommend that you identify an initial list of at least 50 prospective targets. Pinpointing the manufacturers that would be the most likely to produce your product will give you a better chance of making a deal. Plus, if your product falls within a manufacturer's larger line (say, for instance, a new type of bottle warmer for a company that sells baby bottles) your product immediately makes sense to retailers and customers when they first see it. As one buyer recently told me, "a group of related products help tell a story to the customer." Similarly, the more comfortable your target licensee is with the process of manufacturing products like yours, the more likely the company is to consider it. For example, a company who makes stuffed animals would not likely be a good candidate to license a new skin cream. And a company that makes electronics is unlikely to be interested in licensing a plastic exercise device.

So how can you identify the companies that might make a good fit? To start this process relatively easily, spend time in a store where you might expect to see your product sold. Jot down the names from the product packages of manufacturers that produce and sell similar products. You may have also encountered similar manufacturers during your prior market research (review your bound notebook).

Another good way to identify prospective manufacturers is to identify the trade association that serves the industry in which your product would fall. As I mentioned earlier in the book, there is a trade association for nearly every industry. You can find them at www.asaenet.org. Once you identify the appropriate associations, look to see if they offer a list of their members or a list of members who've registered for their trade shows. Jot these names down, visit their Websites, and see the kinds of products they make. You may also wish to attend one of these trade shows as a guest to find more information. Trade show organizers usually provide a list of the exhibiting companies (at trade shows I have purchased CD-based lists for as little as $5 or $10), and you can walk the floor to see the types of products different companies offer. I am always amazed to see how many products on the market don't necessarily appear in the stores where I shop.

Note: Make sure you don't hassle these manufacturers at the show. They're there to meet and sell their products to buyers, and they probably won't wish to discuss your invention at the show. When you find an exhibiting manufacturer that seems like a good fit, pick up their brochure and simply ask who in the company handles product development. Then follow up with that person after the show.

The trade press can also be a resource for finding prospective licensing partners. Look in publications that relate to your industry, and scour the editorial content and advertising for leads.

Another way to find appropriate manufacturers is through online databases. Local public business libraries are often linked to database systems that enable members to search for companies in specific industries. And from your own home computer, you can access www.hoovers.com, which is a great online database service that provides information about many large-size companies. This service even enables you to find companies that have specific key words in their description. For instance, after going to the www.hoovers.com Website, I clicked the "free U.S. site." To initiate a search, I clicked on "Industry Key Word" and typed the word "stroller." The search brought up a listing for "Baby Supplies & Accessories." Clicking on this brought up 10 companies, such as Playtex Products, Inc., with data about each company and a list of related industries. For a fee, Hoovers also offers a database with even more information.

Another resource for information on large public companies is the Securities and Exchange Commission Website (www.sec.gov). This site provides data on all public companies listed on U.S. exchanges. The larger a company is, the easier it seems to be to get information on this site.

Once you've generated your list of possible target companies, you should "qualify" each lead to determine which companies make the most sense to approach. There are a number of factors to consider when developing this list:

- *Size.* While larger companies may be easier to find, and generally have tremendous distribution, they aren't necessarily the best prospects. Instead, smaller companies, which are less likely to have product development professionals on staff, might stand to benefit the most from the labor and intelligence of an outside inventor. Also, smaller companies are typically less burdened with bureaucracy like multiple layers of decision makers across departments. Another plus is that there are more small manufacturers to choose among. Therefore, I recommend fast-growing small or mid-sized companies as your best licensing prospects.

- *Geography.* If there are companies geographically near you, they might be good prospects; especially if it is possible to leverage local contacts to meet the decision makers.
- *Similar product line.* As mentioned earlier, a manufacturer with a line in which your product is a natural fit is a good prospect.
- *Competition.* Your product could potentially help a company face a competitive challenge. For example, if you see one company launch a product that is similar to yours, think about that company's competitors. In all likelihood this competitor has also witnessed this new launch and may be trying to figure out how to meet this competitive threat quickly. What a great time to show up with your product! Also note that competition could work against you. For example, if one of your target companies has recently launched a product that is similar to yours or might make your product seem like yesterday's news, they probably aren't such a good prospect.
- *Ability to reach the decision maker.* If you can, find out who ultimately decides what products to license, how many different people need to weigh in, and what paces they typically put a new invention through. The less complicated, the better and faster the process will be for you.
- *Company policy.* Find out a company's policy for accepting submissions. Also find out if they will sign your nondisclosure agreement (NDA) or if they have one for you to sign. What if they don't have an established policy? That can be either good or bad. It can be good if it means there won't be an abundance of submissions with which you are competing for attention. However, it could be bad if they have a policy, stated or unstated, of only carrying products "invented in house."
- *Manufacturer reputation.* If possible, find out if this company has licensed other products, and then try to contact the inventor to ask them about their experience. Note: regardless of who licenses and

sells the product, the original inventor's name remains on the patent listed publicly at the United States Patent and Trademark Website (www.uspto.gov). When I have called inventors for references in the past, they've typically been receptive to my calls. They usually view me as a fellow inventor and have been forthcoming with the information I was seeking.

Making the Sale

So you've got your research, you've got your prototype and sell sheet, and you've got your target list. Now it's time to make the sale! While some inventors look to other people to do the job (like an invention promotion company), I strongly believe that you, the inventor, are the most qualified person to sell your product to a licensee. Plus, some manufacturers (including my own company) will not do business with invention promotion companies, because so many of them are run by scam artists. We want to hear from you directly!

Your best bet is to begin by following the sales strategies outlined in Chapter 8. In a nutshell, mail your letters, make the calls, follow up, and follow through. And as with any type of sales, the more prospects, the better. This is true for two reasons: first, it is a numbers game. Most companies will turn you down for one reason or another. So the more times you ask, the more nos you get, and the more likely you are to get a yes. Second, and unique to licensing, is that some manufacturers may want to license your product as a defensive maneuver. In other words, they don't want to see their competitor license it. From a licensor's perspective, this is a great tactic as long as you can get a certain level of royalty and sales commitments.

What to Expect

First and foremost, don't expect a million dollar deal. It's doubtful you'll retire based on licensing your first product. In fact, a 2 percent royalty with no up-front payment might actually end up being a pretty good deal. The reality is that while a great idea is an essential beginning for any product, it's just one small piece of its ultimate success. By licensing your idea, the manufacturer assumes the responsibility, costs, and risks inherent in a new-product launch, including steps like mold and pattern development, patenting, production, insurance, regulations, safety requirements and testing, sales, distribution, managing sales reps, handling returns, collections, inventory management, and so on. This is why, to your probable dismay, you won't get a larger piece of the pie.

On the Move

Cheryl Wells, Founder and CEO of Up & Away, Inc., recently licensed her first product, Auto Mobiles, to Infantino, a manufacturer in the infant and juvenile industry with a distribution presence in over 8,000 stores in North America. Auto Mobiles are mobiles that adhere to the ceiling of a car and provide children with visual stimulation while in their car seats.

The structure of her agreement demonstrates how the terms must work for each party. For example, Cheryl really wanted a

Cheryl Wells, inventor of Auto Mobiles, with daughters Tatum (6) and Ashlee (21). Cheryl recently negotiated a successful licensing agreement with a large manufacturing company in the juvenile and baby products industry.

cash advance for her effort. The licensee was not comfortable with that. However, the licensee agreed to purchase Cheryl's remaining inventory at a wholesale price (she had initially sold the product herself). In addition, Cheryl was able to retain distribution rights in Europe, while the manufacturer launched exclusively in North America. And although the manufacturer will make design changes and take over production of the product, Cheryl also retained the right to approve the quality of the new products before they are distributed.

By any standard, the deal Cheryl achieved appears to be a win-win agreement. Even so, it was not without some difficulty. In the five years that passed from Cheryl's initial idea to licensing, she pinched every penny, running her own dental lab to pay her bills, while her invention moved through the process. At the point of licensing her product, her sales had just begun taking off and she had created a terrific brand. She also held a substantial utility patent. After so much effort, letting go of the product was not accomplished without some ambivalence. As Cheryl said, "I felt like I was giving my child up for adoption. I really wanted it to go to a good home." Fortunately, she felt she found a good home with a company that she believes will aggressively sell her product.

Also note there is no set rule or right set of terms when it comes to negotiating a licensing agreement. The perfect agreement is one in which both the licensor and licensee each get what they want. Therefore, the terms are completely negotiable and can vary dramatically. Often times the most successful agreements are those with extremely unique terms that account for the specific goals of the parties to the agreement.

There are some generalities, however. Most ideal for you, the inventor, is to get as much up-front cash, as high a royalty, and as high an annual minimum payment as possible (these terms are explained below). Of course the manufacturer will be gunning for less risk—which means lower up-front payout, lower minimum payment requirements, and as low a royalty percentage as possible. You should understand these basic business terms before entering into a negotiation, and they are explained next. In addition to understanding the business terms, you should understand your legal rights and responsibilities. It is wise to seek the counsel of a business attorney familiar with intellectual property rights when negotiating a licensing agreement.

Reaping the Rewards

Generally, the further along in the development your product is, the more lucrative the terms of your licensing agreement. For example, if you present just an idea to a licensee, you'll probably get less lucrative terms than if you've already secured a utility patent, produced merchandise, and generated sales.

Up-front payment. This is money that the licensee pays the licensor up front, before development or sales even begin, for the assignment of the rights. This can be an outright payment, but most commonly takes the form of an advance against (future) royalties. The amount of up-front payment varies. However, it is not unusual for an inventor to seek an up-front payment that covers the cost of her patent filing. Another way to come to an agreeable sum is to base your payment on projected sales expectations for the first year.

Royalties. These are the payments made to the licensor based on a percentage of the licensee's product sales. So, if you make a 2 percent royalty, that means you'll receive 2 percent of the wholesale price of each unit sold. The typical royalty range tends to run from 2 to 5 percent. Again, the further along or more proven the invention, the less risk for the manufacturer and the more likely you'll get an up-front payment or higher royalties. From my perspective, the royalty is the most important element of the agreement, because if the market responds to the product, the manufacturer will do well and the inventor can earn a good revenue stream.

Annual minimum. This is a contractual term that requires the licensee to pay the licensor a minimum amount of royalties, irrespective of the actual royalties due from sales. To me, the purpose of annual minimums is to ensure that the manufacturer places sufficient effort and resources behind promoting the product. Therefore, I believe that annual minimums are most important in the initial years of the agreement—when the product is being launched—to ensure that the licensee adequately prioritizes this item when deploying sales resources.

(Note: These negotiation points are interconnected. In other words, when an agreement has a high up-front payment, there may be a lower royalty percentage. Or if there is a large annual minimum, there may be a lower up-front payment.)

Exclusivity agreement.   Usually a manufacturer will want to have exclusive rights to distribute the product globally. However, this is subject to negotiation. Depending on each party's motives, the agreement could actually divide up the markets in many ways. Some variations to an agreement could include provisions that provide exclusivity domestically but not internationally. Others might offer the license for certain types of accounts or in certain industries. The length (term) of the agreement can also vary from one year to forever.

Special Corporate Programs

In addition to the systematic approach we've already outlined for licensing your idea to a manufacturer, there are also special programs that you might wish to consider. Sometimes companies will host new product searches where they outline a formal application process. For example, HSN (Home Shopping Network) is running invention search programming. And in March 2005, children's toy store FAO Schwartz launched a program aimed at finding innovative toys called "Inventors' Audition for Child's Play."

One company, The Big Idea Group (www.bigideagroup.net), accepts invention submissions for consideration by their pool of manufacturer and retail clients. Other opportunities exist on a larger scale, including Procter & Gamble's Connect and Develop program (www.pgconnectdevelop.com). Partners in this network seeking to tap into external intelligence include www.innocentive.com, www.ninesigma.com, and www.yet2.com. Another program has recently been launched through the Dial Corporation (see www.dialcorp.com for details). In addition, Staples is now offering an Invention Quest Contest (see http://inventionquest.dja.com.) Be aware that it may be difficult to distinguish companies who are legitimately helping inventors do business from invention promotion companies whose principal ambition is to scam payments from eager inventors.

While I don't discourage you from taking advantage of these programs, I tend to think of them more like invention lotteries. I would encourage you to put the bulk of your efforts on strategically focusing on identifying and directly approaching companies that would be a good fit for your product.

How Patents Play In

Common licensing practice tends to assume that an inventor will secure, or at least file, a patent, copyright, or trademark prior to presenting an invention to a prospective licensing partner. These protections provide the inventor with a tangible asset to offer licensees. From the perspective of the licensee, a patent makes an invention more desirable because it helps prevent competitors from quickly entering the market. It also means that the licensee's own internal product development team cannot launch this product, absent an agreement with the inventor, without some legal risk. In fact, some manufacturers won't even accept submissions that don't have a patent. For these reasons the terms for the licensor tend to be more lucrative when a patent has been filed.

On the flip side, however, it's worth repeating that only 2 to 3 percent of patented inventions ever make it to market, while many nonpatented products do. Plus, as discussed in Chapter 5, quality patenting services are costly. And, in fact, some manufacturers even prefer nonpatented submissions, because they can then use their own legal team to write the patent, as well as incorporate their own ideas or expand on the original idea.

Note that these manufacturers will likely be reluctant to sign nondisclosure or noncompete agreements or similar documents, because, given their practice of accepting nonpatented submissions, it is conceivable that other inventors have submitted similar ideas or that the company could already be working on something similar in-house.

If this is the route you are taking, limit your risk by finding out about the target licensee's reputation. Then realize that if you haven't gotten a patent, there is always some risk that your idea can be stolen...and as I've said before, there is risk even if you have a patent. Weigh the pros and cons of each option as well as feedback from your initial contacts to determine if filing a patent will be worthwhile or not. As of the time this book was written, Mom Inventors, Inc. has licensed three unpatented and one patented invention.

What Will It Cost?

Many inventors pursue licensing because it is a low-cost, low-risk way to get an invention to market. The main costs associated with licensing include collecting information, creating your presenta-

tion, and making the calls—and, of course, the opportunity cost—
your time. The best way to save money is to spread out any costs:

- Find information for free rather than purchase it. For outside
  help, get acquainted with your local business librarian.
- Spend some time every week performing research.
- Make a few calls and send out a few letters every week.

Chapter Wrap-Up

Licensing can be a terrific way to profit from your idea. This is especially
true if you lack sufficient financial resources or the interest to develop the
product yourself. However, make sure your expectations are in line with
reality. Individual licensed inventions will seldom produce enough licensing royalty income for an inventor to retire and move to the tropics. Annual
million-dollar (or even half–million-dollar) license contracts are rare. But,
$5,000, $10,000, and $20,000 contracts are not. Inventors who make their
living through licensing inventions tend to have inventing minds that never
rest, and they get pleasure from coming up with new invention ideas. Once
you go through the licensing process, you may wish to repeat the process
and generate multiple sources of licensing revenue! This is another reason
to view your licensees as partners. They will likely want to see other future
ideas from you.

Conclusion

So here we are. Many of you have read this book to illuminate a path to success. Perhaps an idea occurred to you in the quiet of a moment; you refused to drown that idea in self-criticism or fear, and then looked for a flash of inspiration to bring it all to life. You may have said to yourself, "Why not? I can do it!"

Whether you're inventing the next great widget—or reinventing how you work—virtually all aspects of your life can benefit when you pursue your dream. You'll learn many skills by giving life to your product or service: developing a focused plan, setting up a work infrastructure, conducting research, navigating legal matters, expanding your own creativity, negotiating contracts, and selling or promoting yourself or your business. When you've learned these lessons and you've gone through this process, you may even find that you are a different person.

You now have the essential tools you need—and you're as qualified as any seasoned executive—to invent a product and build a business. Just as I have, you will continue to learn along the way. In the meantime, remember: You are your own best advocate. It's up to you to make it happen … but you are not alone! Tap into your network of friends and family for support, and create a team of experts for all your additional needs.

If you have yet to take action, I encourage you to go for it now! And no matter what you wish to invent or what area of your life you'd like to reinvent, take it on with vigor. You have what it takes to succeed.

In the process of creativity, I have been inspired by a poem called "Success" by Ralph Waldo Emerson:

> To laugh often and much;
> to win the respect of intelligent
> people and the affection of
> children; to earn the appreciation
> of honest critics and endure the
> betrayal of false friends;
> to appreciate beauty;
> to find the best in others;
> to leave the world a bit better,
> whether by a healthy child,
> a garden patch or a
> redeemed social condition;
> to know even one life has
> breathed easier
> because you have lived.
> This is to have succeeded.

My mother always told me: "Leap and the net will appear." I invite you to take that leap today.

Resources

Here are the Website resources I discussed in the book, listed by chapter:

Chapter 1 Taking Your First Steps

www.uspto.gov — United States Patent and Trademark Office
www.onepagebusinessplan.com — One Page Business Plan resource
www.ftc.gov — Federal Trade Commission
www.ftc.gov/bcp/conjline/pubs/alerts/invnalrt.htm — Fraudulent promotion firms
www.uspto.gov/web/offices/com/iip/complaints.htm — List of companies with claims made against them
www.uspto.gov/web/offices/com/speeches/s1948gb1.pdf — Details American Inventors Protection Act of 1999
www.uspto.gov/web/forms/2048.pdf — Downloadable complaint form
www.creativethink.com — site of author Roger von Oech, who wrote *A Whack on the Side of the Head: How You Can Be More Creative*

Chapter 2 Knowledge Is a Mom's Best Friend

www.google.com — Internet search engine

www.yahoo.com — Internet search engine

www.msn.com — Internet search engine

www.askjeeves.com — Internet search engine

www.searchengines.com — Resource to find specific search engines

www.synonym.com — Resource to identify synonyms to help with research

www.onestepahead.com — Juvenile/baby products catalog and online retailer

www.babiesrus.com — Juvenile/baby products online retailer and stores

www.babyuniverse.com — Juvenile/baby products online retailer

www.babycenter.com — Juvenile/baby products online retailer

www.bedbathandbeyond.com — Online retailer of home goods

www.uspto.gov/go/ptdl — Patent and Trademark Depository Library

www.uspto.gov — United States Patent and Trademark office

Chapter 3 From Your Mind's Eye to the Palm of Your Hand: Creating Your Prototype

www.shapelock.com — Reusable plastic to build a prototype

www.thomasnet.com — Resource to locate manufacturers and prototype developers nationwide

www.compassdesign.com — Site of engineer Curt Anderson

www.cc.utah.edu/~asn8200/rapid.html — Information on rapid prototyping

www.rapidprototyping.net — Information on rapid prototyping

http://home.att.net/~castleisland/ — Information on rapid prototyping

http://www.aero3dp.com — Information on rapid prototyping

www.astm.org — Voluntary standards organization

www.cpsc.gov — U.S. Consumer Product Safety Commission

www.ansi.org — American National Standards Institute

www.notionsmart.com — Site that sells attachments to fabric (buttons, elastic, zippers…)

www.protosew.com — Prototype developer for textile products.

Chapter 4 Put on Your Detective Hat: Market Research

www.census.gov — U.S. Census data

www.google.com — Search engine

www.hoovers.com — Database with information about 12 million U.S. companies

www.sec.gov — U.S. Securities and Exchange Commission

www.asaenet.org — American Society of Association Executives (list of associations)

www.thebloomreport.com — News and information for the toy and related industries

www.silverstork.com — a mom-focused research company, dedicated to helping businesses understand the mom market

Online Bulletin Boards

www.parentsoup.com
www.windsorpeak.com
www.babycenter.com
www.ivillage.com
www.clubmom.com
www.theknot.com
www.ultimatewedding.com

Microloans

www.microenterpriseworks.org
www.accionusa.org
www.count-me-in.org

Loan Programs

www.sba.gov/financing/basics/lenders.html — Information from the Small Business Administration

www.blx.nct — Business Loan Express; offers business loans

www.innovativebank.com — Offers business loans

Government Grants

www.sba.gov/financing/basics/grants.html — Information from the Small Business Administration

Chapter 5 Protect Yourself: All about Patents, Copyrights, and Trademarks

www.uspto.gov — Registered patent attorneys and agents

www.uiausa.com — Site of the United Inventors Association, which offers free resources and a wealth of information on inventing

www.patentplanet.com — Offers affordable patent searches

www.wipo.int/treaties/en/ShowResults.jsp?lang=en&treaty_id=2

www.uspto.gov/web/offices/pac/dapp/pctstate.pdf — List of countries that are members of the PCT Treaty

Chapter 6 Getting the Goods: Manufacturing

www.thomasnet.com — Resource for finding appropriate manufacturers in the United States

www.alibaba.com — Resource for finding overseas manufacturers

www.tdctrade.com — Hong Kong Trade Development Council

www.uschamber.com — U.S. Chamber of Commerce

www.usitc.gov — U.S. International Trade Commission

www.ftn.fedex.com — Fed Ex Trade Networks

www.customs.gov — U.S. Customs and Border Protection

www.pantone.com — Site with worldwide standards for color

www.usps.gov/clicknship — U.S. Post Office page for at-home label printing

Chapter 7 Taking Care of Business: Setting Up Shop

www.sba.gov — U.S. Small Business Administration

www.annrankin.com — Ann Rankin, corporate attorney

www.statelocalgov.net — Resource to find the Secretary of State office in your area

www.irs.gov/businesses/small — Site to obtain Employee Identification Number (EIN)

www.nmsdc.org — National Minority Suppliers Development Council

www.wbenc.org — Women's Business Enterprise National Council

www.dunandbradstreet.com — Site to register for Dun & Bradstreet number

www.tannedfeet.com — Informal yet informative business resource

www.tannedfeet.com/home_business.htm — Home business rules

www.microsoft.com/frontpage — Software that allows you to build your own Website

www.quickcart.com — Shopping cart feature to add to your Website

www.quickbooks.com — Accounting program

www.mfsanet.org — Mailing, Fulfillment Service Association

www.uc-council.org — Uniform Code Council (purchase bar codes)

www.score.org — Service Corps of Retired Executives; now called
   Counselors to America's Small Business

www.sba.gov/wbc.html — Women's Business Center of the Small Business
   Administration

www.microenterpriseworks.org — Microlending organizations

www.icann.org — Manages Internet domain name system (nonprofit)

www.internic.net/alpha.html — Lists qualified companies selling domain
   names

www.count-me-in.org — Offers microloans to women

www.innovativebank.com — Offers microloans to women

Chapter 8 Making the Sale: Getting Your Product on Store Shelves

www.tsnn.com — Resource to find trade shows in the United States

www.expedia.com — Site for travel discounts

www.priceline.com — Site for travel discounts

www.mominventors.com — Link to find margin calculation tool

Chapter 9 Blowing Your Horn: Marketing That Works

www.prweb.com — Free newswire service

www.athenafoundation.org — Award program for women in business

www.wellsfargo.com/biz/intentions/women_bus_svcs — Award program
   for women in business

www.stevicawards.com/women — Award program for women in business

www.publicityinsider.com — Bill Stoller, publicity expert, online resource

www.mediabistro.com — Resource for media professionals

www.bacons.com — Bacon's Media Source

www.prnewswire.com — Online wire service

www.prleap.com — Online wire service

www.pressblaster.net — Online wire service

www.hollywood-madison.com — The Hollywood Madison Group,
   marketing company focusing on celebrities

www.backstagecreations.com — Specialty marketing firm that caters to
   celebrity gift baskets.

www.blogger.com — Resource to help you set up a blog
http://mominventors.blogspot.com — Mom Inventors' blog
http://help.blogger.com — Help with setting up a blog
www.lights.com/weblogs — Premium blog resource created by expert
    Peter Scott
http://weblogs.about.com/od/celebrityblogs — Celebrity blogs
www.prsa.org — Public Relations Society of America

Chapter 10 Finding a Partner: Licensing 101

www.asaenet.org — List of trade associations in nearly every industry
www.hoovers.com — Database with information about large-size
    companies
www.sec.gov — Securities and Exchange Commission — another resource
    to find information about public large-size companies
www.bigideagroup.net — Special corporate idea submission contest or
    program
www.pgconnectdevelop.com — Special corporate idea submission
    contest or program
www.innocentive.com — Special corporate idea submission contest or
    program
www.ninesigma.com — Special corporate idea submission contest or
    program
www.yet2.com — Special corporate idea submission contest or program
www.dialcorp.com — Special corporate idea submission contest or program
http://inventionquest.dja.com — Staples product search program

The Mom-Invented Products Mentioned in This Book

www.babiessimplepleasures.com (Meghan Ritchie)
www.fleecebaby.com (Jennifer Fleece)
www.stylease.com (Jennifer Hughes)
www.tabletopper.com (Beth Berse)
www.rideoncarryon.com (Darryl Lenz)
www.toddlercoddler.com (Susan Dunk)
www.upandawayinc.net (Cheryl Wells)
www.naturesbaby.com (Adena Surabian)
www.huggeemissyou.com (Audrey Storch)

www.couponizer.com (Amy Bergin)
www.jlchildress.com (Jan Childress)
www.bottletenders.com (Anissa Fiore & Rebecca Gammelgaard)
www.cleanshopper.com (Missy Cohen Fyffe)
www.gourmettote.com (Leianne Messina-Brown)
www.simplytiffanytaite.com (Tiffany Whitchurch)
www.proudbody.com (Wendy Tuey)
www.mominventors.com (Tamara Monosoff)

More Useful Websites, Associations, and Publications

www.copyright.gov — Government site information on copyrights
www.uiausa.org — The United Inventors Association offers free resources and a wealth of information on the inventing process
www.patentcafe.com — Offers a variety of patent-related services
www.patentsearchinternational.com — Offers affordable patent searches
www.compassdesign.com — Product development engineering firm
www.west-associates.net — Intellectual property law firm
www.slickideas.com — Graphics/retail packaging design
www.orcacommunications.com — Public relations firm
www.translinkshipping.com — Freight-forwarding company
www.ibius.com - International customs brokerage firm
www.inventorsdigest.com — Inventors' Digest, magazine for inventors
www.inventored.org — A nonprofit organization that offers a wealth of information for inventors.
www.wini2.com — Product evaluation and assessment service
www.innovationcentre.ca — Canadian organization assists inventors with market research
www.inventorfraud.com/goodguys.htm — Resource for inventors offering useful information
www.shopathome.com — Resource-listing catalog; include as part of your sales strategy

Useful Books

It Takes a Village, Hillary Rodham Clinton
A Whack on the Side of the Head: How You Can Be More Creative, Roger von Oech

Chase's Calendar of Events, McGraw-Hill
One Page Business Plan, Jim Horan
Guerilla Marketing, Jay Conrad Levinson
Turn Your Idea or Invention into Millions, Don Kracke
Mothers and Daughters of Invention, Autumn Stanley
Profiting from Intellectual Capital: Extracting Value from Innovation, Patrick H. Sullivan

B

Business Forms

Starting a business can feel both exhilarating and overwhelming. Having the tools you need can minimize stress and help you take immediate action. Therefore, we are offering the forms we use at Mom Inventors, Inc., here as a guide.

Keep in mind that nondisclosure and licensing agreements can vary for every circumstance, and differ according to an individual attorney's style and background. Use these forms as a starting point for reference, but do work with an attorney when negotiating any legal agreements.

On the next few pages you will find the forms mentioned throughout the book, in the order in which they were mentioned. You are welcome to use them without further permission with the understanding that you assume full responsibility for their accuracy and function. We hope these forms will help you get started! Also included are three sample press releases announcing significant developments—awards, appointments, new product announcements, and so on—in a company's history.

CONFIDENTIALITY AGREEMENT

Please note that you will be shown information during the course of this group which is confidential and proprietary. This information cannot in any way be shown, discussed, or revealed outside of this room and should be viewed as highly confidential. Additionally, please note that any and all ideas you share within these groups are the property of

_____.

Based on the above, please indicate and sign below, acknowledging you have read and understand the above and that you release any claim on ideas, information, suggestions, or the like shared within the next context of this group.

_____ I have read and agree with the above. (Check box)

_____(Signature)

_____(Print name)

_____(Date)

Marta Loeb
Founder and President, Mom to Max
Silver Stork Research
Mailing Address
XXX-556-1068 (T)
XXX-556-1099 (F)
marta@silverstork.com
www.silverstork.com

Focused on MOMS of Today and Tomorrow

Release form to be signed by participants prior to engaging in focus groups or other types of research-gathering activities.

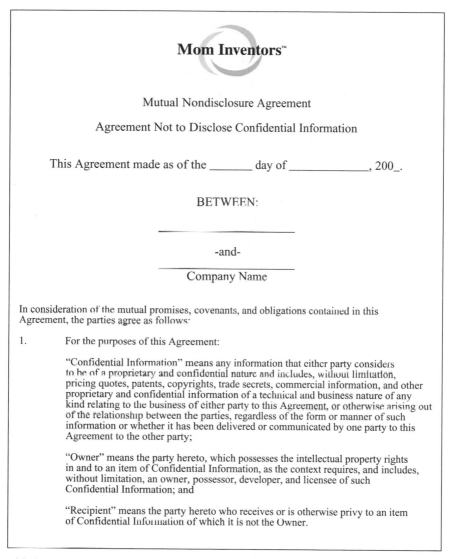

Mom Inventors™

Mutual Nondisclosure Agreement

Agreement Not to Disclose Confidential Information

This Agreement made as of the _____ day of _____, 200_.

BETWEEN:

_____

-and-

_____

Company Name

In consideration of the mutual promises, covenants, and obligations contained in this Agreement, the parties agree as follows:

1.   For the purposes of this Agreement:

"Confidential Information" means any information that either party considers to be of a proprietary and confidential nature and includes, without limitation, pricing quotes, patents, copyrights, trade secrets, commercial information, and other proprietary and confidential information of a technical and business nature of any kind relating to the business of either party to this Agreement, or otherwise arising out of the relationship between the parties, regardless of the form or manner of such information or whether it has been delivered or communicated by one party to this Agreement to the other party;

"Owner" means the party hereto, which possesses the intellectual property rights in and to an item of Confidential Information, as the context requires, and includes, without limitation, an owner, possessor, developer, and licensee of such Confidential Information; and

"Recipient" means the party hereto who receives or is otherwise privy to an item of Confidential Information of which it is not the Owner.

This is an agreement that should be signed by two parties who wish to conduct a confidential conversation, or otherwise share confidential information.

2.   All Confidential Information constitutes the sole and exclusive property and the confidential Information of the Owner, which the Owner is entitled to protect.

The Recipient shall hold and maintain all Confidential Information in trust and strict confidence for the Owner and shall have a fiduciary obligation to use its best efforts to protect the Confidential Information from any harm, exploitation, manipulation, modification, interference, misuse, misappropriation, copying or disclosure whatsoever, except as specifically authorized by the Owner in writing.

3.   The Recipient shall not disclose the Confidential Information of the Owner to any person without the prior written approval of the Owner. The Recipient shall return all Confidential Information to the Owner immediately upon request.

4.   The confidentiality obligations set out above shall not apply to information which:

(a)   at the time of disclosure, is within the public domain, or which, after disclosure, becomes readily and lawfully available to the industry or the public, other than by breach of this Agreement;

(b)   was independently developed by the Recipient, other than by a breach of this Agreement; and

(c)   the Recipient is by law compelled to disclose, provided that the Recipient has forthwith notified the Owner in writing of any such compelled disclosure.

5.   Neither this Agreement nor the disclosure of any information to the Recipient shall be construed as granting to the Recipient any rights in, to or in respect of the Confidential Information of the Owner.

6.   The provisions hereof are necessary to protect the trade, commercial and financial interests of the parties. The parties acknowledge and agree that any breach whatsoever of the covenants, provisions and restrictions herein contained by either party shall cause, and shall be deemed to be, a breach of that partys fiduciary obligations to the other party which may cause serious damage and injury to the non-breaching party, which cannot be fully or adequately compensated by monetary damages. The parties accordingly agree that, in addition to claiming damages, either party not in breach of this Agreement may seek interim and permanent equitable relief, including without limitation interim, interlocutory and permanent injunctive relief, in the event of any breach of this Agreement. All such rights and remedies shall be cumulative and in addition to any and all other rights and remedies whatsoever to which either party may be entitled.

8.   This Agreement constitutes the entire agreement between the parties with respect to the subject matter hereof and supersedes and overrides any prior or other

This is an agreement that should be signed by two parties who wish to conduct a confidential conversation, or otherwise share confidential information.

agreements, representations, warranties, understanding and explanations between the parties with respect to the subject matter of this Agreement.

9. This Agreement shall be binding upon the heirs, executors, administrators, successors and assigns of the parties.

10. This Agreement shall be governed by the laws of California. The parties agree to attorn to the jurisdiction of the courts of California in the event of a dispute hereunder.

11. The invalidity or unenforceability of any provisions or part thereof of this Agreement shall not affect the validity or enforceability of any other provision and any remaining part which shall continue in full force and effect.

12. In this Agreement, words importing the singular include the plural and vice versa and words importing gender include all genders.

IN WITNESS WHEREOF the parties have executed this Agreement as of the date first above written.

_____   _____
Company Name   Company Name

by:_____   _____
   (Authorized Signature)   (Authorized Signature)

_____   _____
(Printed Name)   (Printed Name)

_____   _____
(Date)   (Date)

This is an agreement that should be signed by two parties who wish to conduct a confidential conversation, or otherwise share confidential information.

Shipping Order

Date	Invoice #
4/18/2005	

Bill To

Ship To

P.O. Number	Terms	Rep	Ship Date	Via	F.O.B.	Vendor #	Dept.
			4/18/2005				

Item #	Description	Quantity

Thank you for your order.
Your business is important to us. Please let us know if we can further assist you in any way.

Best regards,
Mom Inventors, Inc.

Address
Phone/Fax
Website/E-mail

This is the document we send to our warehouse to request a shipment.

Mom Inventors™

Purchase Order

To

Ship To
Mom Inventors, Inc.
Address

Date	P.O. No.	FOB	ETA	Terms
4/28/2005	1007		4/28/2005	

Qty	Unit	Description	Unit Price	Total

Total	$0.00

COMMENTS: Please see attached specifications!

_____

Authorized By   **Date**

Address
Phone/Fax
Website/E-mail

This is the document we use to purchase something from a vendor.

Invoice

Date	Invoice #
4/18/2005	

Bill To

Ship To

P.O. Number	Terms	Ship Date	Via	F.O.B.	Vendor #	Dept.
		4/18/2005				

Description	Quantity	Price Each	Amount

Total		$0.00
Payments		$0.00
Balance Due		$0.00

Thank you for your order.
Your business is important to us. Please let us know if we can further assist you in any way.

Best regards,
Mom Inventors, Inc.

Address
Phone/Fax
Website/E-mail

This is the document we use to bill customers.

"Mom Inventors, Inc."
Inventory Stock Status by Item

	Pref Vendor	Reorder Pt	On Hand
Inventory			
Baby Item #1	ABC Company		
Blue		100	212
Pink		100	156
Yellow		100	122
White		100	187
Total Tote Bags			677
Baby Item #2	CCC Company		
Blue		100	287
Pink		100	224
Yellow		100	253
White		100	196
Total Baby Blankets			960
T-Shirts	XYZ Company		
Size Large		20	35
Size Medium		20	27
Size Small		20	42
Total T-Shirts			104

This is the document we use to track inventory.

MAPS
Manufacturing and Printing Specifications

DATE:

SKU #:
PRODUCT NAME:

RE:

Quantity: _____(e.g., 1500 units)
Trim Size: _____(e.g., 5-3/4" x 7-1/2" size of product package)
Card Stock: Weight:_____   Color:_____   Size:_____

Digital Art
You will most likely prepare or have a graphic designer prepare the digital artwork needed for your packaging. This is an example of what Mom Inventors, Inc. typically provides the manufacturer/factory:
- CD-Rom with digital art of both the TP Saver Card and Insert.
- Hardcopy Digital Art Proof of front and back of TP Saver Card (Please note colors and copy are for reference only. Final digital art file is represented by black & white layers printout).

Digital Art File has been prepared as follows:
- Front – 3 Color Line
    PMS #_____(e.g., ### Purple)
    PMS #_____(e.g., ### Yellow)
    PMS #_____(e.g., ### Red)
    Overall High Gloss Coating
- Back
    All copy to print PMS #_____(e.g., ### Purple)
    Please test UPC Code
    Please check broken type – Front and Back
- Please produce two (2) CD-ROMs of the Final Production Run Digital Files that were used for the final job (not from the Press Proof).

Press
Press Proof
- Press Proof Color Goals: match the PMS colors
- Please show two (2) Press Proofs for Customer approval. Customer (you) will keep one and return the other back to the Manufacturer/Factory within 24 hours with comments.

This is the document detailing packaging specifications that we give to the manufacturer/factory as a guide. It can be helpful as a reference point if anything goes wrong with the manufacturing, printing, and packaging. You will have your instructions in writing.

- Final Production Run Color Goals: please match the PMS colors exactly, or as close as possible to the PMS color. Note: color should match the color goal after the application of the coating and on the paper the job will be printing on.

Packing

Pieces packed individually in cartons of _____ (e.g., 12) units with _____ (e.g., 4) cartons per box totaling _____ (e.g., 48) units per box. Each box should then be put in sturdy bulk boxes for transport.

Carton size: _____ Carton weight: _____

Box size: _____ Box weight: _____

Shipment Due Date _____

Manufacturer/Factory agrees to ship_____ (e.g., 1500) complete retail-ready product units

Delivery

Deliver to:
- Company Name _____
- Address _____ _____

    _____

    _____

- Telephone number _____
- Fax number _____
- Cell phone number_____

Please email shipment confirmation to:
- (email address: _____)

Please let us know if you have any questions or recommendations. We welcome your ideas and thank you in advance for your time.

This is the document detailing packaging specifications that we give to the manufacturer/factory as a guide. It can be helpful as a reference point if anything goes wrong with the manufacturing, printing, and packaging. You will have your instructions in writing.

Manufacturer's Mark-Up Calculation in $		
Wholesale Price (sold to retailer)	−	$ _____
Manufacturing/Production Cost		$ _____
Manufacturer's Mark-Up		$ →

Manufacturer's Mark-Up Calculation in %		
Manufacturer's Mark-Up	÷	$ _____
Manufacturing/Production Cost		$ _____
Manufacturer's Mark-Up %		_____ % →

Retailer's Markup Calculation in $		
Retail Price to Customer	−	$ _____
Retailer's Wholesale Cost		$ _____
Retailer's Mark-Up		$ →

Retailer's Markup Calculation in %		
Retail's Mark-Up	÷	$ _____
Retailer's Wholesale Cost		$ _____
Retailer's Mark-Up %		_____ % →

Manufacturer's Gross Margin Calculation		
Manufacturer's Mark-Up		$ _____
Manufacturer's Wholesale Price	÷	$ _____
Manufacturer's Gross Margin		_____ % →

Retailer's Gross Margin Calculation		
Retailer's Mark-Up		$ _____
Retailer's Retail Sale Price	÷	$ _____
Retailer's Gross Margin		_____ % →

©2005 Mom Inventors, Inc.

Worksheet designed to help determine pricing for your product.

TP Saver™ NEW

Baby Proof Your Toilet Paper

For educational purposes only. Facts and figures are purely hypothetical.

Infant and Juvenile Markets
- 4 million new babies each year
- 8 million children ages 1-3 (U.S. Census)
- 35% reported nuisance toilet paper unraveling (March 2002 focus group)
- 2,800,000 U.S. customers today

Pet Market
- 77 million dog and cat households (Pet Manufacturer's Assoc.)
- 20% reported nuisance unrolling (March 2002 focus group)
- 11,500,000 U.S. customers

Easy to Use:
Constructed of non-toxic, durable and easily sourced polystyrene with an elastic band. When the child safety cap is locked into place, toilet paper is secure.

How to Install the TP Saver™:

1. Insert the TP Saver™ into toilet paper tube.
2. Pull the elastic band of the TP Saver™ across the toilet paper roll.
3. Insert the cap into the end of the TP Saver™ and twist cap 1/4 turn clockwise to lock cap.

TP Saver™ Features:
- Child safety cap (locks)
- Easy to use - no assembly required
- Fits standard toilet paper dispensers

Retail Benefits:
- Prevents nuisance unrolling.
- Prevents unsanitary toilet clogs.
- Great potty training aid - meter use.

Consumer Testimonials:
"...great! When can I buy this?"
"...why hasn't someone come out with this?"
"...my kid just flooded our entire bathroom!"
(March 2002 focus group feedback)

Legal Documentation:
- Patent pending
- International treaty on file

For educational purposes only. Facts and figures are purely hypothetical.

Phone • Website • E-mail

The "sell sheet" should include features, benefits, and other pertinent information about you and your product. Use this document when approaching a manufacturer for a potential licensing agreement.

Simple Patent License

THIS AGREEMENT, made by and between Patent Licensor Corp., a New York corporation with offices at _____, New York, New York ("Licensor"), and Patent Licensee Inc., a New York corporation with offices at _____, New York, New York ("Licensee").

WHEREAS, Licensee desires to obtain a license, and Licensor desires to grant a license under the Licensed Patent as defined herein on the terms and conditions specified herein;

NOW THEREFORE, the parties hereto agree as follows:

1. Definitions
   1.1. Licensed Patents
   "Licensed Patents" shall mean the United States patents set forth in Exhibit A attached hereto.

   1.2. Licensed Products
   "Licensed Products" shall mean all products which employ, or are produced by, the practice of inventions claimed in the Licensed Patents.

2. Grant
Licensor hereby grants to Licensee the nonexclusive right to make, use and sell Licensed Products embodying or made in accordance with the inventions of the Licensed Patents.

3. Term
The term of this Agreement shall terminate upon the expiration for any cause of the last of the Licensed Patents.

4. Compensation
Licensee shall pay royalties to Licensor at the rate and in the manner set forth in Exhibit B attached hereto.

5. Assignment
This Agreement shall be binding upon and inure to the benefit of the successors and assigns of the parties to this Agreement. This Agreement may neither be assigned nor transferred, either in whole or in part by either party without first obtaining the written consent of the other party.

6. Warranty and Representations
Licensor warrants and represents that it has the legal right to grant the license set forth herein.

This is a sample licensing agreement similar to one you might sign after negotiating a licensing agreement with a manufacturer.

7. Patent Markings

Licensee agrees to mark all Licensed Products sold or otherwise disposed of under the license granted herein with the words "U.S. Patent No." and the numbers of the Licensed Patents.

8. Applicable Law and Jurisdiction

This Agreement and performance hereunder shall be governed by and construed in accordance with the laws of the State of New York. Any and all proceedings relating to the subject matter hereof shall be maintained in the courts of the State of New York or the Federal district courts sitting in New York, which courts shall have exclusive jurisdiction for such purpose.

9. Enforceability

If any provision of this Agreement shall be held to be invalid, illegal or unenforceable, the validity, legality and enforceability of the remaining provisions shall in no way be affected or impaired thereby.

10. Entire Agreement

This Agreement and the Exhibits attached hereto contain the entire agreement between the parties hereto with respect to the subject matter hereof and thereof and supercede all prior agreements and undertakings between the parties relating to the subject matter hereof and thereof.

11. Amendments and Waivers

All amendments and other modifications hereof shall be in writing and signed by each of the parties hereto. The failure of either party to exercise in any respect any right provided for herein shall not be deemed a waiver of any right hereunder.

IN WITNESS WHEREOF, the parties hereto have signed this Agreement as of the date hereof.

PATENT LICENSOR CORP.   PATENT LICENSEE INC.

By: _____   By: _____

Title: _____   Title: _____

This is a sample licensing agreement similar to one you might sign after negotiating a licensing agreement with a manufacturer.

FOR IMMEDIATE RELEASE

May 26, 2004

TP Saver™ awarded the coveted iParenting Media Award for one of 2004's Hottest Safety Products

WALNUT CREEK, CA, May 26, 2004 — After reviewing thousands of products, iParenting Media has selected the TP Saver™, a Mom Invented™ product, as a celebrated winner of an iParenting Media Award for innovation in the Safety category. TP Saver™ prevents babies and pets from unraveling the family toilet paper. For more information visit: http://iparentingmediaawards.com/winners/3/807-11-26.php.

"We are delighted with the media attention around the TP Saver™ and honored to have our product chosen — more importantly, we are pleased that this product won an award with such a rigorous testing standard," says Tamara Monosoff, inventor of the TP Saver™ and CEO, Mom Inventor's, Inc.

iParenting Media's innovative system of determining the best products in the children's media and juvenile product marketplace utilizes a thorough evaluation process at three outside review sites for each product: a licensed childcare facility/school, a product expert, and a parent. Three separate evaluations by qualified reviewers, along with a final review by the iParenting Media Awards Executive Committee ensures an objective and credible process.

Each review site completes a comprehensive survey supported by a proprietary technical online platform. Submissions are performed online by the manufacturers, ensuring accuracy of information.

iParenting operates one of the Internet's most popular communities for parents and parents-to-be at iParenting.com. The company is the content provider for four national magazines: *Pregnancy, Baby Years, Women's Health & Fitness,* and *Pregnancy Buyer's Guide.* iParenting Editor-in-Chief Elisa Ast All, MSJ, writes a syndicated monthly newspaper column and hosts an A.I.R.-nominated radio show, *"Points on Parenting."*

Mom Inventors, Inc. Established by a mother and inventor in early 2003, Mom Inventors, Inc. is founded on the principle that many of the best and most unique ideas come directly from their target market – Moms. In addition to developing its own brand of **Mom Invented™** products, Mom Inventors, Inc., licenses products, as well as assists and supports other mom inventors in taking their product ideas to market (866-376-1122) / www.mominventors.com.

Tamara Monosoff holds a doctorate of education and is a former member of the Clinton White House staff.

PRESS CONTACT:
Tamara Monosoff, CEO
Mom Inventors, Inc.
Phone
Fax
E-mail
Website

This press release, dated May 26, 2004, announces an award being given to a Mom Invented product, TP Saver.

FOR IMMEDIATE RELEASE

July 14, 2004

Senior Executive of Rapid-Growth Software Firm joins Mom Inventors, Inc.

WALNUT CREEK, CA, July 14, 2004 — Mom Inventors, Inc., a Walnut Creek, CA based company announces that Brad Kofoed, formerly the Vice President of Business Development for leading software company, EVault, Inc. has accepted the position as President and Director of Sales for Mom Inventors, Inc., a dynamic company focused on developing and manufacturing products for the infant and juvenile industry.

"Brad has spent 15 years successfully building global distribution channels. He will be instrumental in taking our Mom Invented™ products to the next level of distribution," says CEO Tamara Monosoff.

"Tamara has done a remarkable job developing and positioning the Mom Invented™ Brand as well as promoting the company concept of "moms helping moms," says Kofoed. "Within three years, our innovative "Mom Invented™ products will have a significant presence in the juvenile marketplace."

Since 2001, Kofoed built EVault's global indirect sales channel and saw revenue growth of over 200% per year. Prior to that, he lived in Hong Kong where he ran Asian business operations for iAsiaWorks. During the Clinton Administration, Brad served as an Advisor to the White House on the President's Council on Y2K Conversion (1997-2000).

Kofoed holds an M.A. from Golden Gate University and a B.A. from Colorado State University. He is active in his community where he serves on the board of directors for the Walnut Creek Chamber of Commerce and has been a leader in the well-known "Think Security First" initiative. Brad is married with two daughters, Sophia, 2-years-old and Kiara, 7 months.

PRESS CONTACT:
Tamara Monosoff, CEO
Mom Inventors, Inc.
Phone
Fax
E-mail
Website

This notice, from July 14, 2004, announces the hiring of a new senior executive.

FOR IMMEDIATE RELEASE

July 26, 2004

Mom Invented™ Brand is recognized by America's Largest Retailers
Mom Inventors, Inc. acquires new major accounts Wal-Mart, Longs Drugs,
and The Right Start

Walnut Creek, CA, July 26, 2004 — Mom Inventors, Inc., a Walnut Creek, CA based company, manufacturers the trademarked Mom Invented™ brand of products for the Infant and Juvenile market, announced new sales of their award winning product, TP Saver™, to Longs Drugs, Wal-Mart, and The Right Start.

TP Saver™ is an innovative new Mom Invented™ product that prevents children and pets from unraveling the family toilet paper.

Beginning in August, the TP Saver™ will be sold to customers in over 400 Longs Drug Stores, Wal-Mart Stores in Northern and Central California, and in The Right Start stores nationwide.

"We are proud to sell to independent infant and baby stores, catalogs, and Websites across the country, but these new accounts take us to a new level," says Tamara Monosoff, CEO. "We look forward to announcing other sales with major chains for our newest product, Shoe Clues™ in the near future."

Mom Inventors, Inc. established by a mother and inventor in early 2003, is founded on the principle that many of the best and most unique ideas come directly from their target market – Moms. In addition to developing its own brand of Mom Invented™ products, Mom Inventors, Inc., licenses products, as well as supports other mom inventors in taking their product ideas to market.

Tamara Monosoff holds a doctorate of education and is a former member of the Clinton White House staff.

PRESS CONTACT:
Tamara Monosoff, CEO
Mom Inventors, Inc.
Phone
Fax
E-mail
Website

This announcement, of July 26, 2004, proclaims the new availability of a product at major retailers.

Index

About the Author

Tamara Monosoff is the mother of daughters Sophia Colette (3) and Kiara Lauren (1), born two years apart to the day.

Some think of Tamara as a natural-born entrepreneur. Her parents still recall the family trip to an art museum where Tamara, 9 years old, spent the entire visit working out the specifics of her dog-washing business plan. While the dog-washing business never took off (something about a dog bite), her entrepreneurial spirit lasted into adulthood. In winter 2003, Tamara launched her company, Mom Inventors, Inc. with the dual mission of manufacturing quality products invented by moms and providing an on-line community for aspiring mom inventors. All products bearing the Mom Invented™ brand can be found in stores and catalogs across the country. The www.mominventors.com Website has been visited by over a million guests in the past few months.

Since launching her company, she has been interviewed by numerous publications and has appeared on the front page of *The Wall Street Journal*, in *People* magazine, and in *The London Times*. She has appeared on NBC's *Today* show with Katie Couric, *NBC Nightly News with Tom Brokaw*, *CNNfn* (financial news), *CNN Live*, ABC's *News Now*, *Inside Edition*, ABC's *Good Morning America*, and numerous local networks. She has been interviewed on live radio shows around the globe including BBC radio–Scotland, CNN radio, and *The Bill Handel Show*.

Prior to both motherhood and to launching Mom Inventors, Inc., Tamara was an appointee to the Clinton Administration and served in both the White House and the U.S. Department of Education. Following her three-year term in Washington, Tamara lived in Hong Kong for 18 months, where she consulted to American companies entering Asian markets and spoke on the subject of women and leadership to such groups as the Hong

Kong government's Commission on Equal Opportunities. She was also the keynote speaker for the American Chamber of Commerce's conference "Women in Leadership: Success Strategies 2000." Tamara holds a doctorate in International and Multicultural Education with an emphasis on women and leadership and a master's degree in Counseling Psychology from the University of San Francisco. However, she has found playing the role of mom has been the most challenging and most important job of all!

Monosoff lives in Walnut Creek, California, with husband, Brad Kofoed.

About Mom Inventors, Inc.

Mom Inventors, Inc. produces products made by and for moms. These products are sold through retailers nationwide. Each product carries the Mom Invented brand, symbolizing the dynamic creativity of moms everywhere and our potential connection to each other. In the process of building this business, an exciting community has emerged.

The Mom Inventors community is growing exponentially each day. Whether you are developing the next new software application, a great new baby product, or any inspiring idea, this Website is intended to provide a supportive environment. As a community of "moms helping moms" you'll find informational resources, a message board, seminars, inspiring stories from our featured moms, a newsletter, and our popular Mom Invented™ Store.

We seek to nurture what mothers do best—solve problems—and in so doing change the rules by which we live. There are 82 million moms in the United States. We represent the largest source of untapped entrepreneurial intelligence in this country. While not every mom will choose to become an inventor, every mom can choose to reinvent her life. Through collaboration (one of our dominant character traits), and by leveraging our hard-earned wisdom and stamina, each of us can design the lives we seek and ultimately change society in ways not yet imagined. As individuals we may not yet know exactly how, but that's the exciting part!

I invite you to join our community and take action. Take the chances necessary to achieve your dreams. Visit our Website at www.mominventors.com.

Special Invitation

Dear Friends,

I would love to hear from you!

It would bring me great pleasure to learn how you've used this book to bring your ideas to fruition.

In addition, we'd also like to consider your story for inclusion on our Mom Inventors Website. Each month, our "Feature Mom" section tells the story of a new mom who has successfully brought her product to market. She shares her lessons learned, roadblocks, and "aha" moment. It's the most popular and inspiring part of our Website!

If you are interested in sharing your story, please visit www.mominventors.com and click on "Submit Your Story."

If you would like to reach me, please send an e-mail to Handbook@mominventors.com or fax 925-280-8224.

Warmest wishes,

Tamara